MW01285501

Praise for

There's Got to Be a Better Way

"A road map to eliminating inefficiencies and busting bureaucracies. Drawing on rigorous research and rich experience inside a wide range of workplaces, Nelson Repenning and Donald Kieffer reveal how to redesign work to do more in less time."

—Adam Grant, *New York Times* bestselling author of *Think Again*

"Repenning and Kieffer are absolutely right: there's got to be a better way to work than what we're doing now! Fortunately, their theory of dynamic work design offers exactly the type of compelling alternative we've been so desperately searching for."

—Cal Newport, *New York Times* bestselling author of *Deep Work*

"The most useful book on creating enduring organizational change I have ever read. This masterpiece shows why, when leaders try to change organizations for the better, they so often make things worse by focusing on fighting fires rather than fixing root causes. *There's Got to Be a Better Way* shows how savvy leaders can, instead, solve the right problems and build organizations that are consistently innovative, resilient, and reliable."

—Robert I. Sutton, *New York Times* bestselling author of *The No Asshole Rule*

"If you want to solve the business problem you thought was unsolvable, look no further than this incisive new book, which presents a smart new way to unlock fast fixes to your once intractable challenges. It's a mindset makeover!"

—Suzy Welch, *New York Times* bestselling coauthor of *The Real-Life MBA*

There's Got to Be a Better Way indeed offers one. Blending expertise in system dynamics and behavioral science, along with decades of real-world practical experience, authors Nelson Repenning and Don Kieffer teamed up to write this groundbreaking new book. In it, they describe a compellingly actionable learning process for solving the most perplexing and persistent problems that plague every large organization. A must-read for leaders in any industry facing complexity, uncertainty, and pressure for results."

—Amy C. Edmondson, author of *Right Kind of Wrong*

"There is a better way! I've seen it, and I promise you it's possible. Overloaded, overregulated organizations are not only wildly inefficient—they are absolutely no fun to work in. In this eminently practical and deeply grounded book, Nelson Repenning and Don Kieffer draw on their decades of experience to show us all how we can build the kind of creative, extraordinarily productive workplaces most people only dream about."

—Rebecca Henderson, author of *Reimagining Capitalism in a World on Fire*

There's Got to Be a Better Way emphasizes the power of dynamic leadership in the fast-paced world we live in. This is a great roadmap for learning how to identify core challenges, embrace flexibility, and experiment with new ideas to refine processes that have been holding your team back. Understanding how to swiftly identify the issue will allow leaders to pivot quickly—or boldly move in a different direction—without the fear of failure. Problem-solving in this way will ultimately drive long-term success and collaboration."

—Joe Eastin, executive chairman and cofounder, ISN

"In *There's Got to Be a Better Way*, Nelson Repenning and Donald Kieffer deliver a compelling road map for overcoming organizational inertia. With a wealth of real-world case studies and a proven framework, the authors introduce Dynamic Work Design—a practical, principle-driven approach that helps leaders unlock efficiency, drive sustainable change, and foster innovation. This book is essential reading for executives seeking to turn workplace frustration into high-impact results."

—Jim Anderson, CEO, Coherent

"Using five fundamental principles, Nelson Repenning and Don Kieffer show how any organization can use their insightful methods to get stuff done faster, better, and with less effort. Repenning and Kieffer bring an engineer's perspective to business problems, giving organizations methods to diagnose and solve their own challenges in ways that uniquely work for them. At Fannie Mae, we applied these methods and improved our company immeasurably. Their teachings worked for us, and they can work for you."

—Timothy J. Mayopoulos, CEO, Fannie Mae

"This book is a must-read for all leaders of organizations—big and small, private and nonprofit, newly founded and well-established. It should be required of all students of organizational behavior. Building on decades of research and consulting, Repenning and Kieffer show how their dynamic work design approach can address long-standing organizational issues while also stimulating a reinforcing cycle of learning and innovation. Drawing on examples from an array of different organizations—industrial conglomerates, research laboratories, hospitals, and even shelters for at-risk women—*There's Got to Be a Better Way* illustrates how their disciplined approach actually works in practice and drives results. This is the very best management book I have read in years."

—Richard M. Locke, dean, MIT Sloan
School of Management

"A masterful book that avoids the buzzwords common to the genre, providing actionable methods for removing frustration points and bottlenecks in order to make organizations more productive and more rewarding to work in. Repenning and Kieffer's methods can help reveal incorrect assumptions and blind spots that stop us from identifying and solving the right problems."

—Daniel Huttenlocher, dean, MIT Schwarzman
College of Computing

"Starting with the Human Genome Project, the Broad Institute has always embraced bold challenges to accelerate biomedicine. Ever since we learned from Nelson Repenning and Don Kieffer about Dynamic Work Design over thirteen years ago, it's been our foundation for continuous transformation of our Genomics Platform. When we applied it at the start of the COVID pandemic, it helped us deliver over 37 million tests, with turnaround under 24 hours and a cost far below commercial operations. It's been essential to so much of what we've done."

—Eric Lander, founding director, Broad Institute

There's Got to Be a Better Way

How to Deliver Results and Get Rid of the Stuff
That Gets in the Way of Real Work

There's Got to Be a Better Way

NELSON P. REPENNING &
DONALD C. KIEFFER

BASIC

VENTURE

New York

Basic Venture
Hachette Book Group
1290 Avenue of the Americas, New York, NY 10104
www.basic-venture.com

Printed in the United States of America

First Edition: August 2025

Published by Basic Venture, an imprint of Hachette Book Group, Inc. The Basic Venture name and logo is a registered trademark of the Hachette Book Group.

The Hachette Speakers Bureau provides a wide range of authors for speaking events. To find out more, go to www.hachettespeakersbureau.com or email HachetteSpeakers@hbgusa.com.

Basic Venture books may be purchased in bulk for business, educational, or promotional use. For more information, please contact your local bookseller or the Hachette Book Group Special Markets Department at special.markets@hbgusa.com.

The publisher is not responsible for websites (or their content) that are not owned by the publisher.

Print book interior design by Amy Quinn
Illustrations by Patti Isaacs

Library of Congress Cataloging-in-Publication Data
Names: Repenning, Nelson P. (Nelson Peter), author. | Kieffer, Donald C., author.
Title: There's got to be a better way : how to deliver results and get rid of the stuff
    that gets in the way of real work / Nelson P. Repenning and Donald C. Kieffer.
Description: First edition. | New York : Basic Venture, [2025] | Includes
    bibliographical references and index.
Identifiers: LCCN 2024046770 | ISBN 9781541704626 (hardcover) | ISBN
    9781541704633 (ebook)
Subjects: LCSH: Workflow. | Task analysis. | Time management. | Organizational
    effectiveness.
Classification: LCC HD62.17 .R47 2025 | DDC 658.5/3—dc23/eng/20250213
LC record available at https://lccn.loc.gov/2024046770

ISBNs: 9781541704626 (hardcover), 9781541704633 (ebook)

LSC-C

Printing 1, 2025

Nelson: To Caroline Repenning (a.k.a. Mom), for a lifetime of support

Don: To Erica

Don and Nelson: To those who work for more than a paycheck

Contents

Introduction

The Better Way of Dynamic Work Design

The modern organization can be an incredibly frustrating place. There is a reason that TV shows like *The Office* remain popular. We see ourselves in the comically exasperating world of trying to work with and through others and are often left feeling exhausted and out of control. One executive we know captured this feeling perfectly:

> I know my organization is in trouble when I start Monday morning by making a list of all the important things I need to do this week. I work my ass off all week, but on Friday afternoon I can't cross off a single item.

Nobody likes when it feels like the system is managing you rather than you are managing it. Worse, our organizations seem to actively conspire against us ever getting anything done. To paraphrase the comedian George Carlin, it often feels like everyone who works for us is lazy and everyone we work for is clueless. If there is a single sentiment that unites the thousands of leaders we have worked with over the past three decades, it is simply this: there's got to be a better way.

There is. In this book, we introduce a new way of working—dynamic work design—that enables you to find your own unique better way so that you are managing your organization rather than it managing you. Using the principles and approach of dynamic work design will allow you to calm the chaos of your organization and help you find new and ever-better ways to deliver results.

Dynamic work design originated in a chance meeting in 1996 at Harley-Davidson's corporate cafeteria, the Rally Point. Harley had recently commissioned an external study of its product development process. Its conclusion: the system yielded products that were LEW, or late, expensive, and wrong. It was time for a thorough overhaul. About the same time, having spent his career in plants with several varieties of LEW systems, Don Kieffer sensed an opportunity to demonstrate a better way of developing new products and bringing them to the market. Don was a manufacturing engineering manager in the engine plant but had been able to talk his way into leading the Twin Cam 88 engine project. The Twin Cam was the first modification to Harley's engine in a decade and the most significant redesign since Bill Harley created the original version of the engine, the Knucklehead, in 1936. The iconic engine, with its clean lines and "potato-potato" sound, was recognized and imitated worldwide, and the Twin Cam 88 was Harley's most exciting project in years. And, while the factories normally had minimal input into Harley's big development projects, particularly in the early stages, the Twin Cam would not be led by a design engineer from downtown headquarters but by a guy from the plant.

Don had spent the bulk of his career in manufacturing. He went to work after high school at age seventeen and ended up running metal-cutting equipment in factories. He quickly built the reputation for solving problems and getting things to work—first machines, then departments, then organizations. Later, he started taking college classes at night and after eight years had a degree in electrical engineering. Harley hired Don as a manufacturing engineer at the Capitol Drive engine plant in 1989. Fifteen years later he was general manager of that same plant and vice president of operational excellence for the company. After leaving Harley, Don took a role as a senior vice president for operations at Intermatic, a private company, with responsibility for thousands of employees and several facilities around the globe.

When we met, Nelson Repenning was a newly minted PhD and had just the day before accepted an offer to join the System Dynamics Group at MIT's Sloan School of Management as an assistant professor. His dissertation research had focused on a question that, to this day, borders on heresy: Do the standard management tools taught in business schools actually have any impact on practice? The answer turned out to be "only occasionally." Despite initially positive returns, most efforts to introduce new management tools and approaches, such as lean thinking and agile software development, fail in the long term—often because the leaders don't foresee the negative impact on day-to-day business as the organization tries to digest a major change initiative. Nelson's research suggested that the answer lay in what he called the *firefighting trap*. As we explain in detail later, when leaders get overwhelmed and lose touch with how the work of their organization really gets done, they focus all their energy and attention on immediate results and risk getting trapped in a permanent state of crisis management.

That day at the Rally Point, our conversation quickly shifted to the problems we were each working on. We were an unlikely pair: a factory rat, as Don calls himself, with a clear view from the front line of how management decisions combine with poor work designs to cause chaos for the people who actually do the work, and an ivory tower academic focused on organizational dynamics. Yet we shared an obsession. We were both convinced that the complex problems we saw had solutions that could make a real difference to both organizations and the people working in them. Don knew how to make things work; Nelson saw the larger organizational dynamics that thwarted those efforts. We started collaborating.

We were deeply influenced by well-known experts who had made a difference for thousands of companies. Don followed W. Edwards Deming, arguably the father of the quality movement in the manufacturing world, and later worked with some of the elder manufacturing masters from Toyota. Nelson had studied with Jay Wright Forrester, the influential MIT professor and founder of the field of system dynamics, and cut his academic teeth in the early days of the organizational learning movement, an effort focused on improving how organizations translate experience into future action.

As Harley (and many other companies) had experienced, large, complex engineering projects often turn into total nightmares. Boeing's recent challenges with the safety of its 737 Max airliner are just one of a long list of examples. The Twin Cam 88 project provided an ideal opportunity to both understand these troubles and find ways to avoid them. True to form, there were plenty of formidable problems during the engine project, including two significant and unexpected delays caused by technical difficulties.

Despite those hiccups, the Twin Cam 88 helped catalyze big changes inside the company. Because of its size, the project broke almost every system it touched, putting Don at the center of helping to figure it all out. He and Nelson worked to understand the complexity of the issues and devise strategies to solve them. The change in mindset they pushed was subtle but important: product development is not a subset of engineering; it is a company-wide process that touches almost every part of the organization. To be successful, all the parts of the company had to work in concert, not as individual, disconnected pieces. Later, Don proposed and led the first project management office, which guided every project through Harley's new development process.

Many forces and people pushed Harley forward. By the end of the Twin Cam 88 project, the company had added a new development center, new technologies, a lot more engineers, and, most importantly, a revamped development process. These changes would eventually yield a fourfold improvement in Harley's ability to deliver new products to its customers. This effort spawned academic papers that won Best Paper Awards and were recognized as the best work in System Dynamics in the previous five years.

The new engine was a huge hit. With a more powerful and more reliable engine, demand and profitability soared. For the first time, performance kits had been engineered and introduced at the same time as the new engine. They were available on day one, boxing out aftermarket competitors and supercharging the sales of the parts and accessories division that already had several hundred million dollars of revenue.

We were hooked. The early results at Harley suggested that there was, in fact, a better way and that, perhaps, if we kept working together, we could develop a set of principles that would help other organizations deliver better results. In 2008, Nelson invited Don to address an executive education session at MIT Sloan. Don was soon named senior lecturer, and the Don-Nelson tag team became a regular fixture in the executive education class-room. Don started a small consulting group when students began asking for help outside of the classroom. Nelson later joined the consulting group, and our collaboration continued to deepen.

As part of our efforts to help companies design better work, we helped BP overhaul its operations and safety procedures after two deadly, high-profile accidents: the explosion at the Texas City refinery in 2005 that killed fifteen people and the Macondo oil spill in 2010 that killed eleven and pumped five million barrels of oil into the Gulf of Mexico. We came to appreciate the chronic problems that BP had inflicted on itself through an inflexible management system focused on financial discipline. In a well-intentioned effort to please the financial markets, BP had created an intricate system of rules and targets that put managers in an impossible bind that could only be resolved by working around the systems that the company had worked so hard to implement. Our work helped BP address these challenges. By 2013, the company reported the best process safety record in the oil industry, a trend that's continued ever since. Only one incident has been reported since 2011, a minor refinery fire in 2022. This record represents a major achievement for a company that many safety experts and environmentalists had written off as incapable of improvement.

Over the years, we have worked with many organizations—large and small, for profit and not-for-profit, in the United States and elsewhere, and in nearly every industry. Many were in fields considered difficult to change: education, health care, banking, energy, and social services among them. We've seen a Boston shelter for at-risk women improve its capacity and client support; a hospital cut the length of stay for patients while increasing the quality of their care; a semiconductor company reduce test cycles from four months to four weeks; and a river rafting company dramatically reduce the time people spent onshore waiting for their turn.

Consulting, teaching, and coaching projects in Sloan's Executive MBA program helped further refine our approach. We began to publish articles.[1] Gradually, dynamic work design—its five principles and its approach to change—emerged as the best description of how we, our students, and our clients were producing such striking results so quickly.

Our main contribution comes in the form of a diagnosis and a solution. As we help organizations solve their problems, we find that those problems are inevitably rooted in managers and leaders who, thanks to being overwhelmed by the day-to-day chaos of getting things done, don't understand how the work in their organizations actually happens. Consequently, in a well-intentioned effort to improve performance and/or to respond to a performance shortfall, they intervene in ways that usually make things worse. The result is a vicious cycle of increasingly restrictive and complex rules and structures and increasingly frustrated and seemingly obstinate employees. To close the gap between what leaders see in reports or hear in meetings and what really happens on the ground, and the dysfunction that emerges from the gap between them, we offer a simple approach and framework to improve the effectiveness of those interventions. Because dynamic work design is based on principles and discovery, not rules and rituals, it can be applied in almost any type of organization. We've seen it work many times over. Dynamic work design will guide you in finding your organization's own better way. One of our earliest users, the Broad Institute (pronounced *Brode*), provides a good example of what's possible.

FINDING A BETTER WAY AT THE BROAD INSTITUTE

Sheila Dodge first came on our radar in the spring of 2012. While she had joined MIT's Executive MBA program two years earlier, her propensity for taking careful notes over competing for airtime with her classmates meant that she didn't initially stand out. A presentation in the final week of the program changed that initial perception.

A molecular biologist by training, Sheila worked for the world's leading genomics research center, the Broad Institute, located in Cambridge, Massachusetts. Established in 2004 as a Harvard-MIT research collaboration, the institute grew out of the Human Genome Project. Its main goal was the genetic analysis of diseases, including cancer and schizophrenia, that did not always respond to conventional treatment. By comparing the DNA sequences of people who had a particular disease with those who did not, the institute hoped to identify the genetic anomalies that were responsible for causing the disease. As her time at the MBA program was coming to a close, Sheila was promoted, moving from managing one area in Broad's lab to overseeing and integrating the three separate groups responsible for data production into a single, cohesive organization.

"We are trying to understand what causes disease in people," Sheila explained to us. "We spend a lot of time and effort building up a reserve of genetic data, and we use those data to try to elucidate what's going on in the human body. Our goal is to transform how medicine happens: how doctors interact with patients, how they understand which drugs to give people, and how they prevent and treat disease." She knew the importance of the lab to Broad's mission of improving public health.

Beyond being responsible for extracting DNA data from tens of thousands of samples, Sheila also had to make sure the lab stayed on the leading edge of technology. Gene sequencing is one of the world's fastest-changing industries, with cost reductions far outpacing those experienced in other technologies, such as semiconductors. The work involved sophisticated processes: highly precise equipment focused on teasing out the DNA from samples and then analyzing the resulting data at a rapid pace and at an immense scale. The data the lab produced supported active research focused on saving lives. Sheila understood the importance of the work and the criticality of both maintaining quality and keeping up with demand.

But there was a problem. Broad had been so successful in popularizing research based on genetic data that it now had more demand for its services than it could satisfy. Everyone in the lab was overwhelmed. Sheila could see that the workflow was erratic and the costs in people's time and the institute's money were too high. Most of the people in the lab worked nights and weekends to try to keep up. Many were burning out. Sheila herself was at her wit's end. She wondered how she could keep holding the lab together and still have a life. There were also hallway whispers among Broad's research scientists suggesting that the lab's work should be outsourced since they couldn't keep up with the demands. She knew they had to improve the workflow, and with a new MBA from MIT and a promotion, she felt pressure to make progress. Her final presentation brilliantly described the problems she faced and offered a compelling vision for what the lab could be. She just didn't quite know how to get from here to there.

We—Nelson and Don—had been solving problems like this for over a decade, but we didn't know anything about a high-tech biomedical lab that produced petabytes (a petabyte is one million gigabytes) of DNA data. Nonetheless, the problems Sheila described sounded all too familiar. Good work design principles aren't about the type of work or the industry; they are about taking full advantage of an organization's available brainpower.

We immediately sensed that the lab's problems were rooted in the inability to get the work flowing, especially across administrative boundaries, a problem we had seen at Harley and many other companies. Sheila's team worked hard to move work through the lab, but each effort, while getting an individual sample closer to completion, created more congestion and more chaos, ultimately hurting the lab's overall performance. We suspected that a few simple changes could reduce the gridlock and get the work moving, and in doing so, both satisfy the growing demand and get people home at a reasonable hour.

As Sheila and her team implemented the principles and approach of dynamic work design, dramatic shifts followed. They quickly improved turnaround times by more than 80 percent and quadrupled their capacity—gains that allowed them to process many more samples and get the results to the customer faster and more reliably. The pace of technology development also improved by over threefold. These gains put the lab ahead of demand for the first time in several years and created the space to develop even more innovative products and services. Broad returned to its industry-leading position. When COVID-19 hit, the institute used its new-found capabilities to transform itself into one of the largest and most efficient testing labs in the country in just a few months. When they see this example, students often ask if dynamic work design will work in their particular industry. Dynamic work design is about the flow of human work, not the work humans do. So, as we sometimes joke, the stuff we teach only works in organizations that have people in them.

There's Got to Be a Better Way is about applying dynamic work design so that, like Sheila and her Broad colleagues, you can correctly diagnose problems, take action, calm the chaos, and actually get stuff done. Think of dynamic work design as akin to undertaking a progressive shift to a healthier lifestyle, one that is systemic and avoids the quick but unsustainable fix of a fad diet. It doesn't require extensive off-site training courses, inspirational speeches, or logo-embossed pens and tote bags. Dynamic work design won't transform everything overnight. Instead, you start solving real business problems and immediately put "points on the board." Ongoing problem-solving builds knowledge and helps calm the chaos of everyday work, making it easier to see the next opportunity for improvement and creating a virtuous cycle of capability development and engagement.

As you use the principles of dynamic work design, you will increasingly act like a scientist or engineer, engaging in ongoing experimentation to continually discover new and better ways for your organization to get its work done. As you begin to make one improvement after another, you'll see how they transform your organization by leveraging the collective brainpower of your people to get real results.

WHY DON'T WE ALREADY WORK THIS WAY?

To get a sense for what working with dynamic work design feels like and why we need it, do the following: Take a moment to recall a meeting that really went well, where you had a breakthrough or finally resolved a thorny issue. Ideas and possible solutions came from every corner, often building on or extending someone else's suggestion. Relevant expertise you didn't even know was in the room, perhaps from a past career or hobby, appeared out of nowhere. Soon there was a novel solution on the table, and it wasn't even clear whose idea it was. It had been a genuine group effort, and people naturally understood what to do next.

Everyone has such a story, and it usually starts with a crisis: a major customer threatens to leave; a mission-critical project is failing; the business is about to be shut down; or disaster or scandal erupts. The situation is awful, but people drop everything and focus on the challenge. Not only do they succeed, but they discover collective capabilities they didn't know they had.

For example, MIT is normally a pretty sleepy academic bureaucracy (we only recently quit using carbon paper forms for on-campus events), but COVID kicked us into a different gear. In 2020, when the students left for spring break, everything was normal. A week later, the MIT campus was shut down, students were left scrambling to find some semblance of normalcy, and professors were teaching from their kitchen tables using webcams. When classes ended in June, MIT saw little prospect for a return to in-person teaching.

Yet to everyone's surprise, in-person classes resumed in September—a major boon for MIT students and faculty alike. It happened because MIT's leaders put everything else aside to do what was necessary to get the students back on campus safely. We developed infrastructure so students and faculty could test for COVID twice a week. Our friends at Broad returned the results of those tests in less than twenty-four hours. MIT's in-house IT department created a custom smartphone app for reporting the results, and the school installed card-swipe terminals at every door to allow access only to those who had tested negative—all within the space of a few months.

Rapid action is not typical at MIT, but this time we got it right. To our knowledge, no member of our community became infected while on campus. The educational experience wasn't perfect, but it was better than doing it all online. The local community also benefited. A liquor store owner told Nelson that his business would have closed permanently if the students hadn't returned to campus. Apparently, the combination of an open college and closed bars was good for business.

Most people who work in organizations will resonate with the sense of momentum that comes from working with a powerful team and meeting a challenge together. Why then don't we work this way all the time? Why do we tolerate the vicious cycle of frustration and failure that so often happens in the conventional workplace? At MIT and thousands of other organizations, once COVID was in the rearview mirror, we returned to the usual thicket of overlapping priorities, competing interests, and near-constant firefighting.

A century of social science research has shown that human actions are heavily influenced by the contexts in which people find themselves. Everyone who has ever tried to exercise more or eat less knows that willpower is not enough. You have to change your environment. Unfortunately, most organizational-change processes don't heed this basic lesson and, despite the best intentions of their champions, actively work against finding a better way. This happens because most organizational structures and processes remain fundamentally static; they can't keep up with the dynamic world they serve.

The Problems with Static Organizations

We all know (and business journalists love to remind us) that the world continues to change at an ever-increasing pace. The key idea underlying dynamic work design is simply that this widely accepted notion of continual change in the external environment is not reflected in the construction and management of most organizations. Put differently, most organizational structures and processes are essentially static, meaning they have not been designed to accommodate a rapidly changing, unpredictable world.

To see how taking a static approach to managing a dynamic world can get you in trouble, consider the history of commercial Global Positioning Systems. When GPS went "mainstream" in 2007, it represented an enormous leap over paper-based maps. By pinpointing a car's location using satellites and linking that signal to digital maps, GPS gave drivers turn-by-turn directions to almost any destination.

However, early GPS versions could be frustrating because they didn't adapt to changing traffic conditions. If, for example, you asked such a system to guide you from Boston to New York City, it used a sophisticated algorithm to analyze existing maps and determine the fastest route between the two cities. But if there was a traffic jam along the route, perhaps due to a car accident or a sporting event, the system had no way of knowing about it and often routed you *into* the backup. The static nature of early GPS systems rendered them incapable of reacting to changes in real time or to anything else outside their programming.

You could try to fix this problem within the static framework by adding rules based on historical patterns. Rush hours, for example, are easy to predict, and the system could route you around cities during them. Adding one new rule, however, usually requires a second rule to deal with exceptions to the first. For instance, rush hour only happens during the week, so the initial solution would needlessly avoid cities on weekends. This could, of course, be fixed by making sure the system knew what day it was and by using different rules for weekdays and weekends. Accommodating sporting events would require inputting the relevant team schedules and making sure you distinguish between home and away games. Construction poses a bigger challenge, and it's probably impossible to predict traffic accidents.

Static organizational structures and processes have the same problems as early GPS systems. The world changes around them, but strategies, budgets, hierarchical reporting relationships, roles, incentives, and internal regulations all make it difficult to adjust the structure or the workflow to meet the evolving conditions. Like the early GPS designers, static organizations try to manage their unpredictable environments by adding complexity. Strategies become more elaborate, reports get more detailed, budgets grow more granular, reporting relationships get increasingly convoluted, and PowerPoint presentations get longer.

But these static organizational structures will never, on their own, deliver the results that you and your company need. Using rules to compensate for incomplete or outdated information creates a world that is very difficult to navigate because work doesn't follow the organizational chart or a process diagram. Instead, work takes an evolving path made up of people from different parts of those structures. People often can't simultaneously meet their targets and follow the rules and structure, thus forcing them to work around the formal system. The consequent insecurity results in lengthy narratives rationalizing why a shortfall wasn't their fault, typically delivered at tedious meetings that take up time, don't help, and often make things worse.

It is demoralizing and frustrating to be constrained by the static processes that define the modern organization. People show up every day, and instead of doing meaningful work, they play Whac-a-Mole, trying to tamp down the latest crisis. Perhaps the most common symptom of an overly static organization is the prevalence of the workaround—a departure from accepted practice that, while temporarily moving the work forward, sows the seeds of the next crisis. Here's an example. Several years ago, one of our PhD students observed a prototype "shake test" at a major manufacturer of heavy equipment. He saw the team bolt down the assembly to a test machine that shook it rapidly in all directions to test for metal fatigue and other possible failures. The project was behind schedule, and as the team leader delivered the assembly to the test engineer, having no other option to resolve his problem, he whispered, "Don't shake it too hard."

How many products are released to the market this way? How many fail in the field or generate greater warranty expense? How many injuries, or worse, can be traced back to workarounds like this shortcut? If the link to the unsafe practice is discovered, what kind of liability might the company face?

You might think we're cherry-picking one bad example, but we've seen the cycle of more rules and more workarounds over and over. In Chapter 2, we'll look at these cases in more detail and explore how organizations evolved to make workarounds so prevalent. A better understanding of static systems and how they get us in trouble gives us the opportunity to change them.

From Static to Dynamic

In contrast to their static counterparts, dynamic systems are those that regularly adjust to their environment. Dynamic systems include all living systems, ranging from microorganisms to plants, animals, and natural ecosystems. Dynamic work design will help you create similar adaptability in your organization. To see the power of this approach, let's return to the GPS analogy.

Today's GPS is a dynamic entity. The technology left the static world for good in 2009 with the commercial introduction of the Waze app.[2] A group of Israeli software engineers working on an automated road map built a system that included real-time traffic data—first messages from volunteer drivers and then real-time analysis of GPS signals from many cars. Now when you ask your GPS system to guide you from one city to the next, the algorithm continually recalculates the route based on all the latest traffic information, not just the map. The system regularly updates your estimated arrival time and suggests new routes if it learns of an accident in your path or of a major sporting event about to finish. The GPS system doesn't need to know the baseball schedule, the city's construction plans, or the recorded complaints from people on a quiet street. It just needs to know what's happening now. The app's ability to adjust to changing conditions makes it dynamic and allows users to update their plans in real time.

Introduced in the twentieth century, the modern hierarchical corporate form represented a major advance over prior organizational structures. Using specialized groups and intricate reporting relationships, it allowed companies to scale to massive global size. However, such organizations were largely built on static systems, which tended to grow less flexible with time and scale. The rules and practices that made organizations successful also made them bureaucratic and slow. When events challenged the world around them, their structures remained frozen, and many once venerable companies are long gone. Fortunately, some organizations experience moments of dynamism. A crisis often brings it to the fore. But after the crisis is resolved, static structures reemerge. Organizational management is ready for a vital upgrade. Instead of waiting for a natural disaster or a big screwup, let's embrace the inevitable gaps between plans and outcomes and put dynamism to work on a regular basis.

Increasing an organization's dynamism often leads to significant gains in performance. It's also fun. It can be incredibly motivating, even exhilarating, to work in a dynamic organization. The difference is palpable when you visit Broad's sequencing lab. People there have always had a sense of mission about their work—they know the research is important. Now, however, they also have the confidence that comes with being in control of their workflow. They no longer hide small crises and workarounds. At every moment, a dynamic structure helps everyone know both the current priorities and the pressing problems. Walls are full of charts that everyone marks up, showing the real-time progress of each complex line of activity.

Startups often succeed because their initial approach to work is highly dynamic. The freewheeling way they work fits the messy, chaotic, unpredictable nature of their reality. Success and growth, however, can breed rigidity as internal controls and structures are solidified. Dynamic work design provides a way to avoid that rigidity by simultaneously adding necessary structure to the work and retaining the dynamism that engaged people in the first place. Dynamic organizations continually draw data from the work environment so that people can respond to change in real time in the same way that today's GPS systems operate.

The principles and approach we set out in this book will help you harness the fundamentally dynamic nature of your organization. They can halt the vicious cycle of workarounds that don't scale and develop your ability to adapt and thrive in a changing world.

When managers use dynamic work design, they often feel, for the first time, that they are managing their organization rather than that their organization is managing them. The workday is transformed. The tasks of goal setting, planning, and budgeting no longer involve lengthy annual or quarterly negotiations, the results of which must then be worked around. Instead, planning and goal setting become part of an ongoing process of identifying problems and sensing new opportunities. Dysfunctional hierarchical reporting relationships and painful review meetings take a back seat to providing guidance, delivering critical resources, and communicating about what is really happening. The question "Who is responsible?" is replaced by "How can we help?" Instead of pushing long lists of tasks that are all ranked "high priority," the tough decisions are made up front.

OVERVIEW OF THE BOOK

In this book, we describe basic skills that you can use right away. They are just the beginning. We also show how those skills combine to produce increasingly sophisticated methods for managing complex problems and organizations in a rapidly changing world. We show how you can change your workplace, step by step, to make it a truly dynamic organization—ready, as Broad was, to tackle the most intense challenges that may come your way.

We designed *There's Got to Be a Better Way* to help you see the possibilities of dynamic work design and to show you how to put our principles into practice. Here is a quick overview of the rest of the book:

- **Chapter 1: When Work Works Well.** Starting in 2012, the Broad Institute gene sequencing lab went from the chopping block to the envy of the industry. In detailing the lab's experience, this chapter introduces the dynamic work design principles and shows how they combine to create an integrated system for managing an organization in a rapidly changing world.
- **Chapter 2: The Firefighting Trap.** An overly static approach to management puts managers in an

impossible bind, trapping them between the need to deliver the results and the need to follow outdated structures and processes. In this chapter, we show how this bind makes us all into *firefighting arsonists*. In a well-intentioned effort to work around outdated structures to deliver results, we trap our organizations in a vicious cycle of declining performance, growing chaos, and simmering antagonism between leaders and those who do the work.

The next five chapters describe each of the five principles of good dynamic work design in detail. The principles underpin and guide the approach. Out of necessity, we present them in sequence, but their use should emerge from the approach: start small, diagnose why the current design doesn't deliver the desired results, run small experiments, and reinvest the gains in the next round of improvements. Every operational problem we have come across in the past two decades can be addressed by one or more of these five principles. The principles will help you diagnose problems and identify solutions. Together, the framework guides you to design work for a rapidly changing world.

- **Chapter 3: Solve the Right Problem.** Human beings are creatures of habit, and in many cases this serves us well. But an overreliance on the instincts built from past experience to guide future activity can blind us to major improvement opportunities. In this chapter, we introduce structured problem-solving to break the biases that come with past success and help you find new levels of performance.
- **Chapter 4: Structure for Discovery.** Humans are always learning; you can't turn it off. Unfortunately,

most work is constructed in ways that constantly teach us the wrong lessons. To see how daily learning can go awry, in this chapter we visit a Las Vegas casino managed by one of our former students. The ongoing efforts by the front desk staff to perform in a poorly designed system resulted in each one of them learning a different way to do their job. The result was a messy, inconsistent process that didn't deliver key business goals. A series of simple interventions, what we call *structuring for discovery*, redirected the team's natural learning processes toward more productive paths and yielded significant gains.

- **Chapter 5: Connect the Human Chain**. Everyone hates meetings, and yet it's hard to imagine work getting done without them. Face-to-face communication is a critical element of the work-design tool kit, but its benefits are routinely squandered by poor design. In this chapter, we visit the supply chain from one of the largest companies in the world, BP. By "rewiring" its organization to make sure the right people met at the right time and in the right ways to move the work forward and solve problems, BP improved the performance of its US supply chain in every major dimension. Putting face-to-face communications in the right places—connecting the human chain—can lead to major gains in almost every organization.

- **Chapter 6: Regulate for Flow.** We all have too much to do. And we intuitively know that such overload impedes our getting work done. The cardiac unit at Yale New Haven Hospital experienced this phenomenon regularly, often having to tend to postsurgical patients in the hallway because of congestion in the intensive care unit. This chapter explains how to regulate the flow of work to avoid gridlock and balance short-run delivery against the long-run health of the process. Yale and many other organizations have used this principle to dramatically improve productivity, create a more responsive system, and lower costs.

- **Chapter 7: Visualize the Work.** Imagine how hard it would be to play soccer if the field was shrouded in fog, and you only saw the ball when it appeared in front of you. That's often what it feels like to be a knowledge worker. Fannie Mae, one of the largest financial institutions in the world, experienced this sensation every month as they tried to close their books. This chapter shows how to make the flow of work evident by creating shared dynamic visual representations. This principle allows everyone in the organization to see the state of the knowledge work system, not just their individual to-do list. To demonstrate this idea in action, we show how Fannie Mae used thirty dollars of string and laundry clips to create a visual representation called the Close Line and cut the time required to close its books by almost 80 percent. A simple technique but a stunning result.

Taken together, the five principles define an organizational system that constantly learns and adapts and creates significant competitive advantage in the process. But you can't implement them everywhere all at once. Instead, the principles need to be combined with the following approach: start small, solve real problems, get the work flowing, and reinvest the gains in further improvement. In the final two chapters, we discuss how to get started, first showing how the Broad team executed a remarkable pivot to become one of the nation's leading COVID testing labs and then offering thoughts on how you can start your own journey toward a more dynamic organization.

- **Chapter 8: The Power of Leading with Principles.** In the spring of 2020, after eight years of steady improvement, the Broad genomics lab was ready to shut down and wait out the COVID pandemic. A desperate phone call from a local physician changed everything. In the space of six months, the team went from never having done a COVID test to being one of the biggest, most efficient testing labs in the country. Dynamic work design provided the foundation for this successful pivot and can similarly help make your organization robust and more difficult to "disrupt."
- **Chapter 9: Getting Started.** You can't install dynamic work design through a checklist of change practices: having meetings where you say the word *quality* repeatedly or declare yourself an agile organization isn't going to cut it. Instead, dynamic work design is akin to untangling a knot: you need to find the first thread to pull. In the final chapter, we help you find the starting point for your journey to a better way. The key is to find a problem that is both small and important, one that sits at the core of your organization's work and for which you can make progress rapidly. When, as we discuss, you can resolve this apparent paradox, you are on your way to making real, sustainable change in your organization.

Leaders at Broad, Palace Station Hotel and Casino, BP, Yale University hospitals, and many others have used dynamic work design to make remarkable accomplishments in their organizations. Dynamic work design's impact on their colleagues has been equally, if not more, important, transforming cynicism and apathy into loyalty and motivation. Organizations will always need talented employees who work hard and smart managers who make good choices. But many of today's organizations do something akin to putting a skilled and talented race car driver behind the wheel of a minivan. Fully leveraging all of the human potential in the modern company requires well-designed work that matches the dynamism of the surrounding industry and environment. Dynamic work design won't overcome every business or life problem, but it will make a tangible difference that lasts as long as you are working.

If you can use the five principles and the approach described in this book, you and your organization will no longer be standing in your own way. Use them and make them your own. And when you generate results, please let us know: visit our website, https://shiftgear.work/dwd-stories/, and tell us your story. There is nothing we like more than hearing from people who have used these ideas and tools to make their organizations work better.

Part I

Obstacles

Chapter 1

When Work Works Well

GETTING RID OF OBSTACLES IN THE WAY OF REAL WORK

B etween 2012 and 2019, the sequencing lab at the Broad Institute achieved a remarkable transformation. Using dynamic work design, the team cut the time required to process a sample by more than 80 percent, quadrupled their capacity, and dramatically improved their ability to meet promised delivery deadlines. They also generated a threefold-plus improvement in the productivity of their technology development, allowing them to deliver industry-leading services, including increasingly sophisticated analytics. Thanks to these changes, the team's track record for winning scientific grants became the envy of the industry.

In this chapter, we introduce the essence of dynamic work design by showing how the Broad team used it to transform their work. Using a simple approach guided by five principles, they were able to increase the pace of science and speed the search for new cures to devastating diseases. Broad's growing operational prowess also enabled a rapid pivot into COVID testing that saved countless lives. In subsequent chapters, we introduce each of the principles in detail, but here we show how the principles combine to create a *system* for organizing work that produces ongoing gains in quality and productivity, the ability to adapt to changing conditions, and more engaging jobs. To see why you need this system, let's start by digging a bit deeper into what happens when you take a more traditional, static approach to managing in a dynamic environment.

THE VICIOUS CYCLE OF GETTING SH*T DONE

When we first met Sheila Dodge, then the newly appointed director of operations for Broad's Genomics Platform, she was not alone in feeling stressed and overworked. Everyone in the lab felt the pressure. Managers and technicians spent their days scrambling from station to station trying to placate angry researchers (some of whom had Nobel Prizes) by rushing their already late samples through the process. Meeting these deadlines, however, often felt like an almost impossible task: each time one set of analyses got rushed through the process, it seemed like two more turned into high-priority emergencies. The delays were growing, and they were falling ever-further behind. And falling further behind meant another difficult phone call with an unhappy customer. The lab was overrun with samples needing special handling. It often took five days of rooting through the storage refrigerators just to find the specific sample that needed to be run. The situation was similar in technology development. The backlog of projects needed to keep the lab up-to-date and on the leading edge only continued to grow, along with the pressure to get those projects completed.

Broad employed some of the smartest people in the world. Everyone had an advanced degree in biology or computer science and several had training in process-improvement techniques. Nonetheless, the days were long, chaotic, and frustratingly disorganized. What were they doing wrong?

Let's start with a typical "day in the life" at the lab. Mornings began with updating the production schedule: the "official" list detailing the order in which samples should be processed. Producing this plan required a painful and often heated negotiation between the project managers (who worked for and represented the interests of the researchers) and lab staff (who had to produce the data) over which samples should have priority. Despite the difficulty of creating the plan, it never lasted more than a few hours. Calls from irate researchers or Broad's founding director, Eric Lander, resulted in new priorities—this sample just has to get done!—and the plan became something that had to be worked around. The team would stop efforts to meet the recently agreed-upon schedule and rush to find the newly prioritized samples and hand carry them through the lab.

Though it had started as a temporary stopgap to placate angry customers, the workaround of expediting late samples soon became a permanent part of how the work got done. The team developed a daily "hot list" of the high-priority samples that needed individual attention. The hot list worked for a while, until the researchers realized that getting their sample on the hot list meant that their sample moved to the head of the line. Soon everything was on the hot list, and it had to be augmented with a double hot list, and later, a triple hot list. Eventually, an "FOE list" emerged to reflect the VIP requests sent in by "friends of Eric [Lander]."

Of course, every time a VIP sample was hand carried through the process, it further disrupted the lab's workflow and further delayed every other sample in process. More delays led to more calls from irate researchers. More calls from researchers led to even more samples needing to be hand carried. The result was a vicious cycle of firefighting in which every expedited order made the process more unstable and chaotic and created the need for more expediting. Expediting samples, initially a temporary intervention to placate one unhappy customer, became the only way to get samples through the system. Expediting had become the process.

When used sparingly, expediting can be a useful response to a changing world, but the team's almost exclusive reliance on it sent the facility into a tailspin, creating an increasingly slow and unresponsive work system. Critically, though they were in the midst of this increasingly adrenaline-fueled day-to-day activity, the lab team didn't view these additional efforts as a problem or even out of the ordinary. They knew that things were chaotic, but isn't that how all real businesses work, particularly when they are in a rapidly changing industry? As Sheila would later tell us, "I thought this was my job. After all, that's what leaders do—they get sh*t done."

The Permanent Temporary Workaround

Workarounds like expediting, though initially planned as temporary, that become a permanent part of the work are found everywhere in modern life—even in places where it doesn't seem, at first glance, like a problem is being solved. We've all been stuck in long lines of cars backed up at a busy exit on the highway. Some people resolve their frustration by moving left, leaving the line, and bypassing the traffic. Once closer to the exit they try to nudge their way back into line.

Jumping to the head of the line is a workaround for a system operating beyond its normal capacity. Drivers who bypass the queue take control and get home sooner. But it eventually makes the situation worse for everyone, including the bypassers. The time required for queue jumpers to renegotiate their positions in the exit lane slows progress for everyone and can result in heated disputes and even road rage as they try to push their way back into line. Everyone who chooses to stay in line can see that the lane-bypass workaround operates at their expense. Next time, they will also likely feel more impatient and will be more likely to try it for themselves.

You can easily come up with your own examples of quick fixes that become chronic. After World War II, in an effort to offset the advantages of wealth in college admissions, Stanley Kaplan started tutoring low-income kids in his New York basement to get them ready for standardized tests as a workaround for underperforming public schools. Today, Kaplan Inc., a permanent fixture on the college admissions landscape, earns more than a billion dollars annually and is just one player in the rapidly growing test prep industry. Not surprisingly, the kids who take advantage of test prep courses disproportionately come from wealthy families. Similarly, for most people, consuming strong coffee or other caffeinated beverages starts out as an occasional morning offset to a poor night's sleep or a long day. Soon, the morning ritual extends to the afternoon and becomes a permanent part of our daily routine. When evening comes and we still have caffeine in our system, sleep is more difficult and ensures that the cycle will begin again the next morning. In business, managers often take steps to achieve a short-term financial target even when they know that such actions undermine the long-run stability and health of their organization and risk pulling their organization into a vicious cycle of decline.

Everybody has to take the occasional shortcut. Applied judiciously, they are critical to navigating the uncertainty of modern life. But when used to excess, they risk tipping your organization into a vicious cycle where workarounds beget more workarounds and the system descends into soul-destroying chaos. Morale, quality, and productivity all suffer. Companies caught in this cycle are ripe targets for upstart entrants. As Broad's lab descended into permanent firefighting, competitors, sensing an opportunity, entered the sequencing game and threatened Broad's viability.

To see a path out of a mess like this we turn to an unlikely source far from gene sequencing, the world of video games.

THE WORLD'S MOST ADDICTIVE TECHNOLOGY

Several years ago, Nelson's son asked him to join him in playing his new favorite video game, *Call of Duty*. Robbie was already quite expert, while Nelson had zero experience. The first outing was a comical disaster. Unlike his son, Nelson couldn't remember what each button on the game controller did, had no idea which weapon to use when, and immediately lost track of where he was on the map. Robbie moved so quickly that Nelson didn't have time to learn anything about battling his son's avatar. Instead, Nelson kept pushing the one button he understood, the one that made his avatar jump out of the way of an attack. While Nelson was trying to jump out of harm's way, Robbie ran circles around him and enjoyed every moment of reducing his university professor dad to an easily beatable opponent. The only lesson Nelson really learned in the first outing was that when he heard his son laughing, jumping or not, his own demise was imminent.

Nelson's experience of being overmatched by his son is similar to that of an established organization confronting challenges from younger, smaller, and far more competitive entrants. In the world of business, "Robbies" can emerge from the creation of new technologies or, as happened to the Broad team, when the incumbent can't satisfy all of the demand it has created. In either case, "jumping" to stay alive amounts to relying on expediting and other workarounds, even though such firefighting comes at the expense of building the capability and skills needed to compete.

So how do most organizations meet this challenge? They launch a massive "change initiative" or a reorganization that starts with a few days of classroom orientation or online training, largely delivered through PowerPoint slides. They then "turn on" or "cut over to" an entirely new system or organizational structure under the assumption that everyone will get it exactly right the first time. Every veteran of organizational life has experienced the disorientation of not knowing what they are supposed to do or to whom they should report—the organizational equivalent of not knowing which game controller button to push. We once worked with an energy facility that tried to implement over three thousand specific changes in one six-month effort. Such changes ranged from physical modifications to equipment, such as adding safety alarms—a clear, bounded project—to "creating a culture of reporting near misses"—developing the norm of reporting accidents that almost happened—something that could take years to cultivate. More time was spent tracking the status of each item on a big spreadsheet than actually implementing them.

The fix-it-all-at-once change strategy has several problems and rarely succeeds. It overwhelms the system with work and, perversely, often pushes people deeper into expediting and other workarounds. When people do carve out the space to make the required changes, the modifications suggested by senior leaders are typically disconnected from how the work is actually done.

For example, we worked with one manufacturing plant that, in an effort to reduce eye injuries, required everyone to wear safety glasses. This change worked great except when work was done in hot, humid areas, where the glasses tended to fog. Technicians were now stuck between a proverbial rock and a hard place: follow the rule to the letter, risk tripping, and do the task with obscured vision or violate the rule. Mandating one-size-fits-all changes often forces people doing the work to make additional, often surreptitious workarounds. Not surprisingly, putting those who do the work in an impossible bind does little to increase their motivation for participating in change.

Video game designers understand learning and motivation far better than the senior executives who launch change initiatives. Modern video games are deliberately designed to keep your interest. At each level, kids (of all ages) learn just the right set of new skills to prepare them for the next, harder level. When they master those skills, they get the satisfaction of completing the level. The next level has a little more challenge and requires learning a few more skills. This isn't done for benevolent reasons, it's the core of an extremely lucrative business model (video games generate almost $200 billion in revenue annually). Kids are drawn to video games because they contain the key ingredients of psychologically satisfying and engaging work: players get to solve problems, develop new skills, and tackle ever-greater challenges. Video game designers intentionally structure each level so that you have to work hard to get to the next one, but not so hard that you give up. The experience can be so intense that some psychologists suggest that this technology is as addictive as gambling, with the same type of dopamine release.[1]

The positive feeling we get from acquiring new skills is what keeps golf courses, tennis courts, and music schools in business. We are quite literally wired to learn. People love the experience of solving problems, getting better, and reaching a new level of performance. Unfortunately, work frequently produces the opposite emotional state, creating painful anxiety when our desire to meet goals is frustrated by needless bureaucracy and competing agendas that are beyond our control.

So, when Nelson wanted to improve, he did what all experienced gamers do and what well-designed games enable. He made some time to practice and started at the game's "training" level. The combination of a simpler environment, slower action, and smaller increments made it easier to learn the skills, one by one, that were fundamental to survival. Figuring out what each button on the game controller did was a good start. Having learned a few of the basics, Nelson moved to the next, harder level, identified some new deficits, and developed some additional skills. Regular games with Robbie gave him the opportunity to test and sharpen his new capabilities and see where he needed to improve. Manageable increments of learning made acquiring the needed skills far less onerous. Now every game lasted a little longer and Robbie had to work a bit harder to win. The more Nelson learned, the longer he stayed in the game. Nelson never matched Robbie's skill (the age differential and the fact that Nelson had to go to work every day may have contributed), but the number of pre-assassination giggles definitely declined.

With dynamic work design, you approach changing your organization the way a gamer learns a new game. You identify a small piece of an important problem, make improvements, generate some quick wins, scale what you have learned, and build new skills in the process. Early successes give you the confidence and the skills to advance to the next, tougher problem. Each cycle is a bit more difficult and offers the opportunity to focus on the next, most important set of new techniques and capabilities. As you generate results, colleagues will wonder what is happening—Where are these results coming from? How did you do it?—creating opportunities for you to cultivate their interest and engagement.

The modern video game is designed so that as you play, your confidence, competence, and engagement all grow together. Dynamic work design helps you create something similar for your organization: an ongoing cycle of performance improvement, motivation, and learning.

AN INTRODUCTION TO DYNAMIC WORK DESIGN

The essence of how dynamic work design helped transform Broad is captured in a single project. It is one of thousands Broad executed over the last decade and highlights both the core approach of dynamic work design and how its five principles combine to support it.

Getting Research Grants to Flow

Research grants are the lifeblood of many academic enterprises, and Broad depends on them to fund its work. Professors in the fields of science and engineering often devote considerable time to applying for such grants and, when successful, are eager to start spending the money. Research grants, however, require significant administration. When awards are received, new accounts need to be created; grantors require careful tracking to ensure that their money is going to the intended activities. To add to this complexity, some large funders allow only a fixed percentage of a grant to go to overhead, a number that typically falls short of what the university or lab would normally charge. *Overhead under-recovery*, as it is called, creates a significant additional burden (and raises the blood pressure of every university administrator).

At Broad, the process of managing research accounts was a perennial source of frustration for everyone involved. Researchers complained that the process of setting up new accounts was too slow, forcing them to wait before they could start work on mission-critical projects. The Office of Sponsored Research (OSR), the group charged with grant administration, was perceived as unresponsive, further irritating the principal investigators who were eager to get work going in their labs. Broad senior leadership was similarly frustrated with the slow trickle of data on the status of the funding from OSR, making it difficult for them to assess the state of the institute's budget and overall financial health. Not surprisingly, there were regular complaints from both researchers and administrators about OSR and claims that its staff didn't know what they were doing and needed to be replaced.

As is often the case when tempers mount, no party was particularly aware of their own role in creating the problem. Eager to start an exciting new research project and not wanting to wait for an account to be open and active, principal investigators worked around long setup delays by charging activity on a new project to an existing account that still had money in it. These incorrect charges created a huge mess that OSR would eventually have to untangle by manually moving the charges from the incorrect account to the appropriate one, and in the process, stealing resources from the work of opening new accounts.

While there were numerous calls to "blow up" the OSR office and rebuild it from scratch, the Broad team took a different tack. Following the video game analogy, they didn't try to solve the problem with a major reorganization or a new software system. Instead, they narrowed their focus to identifying a few key problems, resolving them, and then reinvesting the gains in more improvements.

They chose the process of setting up a new account—a huge area of frustration and the source of the "charging to the wrong account" workarounds. They began by formulating a clear statement of the problem that this process generated. They settled on the following:

New account setup takes too long; 90 percent of the awards take more than twenty days to set up, and it should be less than ten days, leading to frustration, delays in research, and spending on wrong accounts.

As we discuss in Chapter 3, creating a statement that clearly captures the challenge—in this case accounts taking too long to set up—without lapsing into diagnoses or solutions sets the stage for finding improvements that might not be revealed by instinct alone.

With the problem statement in hand, the team began tracking progress against it. A simple, hand-drawn graph on a whiteboard, updated weekly, showed the average turnaround time for research grants and the percentage that met the ten-day target. The OSR team agreed to meet in front of the whiteboard every day for fifteen minutes to review progress and discuss shortfalls (later in the book, we discuss how to use this approach when physical presence is not possible).

Initially, the daily meeting focused on understanding how the work of opening a new account actually got done. Working together, they mapped the sequence of people who touched the work of opening a new account, starting with the person who was notified when a grant had been awarded and finishing with the person who communicated the new account number and supporting information to the researcher. Developing a common map of how the work moved from person to person produced several insights.

Most importantly, no single person had visibility of the entire process, even at a high level. Much as Don discovered when trying to understand product development at Harley, the process of opening research accounts crossed multiple functions at Broad, including the budgeting office and the senior leadership team, who had to approve grants. The failure to look at account creation as a cross-functional process had several consequences. The same data were entered multiple times into different systems that didn't speak to one another. The people in OSR administering individual accounts often did not have the information they needed to do their work and, in an effort to move a grant forward, often guessed at missing items. The rework rate at some steps was over 80 percent, meaning that four out of five grants were returned to an upstream step because of a problem. There were three different checkpoints in the process, but none was effective in finding errors. Finally, they learned that when someone in OSR came across a problem, they emailed the relevant senior leader, who, thanks to an overflowing calendar and email inbox, often took days to respond.

The daily fifteen-minute meeting that focused on reviewing the performance data and building a joint understanding of the process led to rapid improvements. Simple changes to the IT systems eliminated redundant data entry. Having a face-to-face conversation each day allowed rapid information exchange so that people didn't have to wait for emails to get questions answered. In the space of just a month, the percentage of grants that were approved in less than ten days went from 0 to 50 percent. The culture in OSR was already changing as the team grew more comfortable surfacing issues that made their work difficult.

Once the team understood the basic steps required to open a new account, they created a simple system, what we call a visual board, to depict and track the flow of grants through the system. Each major step in the process was represented by a box drawn on a whiteboard. Each new grant was written on a sticky note, and its progress through the account setup process could be easily tracked as it moved from box to box. Now the entire team could see when a grant was stuck—its sticky note wasn't moving—and they used the daily meeting to surface and resolve the issue and get the work moving.

The watershed moment for the project happened a few weeks after the visual board was created. As the team updated the board each day, sticky notes started piling up in the box labeled "account creation," the step in the process where the new account was actually created in the accounting system. One day in the meeting, the person responsible for that step, feeling the pressure of a growing backlog, said, "I'm not getting a lot of value out of this process, it's taking time away from the work I'm supposed to be doing getting that pile of accounts created." This is a typical response. Nobody likes being the bottleneck, and time spent away from working on it feels wasted. But it wasn't her fault. There was more work than one person could do, even if she skipped the daily meeting. A quick negotiation with her supervisor led to another person being moved to that activity, and the work began to flow more quickly.

The team also started tracking the most common "blockers," their word for issues that prevented grants from moving forward. Many blockers could be resolved within the group. For example, making sure that the team members doing the early steps provided all the information necessary for those doing the later ones reduced rework and eliminated lots of back-and-forth on email. It also soon became clear that those in senior leadership—the ones who had complained the most about OSR—were often big blockers. They had to approve each new account, something they could do by responding to an automated email from the research office. More email sign-offs were required if the grant had special features, such as overhead restrictions. But these emails often languished in the bosses' inboxes for days or even weeks. As we have seen many times, unbeknownst to them, senior leaders were a big part of the delays that they were so concerned about.

A quick review of the data revealed that the overwhelming majority of grants were approved, so senior leadership oversight wasn't actually adding much value. Working with those leaders, the team defined clear escalation criteria so that only grants that were particularly risky or unusual were reviewed by the leadership team, and in a timely manner.

In the space of just over three months, OSR was able to deliver 100 percent of the new-account openings in less than ten days, something that had once been thought impossible without an entirely new IT system and additional people. Everyone was pumped about achieving the results, and working this way was a lot more satisfying.

Broad's effort to improve the process of opening new research accounts almost perfectly captures the essence of dynamic work design and its five principles. Start with the existing work, identify where it doesn't deliver required results, engage with people doing the work to diagnose the problem, experiment with interventions to solve the problem, and then reinvest the gains in the next improvement. Don't consider expensive automation until the work flows smoothly across administrative boundaries and all the people engaged in that work understand how it should be done. Resorting to technology before fixing the underlying design risks wasting money and embedding the original problem even deeper in the organization. In the OSR case, reconfiguring the human system was fast and nearly free and resulted in an approach that easily adapted to changing conditions. Using this approach, dynamic work design created permanent and ongoing gains in performance.

An Approach Guided by Five Principles

The dynamic work design approach is underpinned by five principles. These principles guide your efforts to surface and solve problems and ensure that your system is becoming ever more effective and adaptable.

Solve the Right Problem. Human beings are creatures of habit, and left to our own devices, we usually try to solve today's problems with the solutions that worked yesterday. When the account-opening process wasn't working well, Broad's leadership, completely unaware of their own contributions to the problem, immediately concluded that people and technology were the cause. *Solving the right problem* means relying on the basic elements of the scientific method to hold our instinctive responses at bay and being more conscious and deliberate in the search for a solution. Formulating a clear problem statement, free of solution or attribution, like "90 percent of our awards take more than twenty days to complete when it should take less than ten," is the first and most important step. Clearly separating the problem statement from possible diagnoses, such as "OSR doesn't know what they are doing," "Researchers don't care about the accounting," "Leadership is out of touch," or "Our old technology is impossible to work with," slows our habitual responses and forces us to take a fresh look at what is going wrong. It opens the possibility of finding simpler and more effective interventions that deliver immediate results. Effective solutions are often right in front of our eyes, but we are quite literally blinded by our past experience. As the OSR case demonstrates, approaching problems in a more structured fashion offsets the habitual blaming of people and technology and can reveal easy improvement opportunities in the design of the work.

Structure for Discovery. Video games are great environments for learning in part because the targets are always clear and our performance is continuously reported on the screen. How would any sports team play if it didn't know the score or how much time was left in the game? At the outset, the OSR team had no idea how they were doing; there was no single place to see an account's status in real time. They just knew that everyone was mad. *Structure for discovery* is a charge to ensure that, by design, everyone who does work knows why he or she is doing it, how it's going, and is engaged in the process of improving it. At Broad, a daily fifteen-minute meeting dedicated to reviewing progress and surfacing problems revealed lots of easily exercisable opportunities to get accounts opened more quickly, solutions discovered as a natural result of the structure of the meeting.

Connect the Human Chain. Though the business world is currently obsessed with artificial intelligence, work still flows from one human to the next (who may or may not use AI to do that work). The transfer of work from one person to the next rarely works well. People frequently do not get all the inputs they need to do their work correctly. Similarly, most people have only a vague sense of who receives the output of that work or what that person needs to do his or her job. *Connecting the human chain* means ensuring that the right information is transferred from one person to the next. Doing so often leads to significant gains.

Most descriptions of processes we see list what a person does, such as "reviews document," but don't capture what the work is supposed to produce or why the next person in the chain needs the output. In any work chain, the output of one person's work is the input of the next person's. These deliverables are the things that connect the workflow so that it produces the right product or service. "Review document and confirm that the data are entered correctly" better defines the output. Now we know what the outcome is supposed to be and where to look if we find that data are missing or wrong. A problem either signals an error by the person doing the tasks or that the world has changed and the work needs to be modified to keep the system in tune with the evolving environment.

The OSR human chain, for example, was broken in at least two ways. Someone doing a given step in the process often didn't get the information she needed from her upstream colleague, thus forcing her to either guess or send another email to get the needed information. Similarly, senior leaders sitting above the work didn't realize that they were often the bottleneck in account approval. Fixing these broken connections eliminated rework and sped the flow of accounts through the system. The only technology required was a wall with sticky notes to facilitate a productive conversation.

Regulate for Flow. At the outset, the OSR team was overloaded and overwhelmed. Researchers, not wanting to wait for such a slow process, exacerbated the problem by charging work to other accounts, a mess that OSR would later spend precious hours cleaning up, further degrading system productivity. More generally, when work systems are overloaded, like cars on a highway on Friday afternoon, progress comes to a halt. All work systems need a method to *regulate for flow*, meaning that new tasks only enter the system when there is available capacity, thereby ensuring that work is always moving. Regulating for flow both increases productivity (often dramatically) and, when it doesn't, makes the next problem visible, creating a system for revealing the next opportunity for improvement. As the OSR team got a handle on the volume of its work, it became clear, thanks to the pile of sticky notes that weren't moving, that the bottleneck was at the new-account-creation step. Now the entire team could physically see the next problem to solve.

Visualize the Work. There is no "shop floor" for knowledge work. You can't watch accounts moving down an assembly line, nor can you observe scientists manufacturing breakthroughs. In the world of knowledge generation and transfer, the work exists in people's to-do lists, email inboxes, and other IT systems. Putting the first four principles in place often requires a method that allows you to *visualize the work*. Creating a simple visual management system using a whiteboard and sticky notes allowed the OSR team to track the flow of grants and see when and where work was moving and not moving. A good visual management system is more than a scorecard that reports progress against targets. It is a virtual shop floor showing the status and location of each piece of work. Now those doing the work and those supervising it could see bottlenecks and other problems to be solved.

Each of the dynamic work design principles can help you improve your organization's work. The real magic, however, comes in recognizing that when work has been designed based on the five principles, it constantly improves and adjusts to changing conditions. Just as a well-designed video game directs our efforts to the next skill to be mastered, assessing work against the principles naturally points you to the next problem to be solved and directs the right people toward it. With time, the daily OSR meeting became a forum for spotting the next opportunity for increasing the flow of grant awards and directing the right resources to capitalize on that opportunity. Working this way is both more effective and more fun. It can also be transformative.

Transforming the Lab

The lab's efforts to use the approach and supporting principles of dynamic work design started in the summer of 2012. A month after Sheila finished her EMBA, she and her leadership team attended our two-day executive education class on dynamic work design. At the time, as we described above, they were deeply mired in the cycle of fighting fires with endless work-arounds. A follow-up dinner and discussion with Don revealed both the target—get samples through the lab faster—and two potential diagnoses. First, there was no alignment among the lab's overall goals, short-term targets, and actual activities (they had not structured their work for discovery). Second, the lab had way too much work in the system (they had no method for regulating the flow of work).

Both problems were predictable consequences of their success. The lab had grown out of the Human Genome Project, and their initial target was crystal clear: solve the formidable technical challenges associated with analyzing human DNA. But the lab's success created an entirely new industry that now had customers in the form of Broad's researchers looking to process thousands of DNA samples and use the emerging science of genomics to better understand a variety of diseases. In its early days, the Broad genomics lab operated much like a startup, pursuing multiple opportunities simultaneously in the hope of making breakthroughs. Significant growth now required them to operate more like an established business, but they hadn't regularly revisited the alignment between their goals and their actions. Without clear targets, everything looked like a good idea, and like a startup with rapidly evolving technology, there was never a shortage of cool things to work on. Saying yes to all of these opportunities was also an express lane into overload and firefighting.

As working scientists, the Broad Institute lab staff members were accustomed to applying the first principle—solve the right problem—to their work in biology and chemistry. Given the chaos in the lab, however, they rarely directed those skills to the issues that impeded operational performance. Most of the day was focused on getting the next sample out the door, not on figuring out why there was so much instability.

Redirecting their deep skill in structured problem-solving to the performance of the lab (as opposed to specific scientific challenges) required creating an environment more conducive to discovery. An offsite meeting focused on goal setting constituted the first step. Discussions with researchers helped to reinforce the *why* behind their work—they were literally speeding (or not) the progress of medical science—and resulted in three overarching goals for the lab: to provide the best services (premium), to lead the science (pioneering), and to respond to and anticipate the needs of their customers (they made up the word *presponsive* to capture this goal). Each of these goals was translated into annual targets with supporting metrics. Not surprisingly, improving the performance of the lab was on the critical path to most of their targets. A flip chart from a meeting in 2013 shows "all cycle times reduced by 30 percent" as a key goal for the year. A hand-drawn graph added to a whiteboard in the lab tracked their progress. A daily meeting in front of that graph to review progress and surface problems represented their first effort to connect the human chain.

At the outset, it was hard to know which problem to tackle first. The failure to regulate the flow of their work led to a chaotic work environment. To bring the workload under control, the team abandoned the practice of pushing samples from one step to the next without regard for whether the people at the next step were ready to handle it. In its place, they created a specific number of physical "parking spaces" where samples could sit in between each pair of steps in the process. They also instituted a rule whereby a technician in charge of a given process step could work on the next sample only if there was an empty parking space downstream of that operation. If there is an empty box, fill it. If not, don't produce more until one opens. In the meantime, work with the supervisor to find somewhere else to help. As we discuss in more detail in Chapter 6, this approach is similar to the traffic controls that prevent gridlock by restricting the number of cars allowed to enter the highway. It also quickly redeploys people to places where help is needed. Almost immediately, work started flowing more quickly and the number of samples completed increased. Delivery times, and their predictability, also improved.

Visualizing the flow of work using the parking space system made it clear to everyone where samples were moving (the work was going as planned) and where they were stuck. Simple rules for escalating issues when work stopped helped further connect the human chain so that problems now got immediate attention from the person or people best equipped to resolve them. The parking space setup allowed the system to "ask" for help when and where it was most needed. Much as happened in the OSR project, many of the early problems were easy to solve, akin to figuring out the buttons in a new video game. In some cases, the solution involved teaching staff a simple skill ("Handle the vial this way") or trick ("Don't start the robot until you're ready"). In others, an easy modification to the process or its supporting IT system got the work moving. In one case, spending a few thousand dollars on a new piece of equipment, an issue previously hidden by the chaos, effectively doubled the system's output. Problems that required more effort were assigned to sub-teams for a more structured inquiry.

Over the course of the first few years using dynamic work design, the team surfaced and solved thousands of problems. Many of the problems were resolved by a single technician working with a supervisor; a few made it all the way up to the senior leadership team. During this time, one technician discovered a more effective way to use the expensive reagents necessary for a key process step and saved the lab more than a million dollars annually. As the system grew more stable, thanks to ongoing problem-solving and design improvements, overall performance continued to improve.

Using the approach and principles of dynamic work design, the team cut the sample processing time by more than 50 percent in the first year. By 2016, the average time required to analyze a sample and return the associated data to the researcher had fallen from 120 days to less than 20. Even better, the predictability of those times improved dramatically. As researchers gained confidence in the lab's ability to meet its promised delivery dates, they quit calling to complain. The vicious cycle of firefighting, expediting, and other workarounds started to reverse. With less time spent placating angry customers, Sheila and the team could focus even more time on improving the operation of the lab and tackling the increasingly difficult problems that remained.

Eventually, the lab team and project managers kicked Sheila out of the daily meeting—the same meeting that had once been so contentious that she dreaded attending it. Their motives were not selfless. The lab was running so well and capacity had grown so much that they were running out of samples to process. They asked Sheila to shift her focus. "Since you don't have to come to the meeting," they said, "maybe you could find us some more work to do?" This is genuine organizational change and a shift in the culture. The team was no longer reacting to complaints and playing catch-up. They were now in front of demand, creating new lines of business for Broad, winning against the competition, and building a growing share of the sequencing industry. They weren't just competing and winning against "Robbie"; Robbie was on the run.

THE PATH TO REAL TRANSFORMATION

We are both avid cyclists (Don has ridden from the Pacific to the Atlantic, and Nelson is an avid Masters racer). Any regular rider will tell you that the experience of riding in a group differs widely depending on how your fitness compares with that of your companions. Slower riders are at the mercy of the group and can only react when faster riders pick up the pace. If the group accelerates up a hill or carries extra speed through a tight turn, you have to give maximum effort to catch up or risk getting "dropped" and riding home alone. Stronger riders, in contrast, get to deploy their advantages where it suits them (racers call this *burning matches*). If you are good on the hills, then a well-timed acceleration can leave your competitors behind; you are in control.

In 2012, the Broad team was struggling to stay in the pack; "Robbie" was always ahead. Broad couldn't meet the demands of customers for processing samples or developing technology. The team was falling ever-further behind, constantly burning matches to get an important sample processed or a new project completed. You can't reverse a vicious cycle in one move. The only path to real transformation is through incremental, directed problem-solving. At Broad, the work of problem-solving felt like a steady climb, not a sprint. From the outside, however, it looked dramatic, and the results that it generated put them far ahead of their competitors. A few years after Broad started using dynamic work design, visitors from other labs around the world looked at the lab's productivity in disbelief.

In modern organizations, as we'll see in Chapter 2, it often feels as if the system is managing you rather than you are managing it. In our experience, that feeling reverses when you can supply more than people are asking of you. When an organization can't meet the demand for its products or service, it's always tempting to work around the normal flow of work to make sure the most important work is prioritized. Soon those interventions go from being temporary stopgaps to being permanent parts of the process, and they trap the organization in a vicious cycle of firefighting where they can do nothing but react to the next crisis. When, in contrast, the organization gets ahead of that demand, it retakes control. For Broad, taking back control happened in two pieces. The lab team kicking Sheila out of the daily meeting signaled that they could now meet their customers' needs without extraordinary interventions and endless workarounds. Investing in further improvements was no longer a trade-off but something that peacefully coexisted with reliable delivery. Now the team could choose where to invest next. A similar transformation occurred in technology development (which we discuss more in Chapter 7). A process that reliably delivered new technology to the lab not only ensured parity with their competitors but also gave the team space to genuinely innovate. With the ability to decide what to work on next, the lab was now in full control of its own destiny.

Broad's operational transformation had a huge impact on its competitiveness. Their growing ability to process samples and develop new technology put them at the front of the pack. Their use of dynamic work design allowed them to define a rapidly evolving market in ways that suited their strengths. We'll come back to the next part of this story in Chapter 8.

Chapter 2

The Firefighting Trap

WHEN JUST "GETTING THINGS DONE" HURTS A
COMPANY'S ABILITY TO GROW, THRIVE, AND COMPETE

At the turn of the twentieth century, two lifelong friends, working in a ten-by-fifteen-foot shed in Milwaukee, Wisconsin, used a tomato can as the carburetor for the prototype of their company's first motorcycle. Through their shared passion for motorcycles, William Harley and Arthur Davidson built a company that grew to become one of the world's most iconic brands.

Seventy-six years later, fierce competition from Honda and a call on the company's bank loans nearly pushed Harley-Davidson to bankruptcy. To survive, the company laid off 40 percent of its employees, both union and salaried. It stripped out every bit of nonessential cost, and through sheer force of will, launched a new, technically superior V-Twin engine called the Evolution. The company was back in the game. Harley's subsequent turnaround became the stuff of legend (and business school cases). By the late 1980s, the company was making money again, and Harley dealers had long waiting lists, backed by large deposits, to buy new motorcycles. After an initial public offering in 1986, the stock price soared.

The can-do attitude that developed across the entire company during those dark days paid off handsomely. It also became firmly embedded in the company's culture. Was a critical project falling behind? A veteran manager would jump in and get it done. Was there a problem in the company's York, Pennsylvania, assembly plant? Engineers from Milwaukee would be on the next plane with a suitcase full of parts. Was the assembly line not producing quickly enough to meet the schedule? Union and salaried folks pitched in to get back on track. Everyone was justifiably proud of their ability to get things done, regardless of the circumstances.

Similar to the experience at the Broad Institute, Harley's reliance on such heroics eventually strained key business processes. Though the new Evolution engine was more reliable than its predecessor, overall warranty expense remained a problem. And despite the quick response of managers flying to troubled plants, as Harley developed an increasing array of new products, the process of launching them in the factory became increasingly chaotic. For example, one year a faulty taillight design required last-minute changes to the bulk of the product line and cost millions in warranty expense.

When, as noted earlier, senior executives commissioned a review of product development in the early 1990s, the authors concluded that Harley's process yielded products that were LEW: late, expensive, and wrong. The review also identified Harley's most seasoned, most can-do project managers—the ones who had literally saved the company—as one of the core problems. Their heroic efforts to get product out the door, by focusing on resolving the crisis without addressing its underlying cause, created the conditions for new problems to emerge, turning the project managers into unwitting *firefighting arsonists*. Well-intentioned efforts to get things done hamstrung the company's ability to grow, thrive, and compete. The company was getting increasingly good at managing symptoms but was making little progress in fixing the underlying process. Like Broad's, Harley's success in creating demand for their products had somehow trapped it in a state of increasing adrenaline-fueled chaos and frustration.

The firefighting-arsonist dynamic isn't unique to Harley. You've probably seen it in your organization. People work hard to deliver results, but despite good intentions, their efforts often leave more chaos in their wake. Efforts to "get sh*t done" leave lots of issues that impede performance, but those problems rarely get the attention they deserve. It's easy to blame those who constantly work around the system (at least if you aren't one of them), but the situation is more complex.

THE VICIOUS CYCLE OF FIREFIGHTING

Every organization benefits from leaders who can occasionally depart from standard processes to make things happen. These crisis-driven efforts are a kind of organizational medicine that occasionally needs to be swallowed. But the dose makes the poison. Well-intentioned efforts to "just get things done" can mire an organization in a vicious cycle of workarounds, production pressure, and increasingly short-sighted decisions. In this chapter, we show you how to harness those same good intentions to escape the firefighting trap and transform your company through a virtuous circle of growing capability and competitive opportunity. Before getting to solutions, however, we need to explain why firefighting, while debilitating in the long run, is remarkably seductive.

Two Ways of Thinking

Recall the first time you drove a route that you now travel regularly—say, from home to work. That first trip involved investing some effort and attention to detail, perhaps verifying the address and using your (modern!) GPS. During the trip your mind was fully engaged, and you may have experienced a little anxiety, particularly if you were running late or there was a lot of traffic.

Today, however, that trip takes zero planning and minimal mental effort. You might use the driving time to think through an upcoming presentation or to figure out what to make for dinner. Although we take it for granted, the transition from the first trip to the twentieth is remarkable. If you run a mile every day, your body will adapt, but three months later, though it will be easier, it's still hard work. In contrast, when you are dealing with the brain rather than muscles, an activity that once consumed time and energy quickly becomes almost effortless. Why?

The answer lies in psychology. Research has consistently found that we all have two basic ways of thinking: *automatic* and *conscious*. Or, as Daniel Kahneman famously dubbed them, *thinking fast* and *thinking slow*.[1] With repetition, driving to work becomes something you do on autopilot because, roughly speaking, your brain moves that activity from one cognitive system to the other. Understanding the differences between these two modes is the first step toward understanding how firefighting can inadvertently turn into arson.

The conscious-processing mode is the part of our cognitive system that we can direct, as in when you say, "I'm going to think about something." It is the domain of logic. Conscious processing also appears to be the part of our cognitive system that allows us to imagine a future for which we have no past experience. Cognitive scientists call this ability *mental simulation*. As we will discuss more in Chapter 3, this ability to envision alternate futures that are different from our past experience is central to both innovation and finding novel solutions to existing challenges. For example, the first person to envision summoning a taxi from a smartphone had to imagine a world of on-demand transportation despite having no such past experience. This can only be done via conscious processing.

While our conscious-processing function is powerful, its capacity is limited. On that initial drive to work you probably weren't thinking about much else, since your conscious processor was fully occupied. A few days later, however, driving to work is a breeze. You don't need a GPS or a map, and you use the time to think about other things. As a task is repeated, the automatic processor takes over and allows the brain to save its scarce conscious-processing capacity for more novel or complex situations.

The automatic mode operates differently from its front-office counterpart. While the conscious mode tackles problems logically, the automatic mode uses past experience to guide future actions. It follows rules, like "When I'm hungry, I should eat." When you get in your car to drive to work after months of commuting, your automatic processor identifies the task (getting to work), matches it to past experience (all the other days you drove to work), and supplies the actions to get you there. All of this happens with minimal use of conscious processing.

The automatic processor's tendency to use past experience to guide current actions is a mixed blessing. On the plus side, automatic processing is fast. It identifies patterns and reaches possible solutions far faster than the conscious mode can. Base-ball players who can pick up the fastball, traders who capitalize on minute changes in market pricing, and pilots who instantly react to changing conditions all rely on automatic processing. Conscious processing is too slow to execute any of these tasks.

On the negative side, automatic processing tends to be effective only when you receive immediate feedback on the consequences of your actions. For example, when children touch a hot stove and experience pain, they quickly learn not to do it again. When there is a delay between taking an action and receiving the outcome, the automatic processor is less likely to learn the right lesson. For example, when Nelson's two kids were young, getting them to eat their vegetables was a challenge. Claims that "broccoli is good for you" were wholly ineffective, even when accompanied by a dessert-incentive plan. While kids quickly learn to avoid touching a hot stove, they don't absorb a similar lesson about eating broccoli because there is a long delay between eating it and experiencing the health benefits.

If broccoli produced some immediate benefit—like when the cartoon character Popeye eats his spinach—a parent's job would be far easier. Similarly, if using good organizational practices—techniques like defining clear problem statements and using the "parking space" system to regulate its workflow—produced immediate gains, then the leader's job would be a lot easier. But that's not how automatic processing works, and that's where the difficulties start.

Better Before Worse

To see how automatic processing can seduce anyone into unwittingly becoming a firefighting arsonist, let's look at an example where efforts to solve problems quickly can end up making the whole system less stable and at greater risk of experiencing a major failure.

At Harley, every part on a motorcycle has a document called an *engineering print* that precisely defines the part's dimensions and other specs.[2] As Harley pushed to get new products launched in its factories, manufacturing engineers working on the line would sometimes discover a problem with a given part. Perhaps a bracket was just a little too big and, consequently, difficult to install. To get the assembly line running smoothly, the engineer might modify the process of making the part, perhaps adding a step to bend it a bit or round off one of its edges. On its own, this isn't necessarily a problem, and it could be critical to getting the assembly line running at full capacity. But the engineer now faces a decision: Does she stop her work and update the engineering print to reflect the change? Or does she just move to another part that needs attention (the next fire, of which there are always plenty), perhaps hoping that she will remember to go back and fix the documentation later?

It takes just a moment to choose between these two paths, but the consequences play out over weeks or months. If the engineer skips updating the print, the work gets done faster, more problems get solved, she avoids a distraction, and products get out the door quicker. However, accurate prints are critical to effective engineering. A design engineer working on next year's product might use that print when designing or redesigning an adjacent part, perhaps something that connects to the bracket. If the print is wrong, then there is a good chance that the new part won't fit, thereby introducing a defect in next year's model that might require another ad hoc modification—or even an accident or a recall.

Skipping the print update thus creates "better before worse" behavior (see Figure 2.1). The manufacturing engineer experiences a temporary gain in performance, for which she gets rewarded, and the product gets launched sooner. That's better. Meanwhile, the health of the overall system slowly erodes. The more mismatches there are between parts and prints, the more likely it is that design engineers will inadvertently create more defects that will require the expense, stress, and risk of firefighting. This pattern results in a conversation that is all too common on the factory floor: the design engineer asks why a part is not made to the print, and the manufacturing engineer answers that if they made it to the print, the part wouldn't work.

Such better-before-worse trade-offs were everywhere at Harley. More component testing reduced defects but delayed assembling a full prototype. More test miles improved reliability but reduced the time available to work out kinks on the assembly line. Trade-offs like this are ubiquitous in every organization. Every time you postpone maintenance on equipment, delay training, or fail to fully update a customer's information in your Customer Relationship Management system, you have traded an immediate but temporary gain for a delayed but permanent loss (see Figure 2.1).

ACTUAL PERFORMANCE

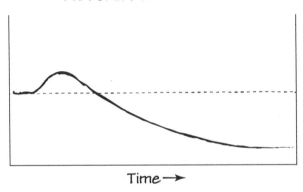

Time →

Figure 2.1. Performance in a better-before-worse situation

At some level, we all know that we should make such trade-offs sparingly. Throughout human history, wise writers have counseled us to balance current rewards against future possibilities. Proverbs 21:5 reads, "The plans of the diligent lead surely to abundance, but everyone who is hasty comes only to poverty." This notion also remains a staple of self-help guidance, captured in admonitions like Stephen Covey's "sharpen the saw." Consistent with this advice, most people change the oil in their cars, pay their mortgages, and go to the dentist.

So why doesn't this happen in organizations? It would be easy to blame the engineers or project managers, but several factors conspire against even the most well-meaning member of an organization.

To start, it's easy to learn the wrong lesson from fighting organizational fires. Recall that automatic processing tends to work best when there is a short delay between taking an action and getting the result. Not taking the time to update the print produces outcomes on two different timescales. Performance improves immediately—the product gets launched sooner—but next year's launch may be even more challenging, thanks to more defects, and leave even less time to update documentation. It's thus likely that the manufacturing engineer will learn to focus on the "better" part (since it happens right away) and not fully consider the "worse" part, since it only happens with a delay. Moreover, postponing or skipping the print update feels good. The product had a problem, the intervention fixed it, and now it's rolling off the assembly line ready to go to customers. We'd all like more of that in our lives. As happens in almost all organizations, everyone responded with praise and appreciation when one of Harley's experienced and dedicated project leads got a project over the finish line. In contrast, engineers who kept their documentation up-to-date were rarely recognized.

Most managers understand that a purely short-term focus can't last forever. Our manufacturing engineer probably ruminates, "I'll get those prints updated as soon as the product is launched." The error comes in not realizing the full extent of the damage he is doing to the underlying process and that said damage will require even more short-term measures. Next year's launch will be even more chaotic and require even more short-cuts. There is always another critical task waiting to be done—one that will also produce important and immediate results. Well-intentioned leaders can easily get stuck in a cycle akin to that of the addict who has a few drinks to get through the day and plans on turning it around tomorrow. The addict doesn't realize that thanks to today's drinking, tomorrow will be that much more difficult.

Managers also overemphasize the benefits of shortcuts and workarounds because they are usually easier to measure and reward than the benefits that come from long-run investments. As one manager we interviewed put it, "Nobody ever gets credit for a defect that never happened." Even if the manufacturing engineers *know* that they are creating future trouble, they will almost certainly be rewarded for their efforts in the present. Their products will get out the door faster, and they will develop reputations for being hard-nosed leaders who can get things done. They may also be promoted faster and leave behind unfinished work for their successor. Countless managers have been lucky enough to be promoted before the "better" part turns into the "worse" part, virtually guaranteeing that the organization won't learn from the full consequences of working this way.

Survival Methodology

Because workarounds and shortcuts work so well and are easy to reward, they often become embedded in an organization's culture. Consider another finding from our work at Harley. To combat LEW, Harley invested considerable effort in creating a new product development process. The new approach was enshrined in a book that they called their *methodology*. Harley's development approach was based on best practices similar to those promoted by other leading companies at the time. Despite this investment, however, projects still regularly suffered significant hiccups that cost time and money. Subsequent investigations frequently revealed that these problems resulted from the engineers skipping one or more steps in the official process.

Why weren't Harley's engineers following the methodology that the company had invested so much money to create? When we asked them, they said that while they aspired to follow the official process step by step, it often was simply not feasible. In some cases Harley didn't have enough of the necessary infrastructure, such as testing equipment. In others, following all the prescribed steps would have resulted in missing an important deadline.

As an informal experiment, we handed their most seasoned project leaders—the best firefighters—an overview of the official process and a pen and asked them to cross out the steps that could be skipped when they were under the gun to meet a deadline. The steps that remained, the ones that had to be done to get something to the market, were remarkably consistent. There were, it turned out, two development processes at work. The official process was written down, which everyone tried to follow but often couldn't because they couldn't get their work done on time. The second process wasn't written down anywhere, but every engineer at Harley knew what it was and how to use it. We started calling this second approach *survival methodology*, because, when under pressure, the engineers knew what they needed to do to survive. Many of them had learned this process when it was necessary for the company to stay afloat; there is no point in focusing on tomorrow when there might not be one. So, they focused on the minimal set of steps needed to get something done. Like the manufacturing engineer on the shop floor, they were rewarded for it. As one of the leads said, "I've gotten where I am by delivering projects under difficult situations. I had a date, and I did what it took to hit it, good, bad, or indifferent."

You probably have your own version of survival methodology. Like Harley's project leads, we all learn to work around an increasingly broken, dysfunctional management system. Sheila at the Broad Institute was so good at it that they made her the lab's manager. Eric Lander, the institute's director, knew that if he asked her to do something, she'd get it done. Resorting to the occasional firefight is not necessarily debilitating and often helps performance. Firefighting flips from helpful to hurtful when it becomes more than a way to get through a temporary hiccup and instead becomes the process. When firefighting is the only way work gets done, it crowds out the efforts to solve problems and build the long-term capabilities that would have prevented those fires in the first place.

Survival methodology is full of workarounds: skipping training, skimping on testing, neglecting data, rushing analyses, canceling meetings, postponing travel, pressuring colleagues to change priorities, staying up late, and inventing new, faster methods on the fly. Sometimes these workarounds represent genuine innovation, but they are largely hidden from view—they are survival methodology—so no one else can benefit or learn from them, and even a great solution creates coordination problems if it doesn't become part of the common approach to doing work.

Blaming the Individuals

Things go wrong a lot in an organization mired in firefighting. Each hiccup has a specific cause—a burned-out bearing or a software bug—and a specific person or team who was supposed to prevent it by maintaining the bearing or checking the software. So what happens when something bad happens and those workarounds and shortcuts are inevitably discovered as the cause?

Unless senior leaders have a deep sense of the underlying work, they are likely to blame the people closest to the problem rather than the slow but debilitating slide into firefighting and inadequate capability. This bias is so prevalent that in psychology it's known as the fundamental attribution error: the tendency to attribute a problem to the person who is closest to it, even if the person had nothing to do with it. We vividly remember a meeting in which one of Don's Harley colleagues claimed that the project leads who managed through firefighting skipped steps because they enjoyed it, likening the feeling they got from departing from the process to sexual release (though the words he used were a bit different).

In most cases, however, this diagnosis is at best misguided and often just wrong. Don's colleagues on Harley's leadership team appeared to have no sense of the impossible bind that the system created for those charged with getting things done. When an organization is mired in the headaches that come with persistent underinvestment in capability (both human and technical) and scant attention to ongoing problem-solving, people depart from standard processes because that's the only way to get their work done. As one manager said in an interview, "We could either follow the process or do the work, and the work wasn't going to wait."

When leaders assume that the problems are due to the actions of specific individuals and teams rather than to a general decline in the health of the system, their interventions tend to worsen an already bad situation. Penalties for problems and shortfalls go up because "those people just need a kick in the pants." The volume of monitoring and reporting increases because "we need to stop people from screwing up." As one project manager Nelson interviewed at Ford said, "I knew my project was in trouble when I was asked to give hourly updates."

It's an almost perfect recipe for an unhappy, unproductive organization and, in some cases, disaster.

FIREFIGHTING IN ACTION

Harley's descent into firefighting, while costly, is far from the most extreme case we have observed. Everything from the current troubles with Boston's subway system to the meltdown of the US housing market to Boeing's troubles with the 737 MAX have similar roots. To see the downward spiral created by endemic firefighting, consider the case of BP's Texas City refinery, a large crude oil processing facility an hour's drive south of Houston.

In March 2005, a devastating explosion at the refinery killed fifteen people and injured almost two hundred others. An investigation by the US Chemical Safety and Hazard Investigation Board concluded that "the combination of cost-cutting, production pressures, and failure to invest caused a progressive deterioration of safety at the refinery."[3] Even more damning, in the years leading up to the accident, BP had conducted several audits that highlighted the declining state of the facility. However, the board's report concluded, the company had been unwilling to make the necessary investments.

At first glance, it's hard to understand how BP could allow this tragedy to unfold. The company seemingly had everything needed to prevent it. BP recruited from top schools, paid their employees generously, and was led by visionary CEO Lord John Browne, who had helmed the company through its "golden period of expansion and diversification."[4] Moreover, the knowledge required to run an oil refinery safely was freely available in the industry and widely circulated within the company. At the time of the Texas explosion, BP was one of the world's largest, most profitable companies. More than in most other industries, the people running oil and gas companies understand the need to invest for the long run. BP would often spend more than a decade and billions of dollars to develop a new oil field.

Many commentators attributed the incident to callous senior leaders who simply didn't value the lives of those who worked in the company's refineries. A closer look suggests that the situation was both more complex and more insidious.

Oil refining is a cyclical business. Refiners are intermediaries between oil producers and consumers. They make money only when the input, crude oil, is cheap and the outputs, gasoline and other products, are expensive. Being caught between two unstable markets causes profitability to fluctuate wildly. When times are good, companies like BP can make billions, and when things aren't going well, breaking even is a significant challenge.

The time period preceding the Texas City explosion, the 1990s, was an unusually difficult price environment for oil refiners. Industry veterans knew that the famine would eventually end and hoped that the feast was just around the corner. But for more than ten years, far longer than the usual down cycle, margins hovered at or below break even.

Starting in the early 1990s, the facility (then under the ownership of Amoco) began cutting costs and postponing capital investments. A retrospective analysis done after the explosion showed that the capital budget had fallen by 84 percent between 1992 and 2002. With the benefit of hindsight, such decisions might seem obviously wrong, but consider what it felt like to manage the facility in 1995. You are, at best, breaking even, and survival is the order of the day. Better days might be just around the corner, but you can't be sure. What would you do? You'd probably do your best to control costs until prices turned up.

Postponing training or an expensive capital upgrade for a year or two doesn't seem like a big deal. Most organizations engage in this kind of cost management every day. You do something similar every time you postpone a software upgrade on your phone or computer. And it worked, at least if no one looked too closely. The facility kept its doors open and its cost-conscious managers were rewarded for their ability to negotiate such a difficult environment.

But the environment didn't get better. By 1999, when BP and Amoco merged, the margin famine had been underway for almost a decade. Consistent with its reputation as a group of hard-nosed managers (BP had been widely praised by journalists and investors for its financial discipline), BP challenged the facility to cut costs by 25 percent. Belts were tightened further. For example, the training budget was cut by more than 50 percent, and the training staff reduced from twenty-eight people to eight. Margins did eventually improve, and the facility began to earn record profits. But after a decade of cutting costs and seeing results improve, BP had "learned" its lesson about how to manage refineries. In a site visit in 2004, less than a year before the accident, Browne challenged the facility to cut maintenance costs by another 25 percent.

At that point, as had been predicted by several audits and reviews, it was only a matter of time before something went wrong. The facility had eroded so significantly that after the incident it took more than two years and billions of dollars of investment to return the facility to safely producing at full capacity. Later, the plant was sold to a competitor for a price that was approximately equal to the value of the inventory (the oil and gas stored there). BP had essentially given it away.

WORSE BEFORE BETTER

Though the Texas City accident is tragically extreme, the decisions that led up to it are not unusual. We have seen versions of this vicious cycle in almost every organization we have ever visited. While, fortunately, in most companies the descent into firefighting doesn't have a body count, it does waste resources, drive away customers, disenfranchise employees, and make work exceedingly frustrating. So, how do you escape it? The answer might appear simple: don't succumb to the pressure to boost performance, and never skimp on the fundamentals. Sadly, once you are in the firefighting trap, executing what can seem like common sense is harder than it looks. To see why, let's return to Harley.

Imagine that Harley decided to purge the system of firefighting and survival methodology once and for all. The project leads who had grown up in the chaotic world of firefighting would be benched, every previously skipped test would be completed, every engineer would attend the training necessary to get up to speed with the latest tools, and every project would follow the official methodology to the letter. They would also do a complete audit of all the engineering documentation and identify all the part/print mismatches and fix them once and for all. Now, what happens?

ACTUAL PERFORMANCE

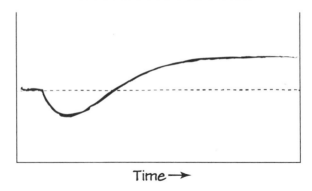

Time →

Figure 2.2. Performance in a worse-before-better situation

The results are shown in Figure 2.2. Just as skipping documentation and training doesn't immediately create defects, performance doesn't immediately improve when you start investing in the health of the system. Instead, time is required for such investments to increase productivity. Consequently, whereas the earlier decision to skimp on future productivity produced a better-before-worse pattern, the decision to increase investment produces the opposite pattern: worse-before-better.

The root of the worse-before-better pattern of behavior lies in the fact that the underlying process doesn't immediately get healthier when you start focusing on it. Starting a fire-prevention program doesn't immediately eliminate fires. Thus, when effort is redirected toward improvement and away from getting products and projects out the door through workarounds, the results take an immediate hit and recover only as the process starts to improve. We have studied and helped facilitate change efforts for over thirty years, and in our experience, the failure to understand and manage worse-before-better is the single biggest reason that change efforts do not succeed.

Just as it's easy to learn that firefighting works, it's easy to reach a similarly wrong conclusion when faced with a worse-before-better pattern. Every time we increase our invest-ment in the underlying process, performance goes down rather than up. If Harley had tried to fix everything at once, new prod-uct development would have slowed to a crawl and the com-pany would have been punished by customers and the financial markets. Even if Harley's leadership was wise enough to under-stand that performance would decline before it improved, they'd still have to forecast both the length and depth of the dip. It is often unclear whether a new tool or technique will work, and so it's always possible that the behavior pattern is worse-before-really-bad rather than worse-before-better.

Understanding worse-before-better conceptually is not enough. Even if their leaders had "gone for it," Harley still might not have waited long enough to determine whether their efforts were worth it. And even if they were patient, their shareholders might not have been. Far too many managers are removed for "poor performance" only to see their successors reap the benefits of the increased investment in capability.

ESCAPING THE DIP WITH DYNAMIC WORK DESIGN

We first started thinking about dynamic work design when we were looking for an alternative to survival methodology. We knew there was a better way for Harley to survive than relying exclusively on firefighting. We could see the firefighting trap at play and wanted to help companies like Harley escape it.

We rejected the approach embodied in most large-scale change programs that attempts to fix everything with one big overarching solution. This can, at first glance, appear sen-sible to an organization mired in firefighting, where every day reveals another problem. "The system is broken," say the decision-makers. "Let's fix everything now." But in a world in which you still have to deliver results, thanks to worse-before-better, large-scale initiatives often contain the seeds of their own demise.

We have seen several companies attempt to fix everything at once. They make significant investments in their underlying processes, only to abandon them when performance begins to degrade. In the research for his doctoral dissertation, Nelson studied Ford Motor Company's electronics division (now Visteon) and its effort to completely overhaul the product design and delivery processes. They changed everything from the computers they used to the suppliers on which they relied. Despite millions of dollars of investment, it took them years to reap the full benefits. Their engineers didn't have time to learn the new tools while also doing their work. As one engineer said, describing the new computers in every cube, "We all now have very expensive paperweights on our desks." (We'll further explore the problems of big initiatives in Chapter 9.)

Rather than jumping into large-scale change at Harley, Don (with Nelson's help) took a more modest tack, one that we still follow today. As a first step, the project leads, including the ones caught in the firefighting-arsonist mode, began reporting to the Project Management Office (PMO), which Don then led. The PMO was more than a tracking function that reported milestones back to finance. Instead, project status was reviewed biweekly, and the goal of the meeting was to surface and solve problems quickly and publicly, so that everyone could benefit. Initially, project leads were not happy. The meeting seemed like additional, bureaucratic oversight that just slowed them down even more. But the meeting soon became a critical venue for surfacing and solving problems and, where possible, removing barriers. New ideas, rather than being private workarounds, were now quickly vetted and, where appropriate, shared across the system. The official methodology increasingly became a living document that reflected an evolving balance of time-honored techniques and newly emerging methods, many created by project leads themselves. Knowledge gained from the meetings was also used to help guide investments in labs, technology, and people that removed real bottlenecks.

The former firefighting arsonists were finally getting the help they needed to get their work done. They responded by increasingly working within the system, rather than around it, and by helping improve it in the process. Don may not have always been their best friend, but they began to put their creative energies into improving their projects in ways that also contributed to the health of the product development process.

As one example, the teams in the plant often complained that the designs they received had lots of problems that had to be fixed on the shop floor. Working together, the plant teams agreed to accept shorter lead times for receiving prototypes in return for designs with fewer problems. To meet this challenge, the design engineers worked to find new ways to uncover problems earlier, pushing the envelope on computer modeling, developing more rigorous testing, and collaborating more with the engineers in the plants. Both teams started to see that better work on the design side saved massive amounts of time once they started building physical products in the plants. The cycle of firefighting was starting to break. The project leads still focused on delivering their projects on time, but now they were doing it in a way that could be repeated and improved upon next time. Each gain was another brick in the foundation of a healthy product development system. The senior leaders, rather than creating more reports and meetings about why things were going wrong, were now supporting the process with expertise and resources when and where they were needed.

The change that Harley experienced wasn't easy. It was the product of lots of hard work from many people. But it did happen, and it is possible in your organization. You'll see how and why throughout the rest of this book as we detail each element of dynamic work design.

Part II

Principles

Chapter 3

Solve the Right Problem

IT'S HARD TO SEE SOMETHING WHEN
YOUR BRAIN ISN'T LOOKING FOR IT

WHAT PROBLEM ARE YOU TRYING TO SOLVE?

In 1999, after Don completed his work on Harley's engine project, he was promoted to be the general manager of the company's Capitol Drive engine plant near Milwaukee (one of two that made Harley engines). The business was doing well. Sales and profits had been increasing for a decade, and there was a two-year waiting list to get a bike. Harley was even doing well in countries outside the United States and was particularly proud that in Japan they were now selling more heavyweight motorcycles than Honda. The market buzz about Harley was building as the company headed toward its one hundredth anniversary in 2003, when 350,000 riders would converge on Milwaukee for a three-day street party.

Don's first year as general manager had, he thought, gone well. Quality and cost improved, the annual new model launches happened on time, and the number of engines and transmissions produced increased steadily. The factory had been cleaned up, with greenery placed along the main aisle, and the team gave tours to more than twenty-five thousand people every year. The place looked good, ran well, and everyone who worked there had reason to be proud. Don was confident that his facility would compare favorably with other manufacturing plants. So, when a representative from Ford Motor Company asked if Harley would host a tour for nearly two hundred participants in a local Ford training seminar, Don readily agreed. His confidence, it turned out, was misplaced.

Ford sent an advance team to audit the facility and plan the tour. After spending four hours examining how the plant operated, the team went to Don's office with a tough message. They wouldn't be using the plant for the seminar because it wasn't up to Ford's standards. In Ford's view, Don's plant was missing many of the basic elements of modern manufacturing. They weren't too kind in how they told him either. The facility "sucked," they said.

The remarks stung. Every indicator, from shop floor numbers to Harley's stock price, said that Don, the plant, and the company were at the top of their game. How could he be so deluded? He was also a bit embarrassed since, as he recalls, he had told his executive team colleagues that Ford was using his plant as an example of good manufacturing practice.

"What am 1 missing?" he thought. Harley had been an early adopter of several innovative techniques in manufacturing, including just-in-time production, continuous improvement, and employee involvement. The company was performing better against its Asian competitors than any other US auto company (which made getting a tough message from Ford all the more difficult). Don had spent most of his working life in factories and, based on that experience, felt the plant was running well. But he was running short of ideas for finding the next big gain required to meet the increasing needs of the company and the expectations of his boss. The comments from Ford fed this concern and were unsettling. He was convinced that he was missing something big.

For decades Toyota has been considered one of the most effective and efficient manufacturers in the world. In the hope that understanding the Toyota approach might help him unlock the next round of gains in the factory, Don tracked down Hajime Oba, one of Toyota's top manufacturing experts, and convinced him to come to Milwaukee. Mr. Oba had worked with Toyota suppliers in the United States for several years to help them learn how to work to Toyota standards and methods. Mr. Oba agreed to visit Capitol Drive in a few weeks.

The day Mr. Oba arrived, Don started with a presentation about Harley, its history, and its recent successes. After a few minutes, Mr. Oba politely asked to forgo the slides. Could they walk through the plant instead? While they walked, Don began telling Mr. Oba about all the great things that had been accomplished. But Mr. Oba didn't seem to be listening. He asked to see the shipping dock and then the assembly line and proceeded to give himself a tour of the plant. Don (much to the amusement of the employees) was relegated to following Mr. Oba and trying to keep up. After about forty-five minutes, Mr. Oba suddenly headed back to Don's office. He went to the whiteboard and drew a detailed overview of the plant, showing how the flow of production moved through the component machining areas, paint shop, main assembly, and shipping.

"This is how I observed the plant to be operating. Is this correct?" Mr. Oba asked.

"Yes," Don replied, thinking that was pretty good for a forty-five-minute walk. "You have it right."

Mr. Oba drew a circle around one area of the assembly line on the whiteboard and made a note next to it. "Please make this change," he said. "When you have finished, call me and I will come back and tell you what to do next." Then he started to leave.

Don stopped him. Not only was Don looking for a much bigger solution than fixing one small problem in the plant, but he also wasn't used to taking orders without understanding why or where they were going. He was the guy who was paid to figure stuff out and get everyone else moving. That's how he got to be general manager. He would need to understand much more about the plan and be convinced that the intervention would be big enough to deliver the results his boss was looking for. When Mr. Oba sat back down, Don began asking him the questions you would typically ask a prospective consultant: How much is this going to cost? How long will it take? How much money will be saved? When and where should we start?

Mr. Oba interrupted him. "Mr. Kieffer, can you please tell me the problem you want to solve?"

Don was a little bewildered by having his question answered by another question, but he played along. "Mr. Oba," he said, "the problem I am trying to solve is that we have made all this progress and yet Ford told me I suck. I want you to help me implement the Toyota production system so we can keep improving."

"Hmm, OK," Mr. Oba replied. Then, after a moment's thought, he said, "So, Mr. Kieffer, you want to implement the Toyota production system?"

"Yes," said Don.

"When do you want to start?" Mr. Oba asked.

"Now, of course, I'm ready to go."

"So, you want to start right now?"

"Yes," Don said firmly, his impatience rising. "Now."

"In that case, Mr. Kieffer," said Mr. Oba, "please answer the question I asked you. What is the problem you are trying to solve?"

The meeting did not end well. Don was frustrated with what felt like a word game. Mr. Oba was not happy either. He had come to help, but Don didn't seem to want to take his advice. So, he left. There was a line of people waiting to work with Mr. Oba, and they would gladly do what he asked.

What Do You See?

Luckily, Mr. Oba had brought several team members with him who wanted to work with Harley. They stayed behind for a few minutes and explained that if Don wanted Mr. Oba's help, he had to work Mr. Oba's way. To get him to come back, they said, you need to define a specific problem in one small area of the shop that we can work on with you.

The interaction left Don a bit thrown. That night, Mr. Oba's question—What problem are you trying to solve?—was stuck in his head and he couldn't sleep. Don had built his career on solving problems quickly and effectively. He had given plant tours to George W. Bush, the Blue Angels, and executives from around the world. He had dealt with the press and was an accomplished public speaker. He wasn't easily rattled, but somehow Mr. Oba had touched a nerve. By the next morning, Don had figured out what was bothering him.

Mr. Oba's question reminded him of his early experience on the shop floor: go to where the problem is happening; understand what is really going on and why; run quick experiments to get things moving; verify you have a working solution; and then make it more robust and permanent. Working this way had been satisfying—and good for Don's career.

But now that he had moved up the ladder, it was no longer feasible to be involved in solving every small problem. As an executive, Don was expected to solve big problems by proposing big initiatives that promised big gains. Installing the Toyota production system in his plant was, Don thought, exactly the kind of big change that he (and Harley) needed to get to the next level (and not suck). It was also the kind of effort that would make his boss feel that Don was acting like a senior leader. Mr. Oba, however, was pushing in the opposite direction, asking Don to define a small, specific problem, do a thorough investigation, and deliver a quick, localized result. Mr. Oba was widely known for quickly turning poor-performing organizations around, but Don didn't see how starting with a very small problem would get him the big results he needed.

Don got a hint of the answer when one of Mr. Oba's team members, Scott Borg, asked him to stand at the busiest location in the middle of the plant and tell him what he saw. After a minute of hesitation, trying to figure out what Scott meant, Don just pointed out what was in front of him. "I see a fork truck driver talking to a machine operator," he said.

"Is that where the fork truck driver is supposed to be?" asked Scott. "And is that what he is supposed to be doing right now?"

Don walked through the plant every day, but Scott's queries suddenly put it in a new light. "I don't know how the fork truck drivers organize their work," he admitted, "or if they even do." Don now had a lot of questions about how fork truck drivers moved material around the facility. Combining a careful look at the work as it was happening with asking better questions seemed to offer a path to more improvement.

THE POWER OF THE PROBLEM STATEMENT

When we teach our dynamic work design course at MIT, many of the students are in the same place Don was before he met Mr. Oba. They have built their careers on solving big problems and getting things done. Most of them also have training in one or more structured problem-solving methods, such as Six Sigma's DMAIC (Define, Measure, Analyze, Intervene, Control). But they are now focused on larger complex issues that impact their organizations in big ways. When we announce that the class is organized around a small problem-solving project and that they need to use a structured approach, they often protest that they are way past small problems and rote methods. We have come to recognize this pushback as a sure sign that, like pre-Oba Don, they are still thinking about the world in static terms. A change like implementing the Toyota production system, they think, is something you do once and then you are done. But Mr. Oba was pushing Don to create a system that is constantly learning and improving. When you think more dynamically, small projects, though they may initially feel insignificant, become the engine driving larger ongoing transformation. When our students finally "get it," the results can be dramatic.

Consider the case of Mike Morales. He took our dynamic work design course about fifteen years after Don met Mr. Oba, when he was president of Corporación Industrial, a Panamanian manufacturer whose products included corrugated boxes.

The basic process of making a corrugated box is straightforward. Large sheets of paper are glued together to create pieces of corrugated cardboard. The pieces are then cut to size, folded, and glued to make a box. In practice, however, mailing boxes entails moving heavy loads among large complex machines, and the process had never been quite as efficient as the management team had hoped. The paper used to make the boxes was often damaged during movement between operations or wasted because of incorrect cutting, a problem Corporación called paper losses. Paper represented 80 percent of the company's production costs, so losses hurt the bottom line.

Much like Don, Mike was an experienced operator and wasn't afraid to tackle hard problems. He likes taking on big challenges, including having successfully summited Mount Everest before attending MIT. Back on solid ground, he and his team were trying to reduce their paper losses. They had recently spent $3.5 million in equipment upgrades and another $500,000 in training. Despite that effort and expense, paper losses had risen from 18 percent to 21 percent the previous year.

When Mike took our class, he decided to take another crack at the problem. We started by asking Mike to formulate a clear statement of the problem he was trying to solve. He tried: "The operators don't know what to do" and "The equipment doesn't work." Neither of these was, however, the real problem. They were diagnoses, revealing Mike's assumptions about who or what was to blame. As he talked through these assumptions, Mike realized that they were just that, assumptions, and he didn't know enough about what was really going on to support them. He settled on a statement that was free of diagnosis or blame: "At 18%, our paper losses are too high." He now had a clear, quantified problem statement and was ready to approach solving it with an open mind.

Rather than gathering data from reports or talking to supervisors, we asked Mike to stand on the shop floor and observe the paper being wasted. It was the same thing Mr. Oba and his team had asked Don to do at Harley. Like most of our students, Mike, having left the factory long ago for the executive suite, pushed back. But direct observation is a mandatory part of the course, so off Mike went to watch boxes being constructed.

His trip to the factory yielded some surprises. While Mike was watching it, the main corrugator machine stopped. The corrugator glues paper together to make corrugated cardboard, and it is the most expensive piece of capital in the plant. It's supposed to run continuously. Assuming it was an unplanned outage, Mike rushed to help get it back online. The operators looked at him quizzically. "Boss," they said, "it's 11:30 a.m., time for lunch." It turned out that they stopped the machine *every day* for a thirty-minute lunch break. Stopping and restarting the machine at lunchtime not only decreased productivity but also increased the likelihood of damaging both the paper and the machine itself. A little additional digging revealed that the lunch break had been instituted years ago as a favor to the local power utility, which had been having trouble with the stability of its grid. That problem had been fixed long ago, but the lunch break shutdown remained.

Mike found other issues. The paper was often too wide, resulting in extra losses from cutting. The paper rolls were often damaged by the forklifts that moved them. Neither of his original assumptions—that the operators or the equipment were at fault—turned out to be true.

The team quickly made changes. They rearranged lunch schedules so the corrugator could run without interruption. They recalibrated the paper width. They purchased new clamps for the forklift so it didn't damage the paper rolls. In less than sixty days and for less than $50,000, the team cut paper losses by six percentage points, saving more than $250,000 per year. In addition, their efforts improved uptime on the corrugator (from 57 percent to 75 percent) and reduced fuel consumption.

Many of the other executives we have worked with experienced similar gains from just focusing on a specific, clearly formulated problem. Kenneth Pedersen, head of retail for JYSK, Sweden and

Finland, one of Don's students at AVT (Association of Visionary Thinkers) Business School in Copenhagen, focused his six-week project on inventory errors at one of his retail stores. He estimated that this problem cost the company double-digit millions of Swedish krona a year, just in the stores in Sweden. His investigation revealed that employees did not have a good understanding of the business targets or why accurate inventory management was important. Moreover, there was no system in place to warn managers when the errors started to grow. The project delivered a 22 percent reduction in inventory errors in that first store.

A few weeks after Kenneth turned in his assignment, he sent Don a note:

> We have scaled up to ten stores and are seeing weekly improvements ranging from 30%–60%. Stock errors have been reduced in nine of ten stores with an average improvement of 22% in twenty-eight days. Seven out of ten stores have met all stock management targets. I met one of the project participants in the hallway the other day. He is an internal auditor, of the old-fashioned type. He had a big smile on his face, and when I asked about the status of the project, said, "Thank you, Kenneth, this is one of the best things you have done for our part of the business." For me, the mindset and thinking of understanding the details of how the work gets done is a very big part of my operational approach. Optimizing stock management and the flow of goods is now a big part of our global business plan for 2024–2025.

THE DISCOVERY MINDSET

Mike's and Kenneth's projects delivered important improvements, but they also raise an interesting question. Why did it take a class project to see opportunities that were so easily realized?

Figure 3.1.

Take a look at Figure 3.1 and ask yourself how you would describe it to someone else.

If you are like most people, you'd say something like this: "I see a white triangle on top of a black triangle, and there are three black circles at the points."

Now look again. Where is the white triangle? Your brain "sees" it, but there is no such shape. Rather, there's a pattern of circles and thick lines that make a space in the center look brighter than the area outside of it, creating the appearance of three edges. This phenomenon is known as *illusory contours*, and it demonstrates the automatic processors' propensity for matching patterns. When the brain receives visual data suggesting the existence of an edge, it tends to fill in the rest of the information.

Illusions also occur in nonvisual form. When a pattern seems to fit our previous experience, our brains tend to process this automatically, adding or subtracting data to conform with past observations.

Mike Morales was a deeply experienced, hands-on manager. His pattern-matching apparatus could quickly supply a solution to almost any problem he faced. When he first became aware of the paper-loss problem, his brain almost certainly defaulted to the time-honored solutions of new technology and more training.

However, while pattern matching brings some features of a situation to the foreground, it ignores or downplays others. Mike had undoubtedly walked by the corrugator during lunch breaks in the past, but he didn't notice or think to ask why it had stopped. He had seen the forklifts move paper rolls many times, but it hadn't occurred to him that they were the source of damage. He just assumed the plant was running the way it should. It's hard to see something when your past experience hasn't conditioned you to look for it.

Prior to his time with Mr. Oba, Don had been in a similar place. He had spent countless hours in his factory and knew it inside and out. He routinely saw the existing ways of doing things as "the way things work." In short: it's your past experience and the way automatic processing turns it into expertise that make it so difficult to see opportunities for improvement. You can't undo your expertise, nor would you want to. So how do you put biased automatic processing on hold so you can take a fresh look?

You need what Mr. Oba was trying to teach Don. You need a *discovery mindset.*

Imagine you are a novice musician, and you want to learn to play a complex piece of music. While you know how to play the piano or other instrument, it would be foolish to try to learn the entire piece at once, and then only test your ability to play the piece at the final performance. Instead, you'd be better off studying the first few measures, identifying any missing skills, such as playing a particular chord or rhythm, learning those skills by playing only those first few measures, and then testing your mastery with someone more experienced (like a teacher).

Then, armed with some new skills and seeing some patterns in this piece of music, you would be ready to take on the next, likely somewhat larger, section of the music, and ready to learn more techniques and recognize larger patterns.

The modern organization, as noted earlier, is a complex, dynamic place, prone to workarounds and firefighting. We can't trust our instincts to anticipate how any given change might reverberate. Trying to change big pieces all at once creates a huge amount of risk. The essence of the discovery mindset lies in starting small, being deliberate, "playing" one measure at a time, and moving faster as you learn.

Mr. Oba insisted on getting an answer to his question "What problem are you trying to solve?" not only to find a place to start but to move Don's thinking back toward the discovery mindset. That's why we press students and the executives we work with to start uncomfortably small and to carefully watch the work they think they already know so well.

Adopting the discovery mindset means holding the "obvious" solutions at bay (produced by automatic processing) until you understand both the problem and the work that generates it. You don't throw money at the problem, launch a big change initiative, or install new technology until you know exactly what is going wrong and have tested that hypothesis.

Keep four things in mind as you pursue the discovery mindset. First, as much as your expertise tells you otherwise, you probably don't know the true source of many of the issues you face. Your deep experience can keep you from seeing embarrassingly obvious improvements until you can find a way to look at the work differently. If these issues have existed for a long time, your employees may think that you obviously (to them) must know that this is how things work and that you like it this way.

Second, improvement goes faster and poses less risk to your organization when you start small. You don't have to boil the Atlantic Ocean to determine that the presence of salt raises the boiling point of water. You don't have to start with permanent changes. Find the cheapest, fastest experiment you can run to tell you whether or not you are headed in the right direction. Once you have demonstrated that it works, then you can think about more permanent, scalable changes.

Third, your organization may need to make big changes in technology or other infrastructure. That said, making such investments before you understand the work and solve all the small problems risks embedding the problems deeper in the organization. Picking all of the low-hanging fruit will leave you with a much better understanding of what investments are actually needed, allowing you to spend your scarce capital budget far more efficiently. As one of our former students, who now is the senior vice president of operations at a major semiconductor manufacturer, likes to say, "There are few ways to waste money faster than automating a process you don't understand."

Fourth, in our experience, real success travels much faster than you might think. When those doing the work find a better way to get things done, they start talking about it. In a project that we discuss in more detail in Chapter 5, Michael O'Sullivan, a vice president at the semiconductor maker Analog Devices, reduced the time required to evaluate the performance of a new chip from three months to twenty-eight days. Just a few weeks later, another project, in a facility three thousand miles away, beat that time, delivering their results in twenty-five days. That second project had not been part of O'Sullivan's initiative, but other groups had heard about it and didn't want to be left behind. Similarly, a few years ago we worked with Standard Chartered bank (we discuss this work more in Chapter 6).

Though they started small, solving real problems and generating real results got a lot of attention. About two years in, our contact sent the following note to his organization:

> Last week we crossed a milestone when we hit 5,000 [problem-solving projects] in the bank. Close to 10,000 of our colleagues are actively using the [problem-solving] methodology and this has created around 150 million dollars in impact to the bank. We managed to do this in less than 2 years since we first started on this journey.

Don't be afraid to start small.

STRUCTURED PROBLEM-SOLVING

The discovery mindset is crucial, but it isn't enough. You need to complement it with a structured method for problem-solving. Fortunately, many excellent options are available. They can all help you systematically structure your inquiries and solve problems. Most people in business are familiar with them. You probably have training in at least one of them.

Though the terms may vary from one approach to the next, all the methods are really just the scientific method repackaged for the world outside of the lab. Consequently, they include the same basic steps: formulate the problem, develop a diagnosis by observing the work (not from just examining the spreadsheets or asking people what is wrong) and engaging with those who do the work, propose a new design, and test that design with a small experiment.

It sounds so simple that you may be tempted to jump into a problem using only the method without the discovery mindset. This will backfire. We have watched far too many managers fail to uncover all the hidden elements of how the work really gets done because they rushed through the steps. Finding innovative solutions requires developing a quantified problem statement that is free of solution or attribution, carefully observing the work, and engaging those doing that work. Others, convinced they already have the right answer, just fill in the forms in reverse, creating a story to match their desired solution.

They often feel clever, thinking they've solved their problem more rapidly and easily than everyone else, demonstrating that they don't need to follow the steps—until the solution backfires or the results fizzle out. Our students who work for large technology-consulting companies often fall prey to this error. They are so convinced that the latest technology will solve the problem (for several years the cloud was the solution to every problem, now it is artificial intelligence) that they reverse engineer the problem-solving steps to yield the technology du jour as the solution. Recently, one student (who shall remain nameless) was well on his way to developing an AI-enabled scheduling system for medical staff in a hospital until he realized, with a little coaching, that a fifteen-minute daily meeting to compare notes on the next day's availability solved the problem far more effectively. Structured problem-solving can be a powerful complement to your intuition, but it must be used in conjunction with the discovery mindset. Just ticking the boxes won't do it.

With that in mind, let's look more closely at the process of structured problem-solving. Since these methods are widely available, we'll focus on a few areas where the nuances of your practice make a difference.

Writing a Good Problem Statement

We have already seen how a poorly formulated problem statement can obscure the real issues by letting automatic processing predetermine the conclusion. It might assign blame, as Mike did at the paper plant: "The operators don't know what to do" or "The equipment doesn't work." It might propose a mega-solution and associated change initiative, as Don did with Mr. Oba: "I want to implement the Toyota production system." It might do both, like this problem statement from a student in our MBA class: "Our invoice processing is too slow due to our outdated IT system. We need to invest in a major upgrade." It might even double down on your own biases: "Those jerks in marketing don't understand a thing about manufacturing. We need to take them out of the scheduling process."

Even if "those jerks" in marketing really don't understand manufacturing, that's probably not the source of your problem. By framing it that way, you'll just end up picking a fight with marketing and focusing on the wrong issue. When your problem statement contains blame or a solution, you've likely allowed automatic processing to take over and risk missing the real problem. Psychologists call this *fixation error.*

We have come to believe (as we titled a recent paper) that problem formulation is the single most underrated skill in management. The key is to carefully and cleanly quantify the gap between the current situation and your aspiration. Research suggests that a clearly stated gap between where you are and where you want to be motivates people to participate. You are helping them assess their progress toward the target. Here are some great examples from our Executive MBA students:

- It currently takes 20 weeks to go from an idea to a prototype that can be shared with a customer (where we are), against a target of 14 weeks (where we want to be), creating a gap of 6 weeks.

- The code produced in each software "sprint" has 22 percent defects (where we are) compared to a target of 10 percent (where we want to be), resulting in a gap of 12 percentage points.
- Trucks spend an average of 90 minutes in the unloading/loading depot (where we are) against a turnaround target of 50 minutes (where we want to be), yielding a gap of 40 minutes.

Back at Mike Morales's Panamanian corrugated paper plant, a well-designed problem statement would look like this:

- At 18 percent, our paper losses are too high (where we are) against the industry norm of 5 percent (where we want to be), leaving us a gap of 13 percent.

Or back at the Broad Institute from Chapter 1, a good problem statement would have looked like this:

- We require 120 days on average to process a lab sample (where we are), but our customers need it in 1 month (where we want to be), and we must close that 3-month gap.

Note that these examples are built around hard metrics. Managers often hesitate to focus on issues like morale or integrity that, though critical to their organizations, are difficult to measure.

Don't shy away from something that matters to your organization, even if you can't yet measure it precisely. Structured problem-solving can be successfully applied to these issues, often with significant results. Consider a project by another former student, Steve Krubiner. When he took our course, he was chief of staff at a Washington, DC, lobbying firm, and his initial problem statement was "My weekly staff meeting demotivates participants and inadvertently discourages participation and innovation."

When we asked him whether all the meetings in his firm were similarly dysfunctional, he replied, "No, we have several regular productive meetings; it's just the staff meeting that is a big problem." This was an important step because it meant that though Steve couldn't yet measure the effectiveness of a given meeting, he could make a subjective judgment about which ones were better than others. We challenged him to find a way to make that subjective sense more tangible, and he came up with a clever solution.

He created a simple web-based survey in which participants could give a numerical score indicating their relative agreement with statements like "attending this meeting is useful" and provide suggestions for improving the meeting. Steve's problem statement went from "My weekly staff meeting demotivates participants and inadvertently discourages participation and innovation" to "My weekly staff meeting receives an average score of 3.5 (on a 5-point scale) against a target of 4.5."

The gap was so obvious that he didn't include it. Moreover, now that he surveyed them regularly and posted the previous week's results on the weekly agenda, the participants quickly suggested several easy-to-implement changes. The meeting's average score quickly climbed to the target.

Note that efforts to quantify a gap, even for so-called soft variables, can lead to far more targeted, effective interventions. For example, one of our clients proposed a large program to solve the "morale problem," including family picnics, rewards, and multilevel "sharing" lunches. When Don questioned the manager about how she knew that morale was a problem, she shot back, "Everyone knows we have a morale problem." Where, Don asked, did she observe poor morale that day: When she had her coffee; while she was doing email; during a meeting? After several uncomfortable minutes of probing, it turned out that the low morale was rooted in a longtime argument between sales and manufacturing. Although many organizations experience similar tensions—Why don't you make what we could sell? versus Why don't you sell what we make?—most companies find a workable middle ground. In this organization, however, it had degenerated into tribal warfare. Don offered a simpler solution. Put the two executives in a room with a good facilitator and don't let them come out until they have a plan they can both support. Then have them present it together to a joint session of both departments. Once the executives started to resolve their differences and work together more amicably, the rest of the organization began to follow suit. No picnics were necessary.

Bite Off Less Than You Think You Can Chew

One of the most common departures from the discovery mindset is taking on a problem that is too large and complex. Putting too many changes in motion on too broad a scale can create more worse-before-better than your organization can stomach. When you lose the connection between the change and the result, the experiment bogs down and the results don't propagate. Trying to solve everything at once risks both missing easy wins and adding new problems.

When you tackle a new problem, try to "scope it down." Look for a specific manifestation of the big issue, where you can make tangible progress fast. Break it down by geography, product line, office, process step, team—whatever it takes.

As a rough guideline, we advise picking something on which you can make progress in thirty to sixty days. Similarly, if you need to include more than six or eight people who are involved with the work, or if it takes more than a few weeks to run an experiment, then you're probably starting too big.

When Michael O'Sullivan at Analog Devices tried to reduce development time, this was his initial problem statement:

- It takes two to four years to develop a new semiconductor, and that has to be eighteen to twenty-four months to stay competitive.

Had he tried to fix this all at once, it would have been years before he knew whether he was heading in the right direction. Instead, he scoped down from the entire development process to a specific phase, known as product characterization, which typically took between six and twelve months. Even that felt too big once he got started, so he focused on a subphase, known as first silicon evaluation, which took three to four months. With that careful bounding, he could demonstrate real results (a 66 percent reduction) in just a few months. With this validated knowledge in hand, Michael could easily propagate his interventions to other projects and other parts of the process.

The Problem Is in the Work

The next step in any structured approach is to identify the problem's source and to explain why it hasn't already been flagged and fixed. The essence of the discovery mindset at this step is to focus on understanding how the current design generates the problem you are trying to solve *as a normal part of its operation* (as opposed to the problem being caused by random external events or someone doing something wrong). Interestingly, we tend to be very comfortable with this idea in the physical world. For example, when Samsung produced a line of cell phones that caught on fire, nobody blamed the user. The problem was clearly in the design of the phone.

When there is a problem at the office or lab, however, we tend to forget that there is an underlying design to the work, no matter how informal or poorly documented it might be. When problems happen at work, we look for someone to blame, and usually it's the person or people closest to the issue. This is the fundamental attribution error (mentioned in the previous chapter) at work. This cognitive error led Mike Morales to focus on training. It must be, he thought, something about the plant operators. He didn't consider the possibility that a poorly designed work system might guarantee that people will engage in bad behavior, even when everyone has good intentions. Focus on the design of the work, not on the people who are subjected to that design.

The best way to conduct this diagnosis is to observe the current work in action. You may think, "But the problem is that there isn't a process!" If work is getting done, there is a process, even if it is disjointed and erratic and is not written down. Before you try designing something new on the whiteboard in your office, pick a piece of work and watch it get done. Go from beginning to end, noting how it moves from one person to the next. You will see the real process, warts and all, complete with all the workarounds, traps, and special circumstances that people deal with every day. Fixing these now-obvious problems is usually very easy and produces immediate benefit without the cost of a massive reengineering project. We coach our students that if they are unsure about how much improvement to target, to use 30 percent, not single digits. The seemingly small but bothersome issues that are easily fixed are probably hurting productivity more than you think. With projects that are properly scoped and run, we rarely see less than a 30 percent gain.

We give our students and clients a simple rule of thumb to guide their efforts: when you go see the work, if you aren't embarrassed by what you find, you probably aren't looking closely enough. When we first offer this guidance, most think that their organization is different and that they won't find much. There are few moments we enjoy more than when students return for the next class session having done their investigations and confess their embarrassment to their colleagues. This is the point at which they start to realize that dynamic work design is about more than fixing a few problems. It is about creating a system for ongoing learning, improvement, and adaptation, one that is constantly surfacing the next problem to go solve.

Once the blinders are off, most managers accumulate a long list of embarrassments. Every year multiple students discover someone who retypes entries into a database from a paper printout, both wasting resources and creating more opportunities for mistakes. In another instance, a student tackled long wait times at his company's retail medical clinics. Investigation revealed that the long lines persisted, even when another clinic a few blocks away had no wait. When he dug into the software running the kiosks that people used to check in, he discovered the ability in the system to automatically suggest a different clinic when there was a long wait, but *nobody had ever turned it on.* The most embarrassing cases often have the highest leverage for positive change.

For instance, when she took our class, Miriam Bredella was the vice chair of the radiology department at Boston's Massachusetts General Hospital. Miriam focused on reducing the time it took to get results from a CT scan back to the emergency room. To understand the work, she watched the doctor on duty read scans. Her investigation revealed numerous distractions, including six telephones ringing nonstop through the shift and residents who would often call or stop by during the busiest time of day, hoping to get help with their cases. No wonder everything took so long. When they moved the phone bank, updated staff scheduling to match demand, and improved communication between Emergency Department and Radiology, the pace sped up immediately, and she was able to reduce the average wait time by over 40 percent.

Another physician, Elizabeth Flanigan, wanted to bring radiology technicians into the neonatal intensive care unit more quickly when a baby was born very prematurely and needed potentially lifesaving medication (the administration of which required imaging). She found that the neonatal team used the text ELBW, indicating extremely low birth weight, to summon the relevant staff. Unfortunately, teams on the receiving end sometimes thought the text meant the baby had a problem with its elbow; no need to rush. Correcting this misunderstanding and a few other operational changes allowed her to reduce the average time required to deliver a critical drug (a pulmonary surfactant) by 40 percent, from an average of fifty-eight minutes to less than thirty-five minutes.

Test Your Thinking

The next step in structured problem-solving is to test your hypothesis by running an experiment. As with your problem statement, keep your experiment small and focused. Don't turn it into a large change initiative. You don't have to change the entire system to see if you are headed in the right direction. Instead, where possible, run a cheap, fast test to determine whether your interventions are solving the problem.

An experiment is more casual and less threatening than a big change, something you can undo if it doesn't work as expected.

Don't order new software or equipment. Simulate the effect of your proposed change using your existing technology or do it manually. If the changes help, then you can decide how much time and money to invest. In our experience, big gains can be had from simple things like staggering lunch schedules to keep the corrugator running or making sure people have a common understanding of acronyms. In Mass General's radiology lab, Miriam tested her hypothesis by having a reading room coordinator triage phone calls and having residents give preliminary reads and provide consultations. When this reduced turnaround times, she moved the phones and changed the staffing protocol.

Don't try to solve everything at once. Propose the minimum set of changes that will help you determine whether you are headed in the right direction. Discovery is an ongoing process. You can always change more later.

I HAVE A PROBLEM

Don's first interaction with Mr. Oba at Harley-Davidson moved him back toward the discovery mindset. He'd had a version of it at the start of his career but, like many executives, had lost it as he moved up the ranks. Now he realized that, even as a senior leader, he needed to get back to discovery and take the rest of the company with him.

A few weeks after the "what do you see" exercise, Don called Mr. Oba again. This time, he had picked a small problem, in an area where only a few people worked, that was disrupting the entire factory. "I'm having a quality and quantity problem in the rotor and stator area," said Don. "It's so bad that it keeps shutting down my main assembly line, throwing the schedule into chaos. Can you help me fix it?" Mr. Oba and his team showed up shortly thereafter, and they started working together, first on the rotor and stator line and then elsewhere throughout the engine plant.

As Don often tells our classes, during that year he went from being a manager to being a lifelong student. There is always a new level of performance to be discovered. As the discovery mindset moved from Don to the rest of the plant, the pace and effectiveness of problem-solving increased significantly and performance followed. For example, one area of the factory was dedicated to making parts for engines that were no longer in regular production. If Harley received an order for a replacement flywheel for an engine no longer in active production, it would take between 90 and 120 days and forty-five different machines to manufacture and ship it. After a year of formulating clear problems and then solving them, the area was able to reduce the number of original machines to seventeen (selling the rest) and both build and ship replacement flywheel assemblies *the same day* they were ordered. They did not accomplish this level of service by building a big inventory of the possible types of completed flywheels and then pulling one off a shelf and shipping it when the order was received. Each one was manufactured and shipped within twenty-four hours of receiving an order.

Don's experience with Mr. Oba and his colleagues ended in an interesting way. Mr. Oba's team pressed to put more and more detailed procedures in place, telling Don that he had to adopt the entire system, not just pieces. Even the mighty Toyota can lose sight of the discovery mindset in favor of doing what worked last time. Don and the employees resisted what seemed like excessive rigor and rules. The goal was to improve Harley, not emulate Toyota's framework perfectly. Toyota didn't develop its much-heralded systems through the rote application of another company's framework. They did it through the repeated application, over many decades, of the discovery mindset to their own unique issues and environment. Don and Mr. Oba's group parted ways, but Harley's improvement efforts continued, and the discovery mindset remained at the center of Don's work.

Soon, Harley promoted Don to vice president of operational excellence for the entire company in addition to his general manager role at Capitol Drive. We began experimenting with the underlying principles of good work design more broadly and across many functions. Although workflows in an office or lab context are less visible than on the factory floor, they experience the same problems. They just show up in different and unique ways. As we'll see in Chapter 4, the practices of effective work are the same whether the organization is in manufacturing or technology or is a not-for-profit group helping the unhoused. Getting the problem right is only the beginning. We also need to design structured ways of working that set everyone up for success, no matter what we are trying to accomplish.

Chapter 4

Structure for Discovery

FROM TUNING INDIVIDUAL INSTRUMENTS
TO PLAYING A SYMPHONY

In any hotel, it pays to manage the front desk carefully. How guests are treated at check-in and how quickly they get to their rooms have an outsized influence on how customers rate their experience.

Check-in is even more important at a Las Vegas casino and resort. Casino resorts cost a lot to build and are expensive to run, thanks to security requirements and the highly competitive nature of the business. A casino full of happy regular customers—eating, gambling, and going to shows—can make a lot of money. An empty casino doesn't last long. Not surprisingly, given the stakes, big casinos are among the most sophisticated businesses in the world in using data to assess performance and evaluate their executives.

So, when Mike Jerlecki, manager of the Palace Station Hotel and Casino, just off the Vegas strip, heard that his front desk email capture percentage, an important metric, was falling behind his peers', his ears perked up. It came up in the weekly meeting of managers of casinos owned by the Station chain and was followed by the report that his restaurant revenues were down. In the casino world, like most places, it's not good to be the one who is falling behind.

Casino visitors often book their stays through intermediary travel websites like Expedia and Orbitz. In those cases, the email address isn't automatically captured by the casino, so the front desk staff have to ask guests for it directly. Email addresses are important for developing customer relationships and repeat business, but asking for them can feel annoying and invasive to customers. Mike's peers at other casinos managed to collect these emails over 80 percent of the time, with some nearing 90 percent. Palace Station, in contrast, averaged just a little over 70 percent. Worse, his casino had just invested $3 million in overhauling its steak restaurant, but guests weren't eating there nearly enough. Mike recalls thinking, "This doesn't look good."

When Mike took our class at MIT, he chose these two targets for his project, both of which he was already under pressure to improve: increase email capture and get more people into the steak restaurant. He suspected that both of these problems were rooted in the check-in process, the first point of contact with customers. Check-in is both the best time to get a guest's email address and the first opportunity to upsell the steak restaurant. But he wasn't sure why those targets were being missed. Was it a lack of staff training? Were the employees not motivated to give the customers a good experience? Was something wrong with the technology? And why had he been caught off guard by these issues at the management meeting?

Following the principles of dynamic work design and coaching from the class, Mike started by observing the work. He wanted to observe what was going wrong as it was happening rather than try to diagnose it by looking at spreadsheets in his office. So, he spent several shifts standing behind the front desk watching his team as they checked in guests.

Senior leaders typically claim to have a deep understanding of the core work of their organization. This assessment is rarely accurate. When we ask them to map how the work moves through their organization, their misconceptions are quickly revealed. Even very successful leaders surprise themselves with how little detail they can offer about the work they think they know well.

Mike was no exception; the experience of watching the check-in process was eye-opening. The first thing he noticed was that although the targets of email capture and restaurant revenue were crystal clear in the executive operating review meetings, they weren't clear to the team at the front desk. Though these two targets had been communicated several times, they had gotten lost in the day-to-day scramble.

Different functions of the casino had asked the front desk to promote and explain the services each one offered. Since the front desk staff were the ones talking to the customers, they had to determine which pieces of information to share with customers who could be travel weary or eager to get to the tables. They learned to juggle these additional, often competing priorities, including explaining regulations on drinking and betting, upselling the many services that the casino offered, and noting the shuttle service that ferried guests around the city. With the best of intentions, individual staff members responded to these requests (and admonitions) as best they could, but each person did it a little differently, using their own homegrown collection of shortcuts and workarounds to jam as much as they could into an interaction that hopefully lasted only a few minutes. Email capture was often missed and promoting the steak restaurant regularly got lost in the shuffle.

Watching the check-in process helped Mike see the challenges his staff faced in getting guests checked in, problems that he had probably helped create and that almost certainly contributed to the casino's performance being behind that of his peers. In reporting what he learned from the assignment to investigate what was going on, Mike concluded, "It is practically impossible for front desk agents to enjoyably and efficiently check a person in to the hotel and achieve all their objectives."

Mike's experience is probably similar to that of many managers. He worked hard and so did his people. The check-in process seemed fine to them. Yet somehow their collective efforts didn't add up to the results that his executive team was looking for. How did the check-in process, the first point of contact with customers, end up so far off the mark? And, more generally, why do the efforts of many skilled, well-meaning people, front line and management, go astray?

LOSING TO MOM (OR HOW THE BEST OF EFFORTS CAN GO AWRY)

The answer lies in a surprising place: learning. Somewhere in the last few decades, *learning* became part of organizational dogma. Large companies have spent billions on training centers, internal universities, and chief learning officers, all focused on using classroom and computer-based training to regularly upgrade individual skills and help the organization learn. While it remains unclear whether these investments have paid off, the learning movement missed a far more fundamental fact: people who do work are learning every day. When we encounter a problem, we make an adjustment. A good result reinforces that action; a bad one leads to another adjustment. Whether we like it or not, automatic processing (discussed in the previous chapter) is constantly encoding experience to guide future behavior. But without a common structure to guide that learning, everyone learns different things based on their individual actions. In many cases, it's easy to learn things that do not contribute to organizational success or that cancel out an action someone else has learned to take.

For example, thanks to poor work design, each member of Mike's team, despite being well trained and motivated, had learned their way into a different version of the check-in process, often drawing lessons from one or two very good or very bad experiences. If a staff member had experienced a guest violating state and city regulations, she learned to start the interaction by explaining gambling and drinking regulations. In contrast, a staff member who had a positive experience when she suggested a show or restaurant would start every interaction there. People who checked in weary travelers in the wee hours of the morning were less likely to emphasize email capture.

To see how daily learning can go awry, here is an example that probably hits close to home for anyone who has ever tried to master a complex physical skill. Nelson's mom, Caroline, is an accomplished golfer, having made the cut at the US Senior Amateur Golf Championship and once boasting a scratch handicap. In the hope of holding his own while playing together, Nelson wanted to improve his game. He practiced every chance he got, but the extra practice didn't make him better. In fact, he got worse. Why? Much like Mike's staff, he lacked a clear design to guide his efforts and thus was learning the wrong things. Upping the effort devoted to practicing in a poorly structured learning environment just deepened an already bad habit.

Nelson had two problems. First, having watched too much professional golf on TV, Nelson fixated on hitting his shots farther. This aspect of golf is not only satisfying but also easily judged on the driving range and frequently highlighted by sports announcers on TV. It doesn't, however, make a big difference in your score. Any golf pro will tell you this is a counterproductive target, particularly for middle-aged amateurs. If you want to shoot better scores, it is far more productive to focus on keeping your ball out of the water hazards and away from the woods. Second, his practice was based on a flawed diagnosis of what was wrong with his game. What Nelson thought he was doing in his golf swing and what he was actually doing were two different things. As he would later learn thanks to some video, Nelson was unaware of a fundamental flaw—a major head movement during his back swing.

The more he practiced, the more his poor swing became embedded in automatic cognitive processing. Worse, the natural adaptation that comes with repetition yielded an increasingly complex set of compensating movements—the golf equivalent of workarounds—and habits that took years to unlearn. His problem was not the difficulty of learning the swing he saw on TV. It was his lack of knowledge about his own swing and what was wrong with it.

The front desk team at the Palace Station Hotel suffered from a similar syndrome. Based on their individual experiences, usually heavily influenced by a particularly difficult customer or complaint from another manager, each of the front desk staff members focused on slightly different targets. If you'd gotten yelled at a few times by a tired guest, you focused on getting them to their room quickly. If a guest got caught violating gambling rules and you got a lecture from the state gambling commission, you'd be sure to explain the regulations every time. Without clear targets, everyone learned to do their job a little differently, which didn't deliver what the business needed.

Learning was further hamstrung by the fact that many of the check-in procedures and tricks had long since been consigned to habit. As we see regularly in repetitive work, thanks to automatic processing, people aren't entirely conscious of all their actions and often can't give an accurate description of what they actually do. Sometimes a local adaptation represents a genuine improvement, but often there is no structure through which to vet and then share such innovation. Experienced check-in staff, for example, often learned to assess travelers' moods right away—"Did you have a long flight?"—and then adjust accordingly, perhaps skipping the lecture on gambling regs in favor of getting them to their room or the restaurant. Rookies might learn a similar lesson from experience, but they might not. It was random.

There is no learning budget big enough or training course long enough to offset the natural adaptation that comes from people trying to make a poorly designed, poorly managed system work. Trying to correct the learning that happens every day at work with a few hours or days in the classroom is akin to sending an alcoholic back to their favorite bar after rehab.

Making sure that people learn the right things on the job requires the set of design elements captured in the dynamic work design principle *structure for discovery*.

STRUCTURE FOR DISCOVERY

When Mr. Oba, as we saw in the previous chapter, pushed Don to articulate the problem he was trying to solve and then to tackle it using a structured approach, Don got to choose which issue to tackle. But, as the hotel front desk example highlights, you can't let everyone in the organization use their own scorecard to decide what problems they work on and how to solve them. Instead, fully capitalizing on the power of learning and problem-solving requires directing it to the issues that really matter. Structuring for discovery means getting everyone playing the same game with the same rules so that everyone is learning together. It creates a work environment with clear targets, whose intent is well understood so that everyone sees both what is working well and the same gaps between reality and aspiration. When individual discovery takes place within a common structure, it's more likely to move in a common direction.

To see this principle in action, let's return to Nelson's effort to improve his golf game. The first issue was that he had the wrong target: hitting longer drives. Better scores lie not in long distances but in keeping the ball out of the woods, sand, and water and having good skills in the shorter shots (particularly putting). A conversation with an instructor led Nelson to two supporting metrics to achieve a lower score. The first, no double bogeys (golf jargon for two more shots than you should take on a hole), required keeping the ball out of hazards. The second, no three putts, focused on skill in the shorter shots—putting and chipping. Both targets focused on accuracy not distance and were easy to track. Meeting those targets would allow him to achieve the larger goal of shooting better scores.

Better targets needed to be complemented with a more accurate assessment of what Nelson was actually doing (not what he *thought* he was doing). A lesson with an instructor and a little video revealed a flaw in Nelson's swing, an unconscious head movement that needed to be fixed. Now his practice was directly connected to the target rather than to just randomly hitting balls at the driving range, hoping to somehow magically discover the "secret" of better golf.

Regular video feedback (easy on a modern smartphone) and occasional check-ins with the instructor allowed Nelson to gauge whether he was making good progress. If not, then he could adjust. He hit far fewer golf balls but got a lot more out of each practice session. Nelson eventually lowered his handicap by seven strokes and is now at least occasionally competitive with his mom, though she continues to play remarkably well for someone in her eighties.

The same learning loop that works for golf or any other complex skill applies to the workplace. An effective work design lets you see progress against the targets you've chosen and quickly reveals issues preventing you from reaching those targets. It ensures that you are constantly making conscious choices on the best activities to execute. A work structure built for ongoing discovery coordinates local learning so that newly discovered solutions quickly become shared knowledge that moves the organization toward its common goals. Such structures share three key elements:

1. Clear targets and shared intent: a set of quantified targets and a shared understanding of why they are important to the organization.
2. Activities: an explicit and clear statement of the actions that the team believes will deliver the targets.
3. Feedback: a regular, clear, and quantified assessment of whether the activities are delivering those targets and addressing issues that emerge.

Targets and Intent

To see the importance of developing a shared understanding of the targets and the intent behind those targets, consider an episode during Don's Twin Cam project at Harley. Senior leadership had given the development team a target (among other goals) of delivering an engine with 10 percent more power than its predecessor. But when the engineers began to face real design choices, they needed more clarity. "More power" could mean more horsepower, the power you *read* in the spec book and measure at max rpm, usually only important on a racetrack. Or it could mean more torque, the power you *feel* in your butt every time you accelerate. Optimizing one of these two metrics at the expense of the other requires different designs for the camshaft, pistons, cylinders, and ignition system.

Much as happened with Mike's front desk team, without clarity from the executive team, this trade-off would have been made deep in the organization, far from those who knew what the customers wanted and far from those who were supposed to decide what the customers would get. Different sub-teams could easily have made this trade-off in different ways. When Don asked the leadership team for clarity in a review meeting, they started arguing with one another. There were clearly unresolved differences of opinion and gaps in understanding. Finally, Willie G. Davidson, grandson of one of the founders, motorcycling world icon, VP of styling, and a former racer himself, said, "When I'm at a stop sign next to a guy on an Evo (the current engine), I want to beat him by two bike-lengths as we pull away." This was a clear vote for a low-end, "torquey" engine so that the customers could feel the additional power with every twist of the throttle.

For riders, Willie's image was rich with Harley culture, information about the engine design, and insight into the customers. It created a visceral and emotional understanding of what was required, and it contained enough data to translate it into a design. Now everyone understood the target and the intent behind it. Had this conversation not happened, Willie G. probably wouldn't have been happy with his first test ride and a costly redesign would have followed.

Structuring work for discovery means that everyone sees and shares the targets and the intent behind them. It quickly yields a common focus on the activities that need to be done next. As we saw with both Mike's and Don's teams, despite leaders' best efforts to set targets, most people have only a vague idea of why they are doing what they are doing. Unclear targets that lack an underpinning intent make it hard to see how their actions directly affect the results. If the targets are not precise enough or the intent behind them is not clear, people don't have a good guide for the small decisions they need to make every day.

The lack of a clear target underpinned by a genuinely shared intent creates a familiar set of problems. Clever employees optimize a particular metric, which is often tied to their compensation. If they don't know *why* that metric is important and how it relates to other targets, they end up damaging the organization. Examples range from salespeople who give overly generous discounts to maximize volume without understanding the impact on production, to R & D managers who skimp on product testing (like shake tests) to meet a deadline without directly feeling the longer-term effects on quality and customer satisfaction. We once worked with a food manufacturer that, on the last day of its fiscal year, pushed railcars full of cereal just over its property line, which the company's accounting rules then recognized as successful shipments. That local manager's results looked great. But those cars were moved back on-site the next day. The associated sales would then be decremented against the new year's performance. The resulting revenue swing was over $100 million from the last month of one fiscal year to the first month of the next. But that was a problem for next year and maybe the next guy or gal.

Clearly communicating the intent underlying a target is particularly important in a complex environment. People regularly find themselves having to make choices on how to meet a target. Knowing the "why" behind a target helps them make these choices correctly. During the Harley engine development, oil pressure tests were regularly run in the lab. One of the goals for the new engine was to eliminate a flaw in the previous design, the "low oil pressure" light that constantly went on at stoplights when the engine got hot and the oil thinned. The target was to increase the oil pressure at idle so that even on the hottest days it did not trigger the low oil pressure warning. This had been a big customer complaint in the previous engine (normally a low oil pressure light on the dash is not a good sign) and something the Twin Cam team wanted to address.

The problem was the result of a design flaw that couldn't be fixed without a major design change. The Twin Cam team used a totally different oil pump design, one that gave the engineers much more control over the pressure. When the first prototype engine was built and put on a test stand to see how it performed, the technician was given the pressure specs, including the pressure at idle. He was not, however, given the intent behind those specifications. The engine passed the lab test with flying colors.

After the testing was complete and the engine was mounted in a frame for a test run, Don took it for a long ride on a hot day. He pulled up to a stoplight, the engine slowed to idle, and the engine oil light came on. After months of designing, building, and testing, this was not what he had expected. When he returned to the lab, he asked the tech how the light could still be going on when the engine had performed well in the lab. The tech replied, "Oh yeah, the pressure always dropped too low and the light went on. But the test spec called for a certain pressure at idle, so when it was too low, I just turned up the idle until the pressure got to the spec." The engineer assumed the pressure spec at idle was needed to test the rest of the system, not something needed to address an important customer complaint. So he just raised the idle speed to meet the pressure specification, thinking he was doing exactly what the engineer wanted. He had met the target but not the intent behind it.

You most certainly have your own examples of problems emerging when people are told to just do their job without giving them insight as to what that job is supposed to accomplish.

Leaders often invest heavily in clarifying intent for large organizations with aspirational statements about vision and strategy. "Today Tastes So Good" (Kentucky Fried Chicken), "Enjoy Better" (Time Warner), and "Quality Is Job One" (Ford) are just a few examples. Often, they are effective at setting the right tone and helping people develop supporting targets. But just as targets absent intent can lead to trouble, so, too, can a clear intent create problems if it is not tied to specific targets. Nelson knew he wanted to beat his mom at golf (or at least compete). But without a good target to work on, his efforts just kept making his game and his scores worse.

Consider another case in which a structure for discovery was not fully in place. As "a day shelter community for women experiencing poverty and homelessness," Women's Lunch Place (WLP) has a clear and compelling intent that the entire organization enthusiastically shares. Open from 7:00 a.m. to 2:00 p.m. six days a week, WLP typically serves 2,200 unique guests every year and provides almost 150,000 healthy meals—numbers that grow every year. WLP uses the meals as an opportunity for advocates to connect women who experience homelessness, addiction, and domestic abuse to the resources they need to live safe, healthier lives. In 2023, WLP provided over ten thousand advocacy sessions to help at-risk women navigate the byzantine systems of city, state, and federal resources.[1]

But the advocates found themselves increasingly overloaded. WLP had no system for matching guest needs to the expertise of advocates. Some guests just needed a subway pass, a request easily handled by an administrator; others had complex situations that required experienced counsel. Doris, WLP's most experienced advocate (a true wonder woman if there ever was one), sometimes managed over 140 cases simultaneously, almost four times more than some of the newer advocates. Advocates were so busy that, like Mike's front desk staff, whatever they learned about helping these guests was not transferred to other advocates. Problems were solved with individual workarounds. Everyone was working full tilt to figure out what a guest needed and to provide that help.

As the load grew, it became ever more difficult for WLP to track each guest and document their progress. The lack of clearly documented gains made it difficult for them to raise the additional funds so desperately needed to meet the growing demand. A business school strategy textbook would tell you that they needed to focus, serve fewer "customers," and use the freed-up resources to more clearly document gains for the guests that remained. But when the customer in question is a victim of domestic abuse, it's hard to say no. WLP was trapped by its own success.

Working with students from our Executive MBA program, WLP began developing specific targets to capture the shelter's intent. Using a straightforward interview protocol, the students called their first version a *risk score*: Did the guest have a place to live? Did she have regular access to food? Was she at risk of domestic abuse? And so on. The target became to lower a guest's risk score until they could live safely on their own. Later the team reframed the risk score as a *strength score* and started codifying the actions necessary to move a guest from one level to the next until she no longer needed WLP's services.

The strength score highlighted the resources most critical for an individual guest. Experienced advocates were no longer spending time trying to figure out what was needed or providing more basic assistance, like getting subway passes. The entire system was now more effective and efficient. Working in a shelter can be difficult and draining, and it can feel like you are constantly losing ground. The strength score sped progress and allowed the team to see what was needed and to quickly provide the specific resource. They began to build on what was working and fixing what needed to be improved. It was motivating, and Doris could now do the complex work she did best, while others were able to contribute to simpler tasks. The strength score also allowed WLP's leadership to evaluate the allocation of cases across the available advocates.

The improving scores also gave WLP the data they needed to gain critical funding. They showed demonstrable improvements in the quality of life experienced by their guests. In a recent review, Michelle Wu, Boston's mayor, highlighted WLP's approach as exemplary and urged other Boston support organizations to consider something similar. A simple triage step helped WLP see the specific targets that had to be met for each guest to deliver their stated intent and helped them meet that intent in a more organized and effective way.

Clarifying targets and their intent is a two-way *social* process. If the communication is only one way, such as through a large presentation or in a private discussion ("What don't you understand about hitting the target I gave you?"), without back-and-forth to test the boundaries of meaning and highlight possible issues, the targets are likely to be interpreted in ways the leaders might not like.

Here's an exercise you can use before work starts to ensure that people understand the targets they face and the intent underlying those targets. It comes from our client work—in this case, with Don as the primary consultant. The client asked that we not use its name.

After decades of success, a midsize company in Wisconsin did not have an extra square inch of space to keep expanding the manufacturing portion of their small appliance business. They were worried about meeting demand in the near future and decided to build an additional facility a few miles away. Though they had assigned over fifty employees to the project team, after six months they were already three months behind schedule and the project manager was under growing pressure. They called for help.

After two days of investigation, Don realized that the targets were not clear. Most of the planned activities were in people's heads rather than written down in the project plan, and there were differing opinions about the status. Team members were working at cross-purposes and quietly complaining. Don gave his assessment to the project leader and the CEO and suggested they go back to square one and relaunch the project. He proposed starting with a meeting of the company's top ten executives to get them on the same page about the targets and intent of the project. This would be quickly followed by a full project team meeting led by the CEO. Then the plan could be rebuilt and the project set on a better course. The CEO was a good leader and communicator, and he needed this facility up and running as soon as possible. He agreed with the assessment and with Don's proposal.

At the start of the first meeting, Don opened by asking the executives, including the CEO, to each take ten minutes to write down the goals of the project and why the goals mattered. When the ten minutes were up, the executives' responses were taped to the wall. Everyone walked around and examined each other's answers, which to their surprise included a "secret" goal from the CFO. Although everyone agreed that they needed to expand and add a new facility, it was suddenly clear that, much like Mike's check-in staff, the executives were all over the place and were pushing the project team in different directions. The room fell silent. They saw how gaps in thinking on the executive team led directly to the problems the project team was having. If the executives were not on the same page and were giving different directions to their teams, how could they expect a multifunctional team of over fifty people to be any different? The CEO immediately organized the second meeting to bring the executives and the entire project team together.

Don asked the CEO to open the next meeting by clearly restating the targets and the rationale for the project to the fifty-plus people on the project team. Don limited him to one slide and ten minutes of time. It wasn't easy to get the key information boiled down to one simple slide, nor was it easy to talk through it in just ten minutes. But when the day came, he was ready, and he did it well.

In most sessions where the boss gives a big presentation, she closes by asking if there are any questions, and awkward silence usually follows. Sometimes the question gets valuable discussion going, but it's often quiet or the questions are softballs. Nobody wants to speak first or challenge the boss in public.

To ensure two-way communication, Don prepped the audience at the outset. "You all have sticky notes. While the boss is speaking, I want each of you to write three questions about what you hear. If you are having a hard time coming up with questions, ask for every Friday off. The answer will be no, but it will get you writing. I want three sticky notes from each person. You can ask any question. You can challenge any statement. Just be respectful of one another. Don't sign your name; we don't care who it is from. We want to hear the real questions and get to real answers . . . today."

This got everyone's attention. They listened carefully to every word, making sure they understood. At the end of the ten-minute presentation, the employees posted their questions and challenges on a whiteboard. They took a break while the CEO and Don read all the notes, grouped all the similar questions, and prepared to answer them.

When the group returned, the CEO began responding to each question and challenge. Some were answered with a yes, a no, or a quick explanation. For others, the CEO didn't know the answer. So, he and his executive team worked through any differences of opinion and got the answer hammered out right there, something employees rarely got to see. Some required explanations of unfamiliar terms. Business buzzwords were explained or dropped after a good laugh. Some questions challenged the need for more production or underlying assumptions about the business, the competitors, and the product lines. Some questions highlighted issues the CEO hadn't thought of or that he was surprised his employees were even asking about. Every single question and comment was either answered in the room or set aside for investigation and a written reply within two weeks.

Now the team understood exactly what they were being asked to do and why; they understood the targets and the intent behind them. They had surfaced *their* issues to leadership and gotten direction. The leaders now understood where their support was needed. Over the next two days, the team redesigned their project plans, adding almost two hundred additional activities. By the end of the approximately twenty-month project, the team not only made up the three months they had fallen behind but also finished three months ahead of schedule, including completing a small overseas plant that was not part of the initial project.

We named this exercise Barbeque the Boss: intentionally putting the boss on the spot in a respectful and fun atmosphere and signaling that it is OK to ask challenging questions. It has proven to be a simple and powerful exercise to make sure everyone understands the intent underlying an organization's targets and that the leaders understand the challenges faced in meeting those targets.

Activities

Getting people to consciously articulate the activities that they do day in and day out, activities they believe will deliver the targets, is the second element of structuring work for discovery. Humans are creatures of habit, and though we would like to think otherwise, we often do things today because we did them yesterday. Discovering new, better ways to work requires bringing those habitual activities and responses out of the fast automatic thinking into the conscious realm, where everyone can see them. Are these habitual activities still the best ones? Is something missing? Are they conflicting or overlapping? While Nelson might have been initially aware of moving his head when swinging his golf club, the movement quickly faded into the realm of unconscious habit. In fact, Nelson denied he was doing it until his instructor showed him a video. Once we know what we are actually doing and have to explain why we are doing it, it's far easier to assess whether what we are doing is the right activity.

Workplaces are full of bad habits. Some are new work-arounds designed to compensate for emerging issues. Others are old routines that, while once appropriate, are no longer needed and may be downright counterproductive. Here are a few examples:

- One of our Executive MBA students, who worked at a tech company, discovered an administrator who printed and filed every piece of engineering documentation that came across her desk, even though the information had been captured in a secure online repository for several years.
- Forklift drivers at a home improvement retail chain moving fiberglass ladders damaged the bottom ladder on *every single pallet*, wasting millions of dollars' worth of product. They were just following the protocols that had been in place when the ladders were made of metal.
- The Broad Institute kept multiple hot lists that pushed samples to the top of the queue.
- BP's Texas City refinery favored cost cutting over safety in many small decisions, even though the executives knew safety was the most important priority.
- Harley's firefighting arsonists rushed to solve problems at the factory, even when their efforts left the underlying problems unresolved and made subsequent launches more challenging.
- Corporación Industrial's paper plant in Panama shut down the equipment for lunch breaks even though the

shutdown created wear and tear on the equipment and wasted paper.

Bad habits often live on because they have short-term rewards. The hot lists helped a few of the institute's top researchers get their samples through the system more quickly. Cost cutting at the refinery translated into higher bonuses. Harley's firefighters were treated as heroes when they delivered tough projects. The paper plant's lunch break had once helped the local power utility. After a while, people don't even realize what they're doing—until something forces them to look again with fresh eyes. You want that "something" to be a deliberate process that you create, not a catastrophe like BP's refinery explosion.

There are a variety of ways to make planned activities more visible and front of mind. For example, you can ask people to document their choices or ask them to explain them to others (either verbally or in writing). This approach likely works because explaining an action helps activate more conscious action (anyone who has taught a teenager to drive will understand this intimately—"Press the brake, smoothly!"). Similarly, having a short discussion each day with a supervisor or even writing a to-do list can help break counterproductive habits and facilitate a more conscious, deliberate choice of the day's activities. Recent neuroscience research suggests that the act of writing by hand activates a larger range of brain circuitry than typing does and may cause people to process information more fully.[2]

Discussion about activities also provides opportunities to align the work across people and functions. A surprising number of companies get stuck when even the highest-level leaders aren't aware of the hidden conflicts among them. We saw this at a Barbeque the Boss–style meeting in a large pharmaceutical company. Like many firms in the industry, the company was struggling with declining productivity in its research and development efforts. New drugs were taking longer to develop, and costs were skyrocketing. As the team was taking stock of the projects underway, it became clear that the legal and compliance team was investing heavily in one particular project that was no longer a priority. When the chief science officer discovered this, he was visibly upset. He and the rest of the management team had moved the project to the back burner, something he felt had been clearly communicated to everyone. He was mad at the legal and compliance team, but his anger was misdirected. People rarely intentionally disregard clear, visible direction, particularly when they have had an opportunity to ask questions. The fault lies in the work design that didn't confirm that this decision had been received and understood.

We see this problem every day. Senior leaders spend days or weeks developing strategies and then communicate those choices one time, in a large town hall–style meeting or email. But the modern organization is a big, messy, complicated place with lots of information going back and forth. Successfully communicating a major change in direction requires multiple efforts, including checking with the recipients to make sure they understand the implications, following up to ensure the change is being implemented as intended, and surfacing any unforeseen issues. The ensuing conversation with the legal and compliance team was difficult, but it helped the company's different management functions finally align around a single set of priorities.

Mike's team at the Palace Station Hotel used a different but equally powerful approach. With their newly clear intent and targets in hand, the team started discussing best practices for checking in guests. Now they were using a joint two-way conversation rather than Mike just telling them what to do. Integrating innovations into standard work sequences—whether they appear as checklists, procedures, or work instructions—is one of the more powerful elements of the work design tool kit.

Both research and our experience suggest that up-to-date standard procedures are most effective when the people who have to use them have a hand in their creation and continued evolution. In Mike's case, creating the initial common checklist required each person to surface and explain why they did what they did so they could make all the best ideas available to everyone. For example, they discussed how to make a quick assessment of whether the guest might be tired and want to go straight to his room or was excited to get right into the casino ("Can we have your luggage delivered to your room?"). Similarly, simple language changes made asking for email addresses seem less invasive ("What's the best way to stay in touch with you in the future?"). These and similar conversations quickly revealed best practices and helped participants identify activities that, though they weren't contributing to the targets, had long since become automatic. The discussions also allowed Mike to chime in and reinforce the message, emphasizing, for example, the need to fill the steak restaurant when the team had failed to give it sufficient attention. The discussions also helped him learn a few things along the way about the work, his employees, and how to improve as a manager.

Regular, Frequent Feedback on the Results of Activity

The final element of structuring for discovery comes in assessing the outcomes of the work. A gap between goals and targets usually means that something went wrong or there is something that people don't know. Perhaps people didn't fully understand the technology or maybe the environment changed. Either way, managed correctly, such shortfalls provide critical opportunities to make adjustments and close gaps. Closing gaps between goals and targets in real time, when they are small and the data are fresh and available, is fundamental to effective learning and discovery. Our MIT colleague Steve Spear, one of the leading scholars of the Toyota production system, likes to say, "A defect is the system's way of telling you that you don't know something."

Though reviewing results on a regular basis is a foundational process in many organizations, the review process is often broken or operates at too high a level and too infrequently to be useful. A few years ago, one of our students, a surgeon in a children's hospital, focused his project on reducing the number of times a nurse or a doctor got accidently stuck with a needle or cut by a scalpel in the operating room. Such events hurt staff and cost the hospital time and money. After each event, the surgical team needed to take a blood sample from the patient to test for infection, a procedure requiring the consent of the child's parents. Asking already stressed parents for additional consent because of a medical error was, not surprisingly, one of the doctors' least favorite tasks.

At the outset of the project, though such cuts and punctures happened at least twice a week at the hospital, the doctors and nurses involved considered these accidents onetime incidents. As the project revealed, nobody was aware of the frequency with which it was happening across the hospital. As we have seen in many projects, just posting the data led to significant improvements. Once the surgical teams had data on their performance, they started adjusting procedures, following best practices, such as saying "Sharp coming through" when passing a scalpel, and making everyone more aware of their actions. Improvement followed quickly.

Enabling people to continually discover better ways of working requires regular information about their progress toward their targets. The more immediate the feedback, the better, such as the feedback Nelson experienced when playing video games with his son Robbie (see Chapter 1). As a simple diagnostic, we often ask people, "How do you know if you are ahead or behind right now?" Some work meets this element naturally. In manufacturing you can often see the results in real time: a car comes off the assembly line or a book from the printing press. Assembly-line workers in a well-designed factory can often easily see whether they are meeting their targets. Similarly, sales professionals often get clear feedback on how they are doing relative to their goals.

In other types of work, particularly knowledge work, key measurements are often reported too slowly to be useful or are obscured in the form of periodic and highly polished updates. We once read a ten-plus-page monthly update on a major multimillion-dollar project that gave a glowing report of teamwork and technical advances. Buried in a single sentence in the middle of the report was the small bit of information that the project was four months behind schedule. Burying such negative information in a sea of positivity, while all too common, only delays the actions necessary to get back on course. When developing new products, for example, errors surfaced early can often be fixed with a mouse click. When that same error is discovered later, it can cost millions of dollars to correct. The project with the glowing report and the buried lede ended up being over a year late.

Not only do long delays between action and outcome corrupt the learning process and hurt results, but they also sap motivation. Imagine how difficult it would be to learn to play tennis if you didn't get to see where your shots were going and then, weeks later, got a written report detailing where they landed. If you asked a senior executive how she did in executing the strategy that day, she would probably laugh at you. At first glance, the question seems absurd. Nonetheless, how *do* executives know whether they are doing a good job? How do they know whether what needed to happen today, or this week, to execute their strategy actually happened the way it was supposed to and yielded expected results? They certainly look at sales and profit figures, but those indicators can lag weeks or months behind and are influenced by numerous other forces. In most organizations, it is very difficult to attribute current success to specific strategic choices. Organizations that are out of touch with the specifics of the work can be easily misled on the key elements that are really driving their results.

This is a situation ripe for what psychologists call *superstitious learning*, where people attribute success to their own actions when, in fact, the outcomes were dictated by other forces. Nelson learned all sorts of wrong lessons as he tried to fix his golf swing based on flawed perception. Similarly, consider the challenge facing the leaders of Peloton Interactive, a manufacturer of popular home exercise bikes. The company's stock price peaked at over $150 per share early in December 2020, when everyone was deciding what to purchase for the first holiday season of the COVID pandemic. Was this strategy or luck? It would be all too easy for executives to attribute their success to their own acumen, believing that their success would continue because of their brilliant game plan. Eighteen months later, however, that stock was worth less than $10 per share. Relying on external, lagging metrics that don't reveal the underlying mechanics can break the connection between action and result, making learning very difficult.

There is a better way: construct clear targets, the intent behind them, and their supporting metrics. Make sure that the key activities and the underlying assumptions about the results those activities will deliver are clearly visible. Treat the activity set as an experiment that will help you discover what works best and will reveal issues and impediments. Check frequently to see if the results happened as predicted and note what you learned. Most executives are accustomed to getting weekly and monthly reports on how the organization is doing relative to its targets. But unless they care about the *how*, about the activity sets and experiments that drove the results, they limit their organization's ability to discover and innovate. Instead of focusing on constant experimentation and feedback, they focus on people, rewarding them for good results and blaming them for bad ones, regardless of the real causes that may or may not be connected to what those people did or had to do. A terrible result driven by factors out of anyone's control might have been much worse were it not for the brilliant action of the manager. But in many cases, if the result is bad, the manager gets punished.

You can't command innovation, but you can create the conditions from which it will emerge. Turn every plan into a series of small experiments. Let the objective feedback guide your understanding. Structuring the work for discovery helps weave your targets together, aggregating all the activities and assumptions behind the targets into a big engine of constant experimentation. In such an environment, individual learning becomes genuine organizational capability, and a foundation for ever-better results is established.

Mike probably couldn't see immediate changes in repeat business, but he could certainly track email capture. The underlying assumption being tested was "The more effective the marketing is, the more repeat business we will get. A key to effective marketing is the ability to reach out to current customers using email." In our experience, senior leaders often move too quickly from one big idea to another. If the big idea doesn't immediately deliver the results they want, they start looking for the next big thing. When executives monitor only whether or not a strategy or change effort is hitting its milestones, they don't assess whether the underlying activities are being executed properly. If you can't answer questions like "Is the plan working?," "What parts helped, and which ones didn't?," and "What have we learned?," how can you have any hope of learning from experience or adjusting to a rapidly changing world? Without genuine attention to learning from experience, the next big thing rarely works any better than the last big thing.

With regular feedback in place to reveal advances and shortfalls based on a specific set of activities, effective discovery requires engaging those who do the work with those who manage the work to capture new ideas and uncover issues that block progress. In our experience, it's essential, but few companies do it well. Instead, when a target is missed or a problem occurs, leaders try to solve the problem without even talking to the people closest to the work. At one energy company, the employees called this *seagull management*: when there was a problem, perhaps a safety issue or a revenue shortfall, "senior leaders swoop in like a flock of birds, shit on everything with their 'brilliant' solutions, and then leave."

Seagull management not only is ineffective but also limits access to a critical source of information. Those who do the work usually have the best understanding of the details of the actual problem, even if they don't know the best way to solve it (which they often do). Remember automatic processing: performing day-to-day tasks leads to a deeper understanding of them. Moreover, those doing the work often are the only ones who know

"where the bodies are buried"—only they know all of the undocumented, surreptitious workarounds and adjustments needed to
get things done. Those who do the work know *how*, but they
become much more effective if they also know *why* and participate openly in the design of the *how*.

When you don't engage those doing the work in the design
of the work, you lose access to a huge collection of knowledge.
There are often significant impediments to getting work done
that those on the front line know all too well but don't get
attention from more senior leaders. After Harley, Don worked
at a privately held manufacturing company called Intermatic.
One day Don discovered that a balky printer on the shipping
dock frequently delayed the work of almost a dozen people at
the plant. When the team member was asked why she hadn't
replaced it and added a backup, she said no one had ever asked
them what was wrong. She assumed the boss knew about the
problem but didn't want to spend the money to resolve it.
She wasn't empowered to spend the money, so the team just
dealt with it as best they could. You'll read the full story in
Chapter 9.

There's a further consequence of not including the people
who do the work in its design or in solving the problems they
face: it makes people hate their jobs. Perhaps the most basic
feature of human psychology is simply that we don't like being
told what to do, particularly when we don't know the why
behind the instruction. As we saw in Chapter 1, people get
motivated and enjoy tasks more when they play a part in determining the outcome. Highly repetitive work, like working
on an assembly line or processing invoices, poses a particular
challenge. Once the job in question is mastered, there are few
new patterns to match, and the work can get boring. Managers
often assume there is no need for employees to think about the

way the work happens and expect them to just do what they are told or to just follow the procedure.

The architects of the Toyota system solved this problem by changing the job description from "Do the work" to "Do the work and help us discover a better way of doing it." One Toyota manager told Don, "We call this 'patience with energy.' Our assembly lines are very refined, so it is hard to find the next place to gain even a few seconds. Our employees know the system well. They always have the customer in mind and are constantly looking for ways to make their jobs easier and more productive. So, we don't have to tell them what to change. We wait patiently for them to make a suggestion. Then we immediately check it out and implement it as fast as we can. The employee loves this immediate response, and it motivates them to come up with another idea."

Bolting wheels on a Toyota Camry may never occupy the mind like doing complex surgeries does, but engaging people in ongoing discovery of even the smallest improvement makes their job considerably more satisfying, especially when management pays close attention to their suggestions. It also allows the organization to capture and leverage the tacit knowledge that employees would otherwise take with them when they leave.

At the hotel, Mike completed his new design by instituting a brief daily huddle in front of a new scorecard on the bulletin board in the breakroom. With a frequent feedback mechanism, participants could see yesterday's results relative to the targets and to the predictions associated with changes that they had made. They focused on highlighting new actions that could be incorporated into regular work and on where an experiment could be designed to test a new idea. The numbers rose quickly, and the employees loved it. It was not only more productive but also better for the guests and more fun.

Through these discussions, the team quickly refined a common approach to the check-in process, expanded their tool kit for resolving complex cases (we will discuss the design of these huddles in more detail in the next chapter), and continued to run small experiments to improve further. As just one example, they figured out who spoke what language, increasing the chance that a guest from Mexico might be matched with a Spanish-speaking member of the team. (We'll cover more about charts and visual tools in Chapter 7.)

IMPROVEMENT AND LEARNING ARE PART OF THE DESIGN

Whether leaders like it or not, humans are constantly learning, adapting, and trying to improve. You can't turn it off. Designing effective and engaging work requires thinking carefully about what people learn, not just in the training center but also on the job. Structuring work so that new knowledge is regularly discovered starts with clear targets and a shared sense of the intent of the work and is followed by supporting metrics and an agreed-upon set of activities that form the plan. Looking at these elements together, by everyone at the same time, helps ensure the plan is not overly bound by habit. Effective learning and improvement happen when those doing the work and those managing the work can, together, clearly see where they have advanced, where they have fallen short, and where they can make the next round of improvements.

At the hotel, Mike used the structure-for-discovery principle effectively. He focused on two key targets: email capture and restaurant covers (guests served). Conversations with the team clarified these targets and their place within the larger plans to improve the work of check-ins. Daily feedback on progress against those targets and regular discussions to capture better methods and resolve newly revealed gaps created significant energy in the team. With time they discovered a better, more common approach to the check-in process, one that eliminated several unneeded steps and pulled from the tips and tricks that individual members had developed in their own work. Later, the team took the initiative to develop fun short videos to train new desk staff in the evolving approach.

Over the course of the two-month project, email capture rose from 70 percent to over 90 percent of check-ins, and the team added over a thousand covers per month in the steak restaurant, increasing revenue by almost $100,000. For several months, Mike was the envy of his peers at the weekly cross-casino performance review meeting.

Note two key elements in building effective discovery processes. First, conversations between those who do the work and those who lead them are central to success. It would be easy to conclude that, in fact, design is unnecessary. We just need talented leaders who manage by walking around. While it is good for leaders to connect with employees at all levels and to go see work being done, it is impractical for a CEO of a multinational company, or any busy manager, to have a careful conversation about targets, intent, and activity plans with tens, hundreds, or thousands of employees with informal walkarounds. There are no substitutes for carefully building the shared view of targets, intent, and activities through multiple layers of an organization. Nor do these casual walks reveal much about the status of the work. In contrast, conducting a deep investigation to help resolve a specific problem that is creating a gap between targets and outcomes can be a powerful leadership intervention. Without the context provided by a clear work design, leaders are unlikely to help surface real issues or contribute to the development of innovative methods. Discovery needs structure.

Every experienced leader eventually learns to be careful in what they ask for in casual conversation. Innocuous questions can easily be interpreted as commands, and offhand comments can become gospel. At Intermatic, Don loved to relive his shop floor experiences by walking through the factory every day and interacting with the employees, often talking about their issues and possible ways to solve them. But after a while, Don's head of manufacturing, Dan Glusick, who was highly skilled in these methods, asked Don to stop taking those walks.

Dan had worked with Don for years at Harley and was an excellent leader. He was also meticulous in structuring the work of his teams. Don's casual conversations with employees were often taken as a directive to change what they were doing and disrupted plans Dan and his production team had worked hard to develop. Don wanted to continue the walks, finding them critical to building connections with his employees, but he did agree to end each walk with a short debrief. Now Dan could decide if Don had uncovered a new problem or had inadvertently caused a new one.

To be effective, the questions leaders ask and the conversations they have must be part of a larger structure focused on achieving the organization's goals. Random conversations can just as easily do damage as make things better. As one perceptive staff member cautioned us when we were coaching his senior leadership team, "Be careful, these guys are like nuclear weapons. Aim them the wrong direction by just a few degrees and you could accidentally take out a whole city." Focusing senior leadership on the issues that matter most requires careful design, not random walks. Dynamic work design offers a structured way for leaders to make sure they are on the same page as their leadership team, who then have similarly structured ways to connect with their direct reports.

Structure for discovery is about making sure that everyone is always on the same page about the organization's targets and the intent behind them. The activities planned to achieve those targets are framed as an experiment that tests the hypothesis "These are the best activities to meet our targets and close any gaps." Frequent checks to see the result and what can be learned allow a team or an organization to harness the power of individual learning and to hasten the discovery of new and better methods.

In the next chapters, we will show how to optimize the organization by integrating the first two elements of good work design and the role of leaders.

Chapter 5

Connect the Human Chain

PUTTING PEOPLE BACK IN THE WORK

Mark Schwiebert knew dynamic work design was starting to take hold in his organization when, for the first time, he saw Ron smile.

As part of the purchasing team at BP's Toledo refinery, Ron was responsible for ordering the parts and services the plant needed. You probably have a Ron in your organization: he or she has been there for what seems like forever and, thanks to a wealth of experience, is the go-to person who can get almost anything done. But the Rons of the world can be grumpy. They feel they are the only ones who do "real work" and often complain that everything is broken and that leaders have no clue how the work actually gets done.

In Mark's previous encounters, Ron was always unshaven, his face locked in a perpetual scowl. While polite, he gave the impression that he was angry and frustrated. During Mark's previous visit to the refinery, Ron told him that he planned to take early retirement.

But on this visit, a freshly shaven Ron was smiling. He grabbed Mark by the elbow. "Come look at this."

A graph on Ron's wall showed noticeable improvement in the fraction of purchase orders (POs) that went through the system without requiring rework. For the last year or two, the purchasing staff, composed of Ron, three other employees, and a couple of contractors, had been under a lot of pressure. They routinely worked late and finished going through their email when they got home. Only a few months ago, purchase orders took several days to process, and suppliers regularly complained about not getting paid. But now most requests met the team's new target of "in by 7:00 a.m. and out by 2:00 p.m.," and the percentage of suppliers paid on time had risen from 65 percent to over 90 percent—one of the highest rates in the company. Shipment delays due to credit holds had disappeared. The purchasing team was now keeping up with their work and getting home at a decent hour.

After congratulating Ron on the good results, Mark said, "Ron, I know you're planning to retire soon, and I wanted to thank you for what you've done to get these results and wish you the best in your retirement."

"Are you kidding?" Ron said. "Mark, I'm not going anywhere. We are finally getting things done and we are making a difference here. I've pushed my exit date out at least a year."

This had not started out as a story with a happy ending. A year earlier, Mark had been promoted to head the procurement function for BP's North American fuels organization. It was an exciting career move. The group he now led spent billions of dollars a year getting parts and services delivered to the operations from over 5,000 suppliers. They served a business with more than 5,000 employees who operated 3 refineries, 4,200 miles of pipeline, 21 terminals, and nearly 17,000 gas stations, 7,000 of which BP owned. In good years, the business generated over $3 billion in profit.

Mark had also become the chair of a major council in his professional organization, the Institute for Supply Management, and he hoped to leverage his experience to transform BP's supply chain. When he was promoted, his new boss asked for an initial meeting. Mark was excited to share his plans and was expecting to be welcomed to the team as a valued contributor. The conversation did not go as he had anticipated.

"Mark," the boss said, "every one of my refinery managers is upset with your group. Procurement is broken and you need to fix it. Now." The list of complaints was long. Ordering parts through his group was cumbersome, and material often showed up long after it was needed. Service contracts routinely ran over their spending limits. Suppliers were routinely paid late and sometimes refused to deliver parts or come on-site until their account was settled.

Mark immediately began thinking of system-wide fixes and how he'd justify their cost. But his boss seemed to be reading his mind. "Don't ask for a new IT system or more staff. Our facilities are way down the list for IT upgrades. Thanks to the market downturn, our margins are falling, and I'm under a lot of pressure to reduce expenses. I'm asking every functional leader, including you, to reduce their operational spending by ten percent." After that conversation, Mark figured that he could probably forget about being a visible leader at BP. His dream job was beginning to feel like a bit of a nightmare and just keeping it would be a challenge. The procurement group was struggling to get the basics right, and the refining organization's management was justifiably upset.

Mark met with his team at the central office in Chicago. "Why," he asked, "are we performing so poorly?" The answers were typical and contained more than a few grains of truth.

"Everyone is overworked," said one team member.

"The IT system is broken," said another.

"There are screwups everywhere," said a third.

Since more staff and IT upgrades were off the table, Mark needed a different approach. He asked us for help.

A few weeks later, Don and Mike Plancon, a director on Mark's central staff, visited Toledo and met the people running the refinery's procurement function, commonly called purchase-to-pay, or P2P. The procurement manager started by showing Don and Mike the official P2P process document. It contained 144 individual steps, starting with entering a request into the system and ending with paying the supplier once the delivery of the part or service had been verified. The process was so long that just printing it, with the steps and linkages, took five pages. Don had to tape them together so he could see the whole thing at once.

Following the lesson he'd learned from Mr. Oba, the Toyota expert who had helped Don at Harley, Don asked whether, instead of listening to a long explanation of each of the 144 steps, Mike and he could go see the people who were doing the work. "Who receives the initial request for parts or services from the refinery? That's the first step in this diagram. Can we talk to them?"

"Go talk to Ron," one of the managers said. "He's been here forever and can tell you anything you want to know about how it all happens."

They walked to Ron's office. Ron was busy and didn't seem too happy to have visitors asking a lot of questions, especially one who was part of Mark's staff and the other a consultant. A consultant usually signaled a new initiative that would take time to implement but would not help actually get work done.

After introductions, Don started off, "Tell us about a typical day. How many requests from the refinery do you get and how do you process them?"

"I don't know, we each get maybe twenty or twenty-five new requests a day."

"Can you show us a request that goes well and what you have to do to turn it into a PO?"

Ron showed them a filled-out form on his computer screen. "I got this one first thing this morning. The system is out-of-date and doesn't allow people to enter all the information I need, but this person always sends me the extra information by email. If the email has everything I need, it only takes about five or six minutes to turn it into a PO."

Don did the rough math in his head. At twenty to twenty-five purchase requests a day, with each one taking less than ten minutes, if Ron starts work at 7:00 a.m., he should be done by 1:00 p.m., even with coffee breaks and lunch. But the procurement team was working ten hours a day and doing emails at home, and they still needed temps to help.

He asked Ron to show him a request that didn't go well.

"If I don't get all the right information, like with this one," Ron said, "I have to send an email to the requester across the street in the refinery." It usually took a few days to get the needed data because the operators spend most of their time out in the refinery and away from their desks. "The longer the back-and-forth goes on, the more pressure I get to put the order in the system. Sometimes we enter information knowing that not all of it is right just to get something in the system, hoping it is good enough for the supplier to deliver."

"Guessing," Ron continued, "usually creates trouble. If the system doesn't immediately reject the PO for lack of information and the supplier is able to deliver it, then it usually rejects the invoice later because some information, like the quantity, the unit of measure, or the tax category, doesn't exactly match. When this delays payment, the suppliers start complaining to accounts payable [AP], who call us to get it straightened out. We get these calls all day long. Usually it means the supplier won't ship until they get paid, so we stop what we're doing and solve it as best we can. But it could be an issue that is weeks or months old and takes us a lot of time to dig in to find exactly where the problem is. There's a huge pile of issues waiting to be resolved; each one has the possibility of dragging on so long that the supplier will stop delivering, causing another mini-crisis." The whole team—four full-time staff and two temps—spent their day switching back and forth between processing new requests and trying to keep payments flowing to suppliers so they would keep delivering parts and services to the refinery.

Mike, starting to feel bad for Ron, offered a few suggestions. "Don't worry about me," Ron interrupted. "I've had enough." He mentioned that he had already told his manager and Mark of his early retirement. "Someone else can deal with this mess," he said (though he used a more colorful word than *mess*).

WORK FLOWS WHEN PEOPLE CONNECT

Ron was a dedicated longtime employee who had spent much of his career fighting fires, doing whatever it took to make sure that parts and services were delivered on time and that suppliers got paid. The system hadn't always made work this difficult. When the computer system was first installed, it automated a lot of steps and sped up the process. But over the years, as procedures changed and the operation grew more complex, the system didn't keep up. Little issues grew into major impediments, and the backlog of orders and invoices rejected by the system continued to grow. More and more time was spent fixing bad POs instead of processing new ones. It was frustrating, but to Ron and his colleagues it just seemed like an unavoidable part of procurement in a big company. In Ron's view, a better way would only come with a big investment in an upgraded IT system. And he knew his facility was scheduled for a major IT overhaul . . . in five years.

Ron's assessment wasn't wrong, just incomplete. Everyone *was* overworked and the IT system *was* broken, but that wasn't what kept them from processing orders and payments on time. The real cause for the late deliveries and payments was the same one encountered at the Broad Institute, Mike's hotel, multiple hospitals, Harley-Davidson, and just about everywhere else. Although BP carefully designed both the organizational chart and the computer system to increase productivity and support its complex business, they hadn't paid similar attention to the set of evolving human interactions needed to move a purchase order through the system.

The official description of the P2P process (the one that Don had to tape together) showed how the work was supposed to flow, what systems were connected to other systems, and what departments were involved. It didn't, however, show the chain of people who moved work from one step to the next. And, as is typical of static designs, there was no mention of how things could go wrong or what to do when they did. Trying to use the official process was like trying to drive in a rapidly growing city using a fifty-year-old map. Ron and his colleagues found themselves spending more and more time dealing with a growing traffic jam of orders and invoices rather than redesigning their work in ways that would give them a more modern "GPS system." They needed an approach that created the interactions necessary to compensate for the increasingly outdated IT system.

Though they have IT and finance, organizations are not primarily IT or financial systems. Organizations are human systems built to connect people, to wire them together so that work gets done. Though it may be supported by sophisticated technology, turning a good idea into a product or delivering a service to a customer requires coordinated human effort. When managers confuse the design of support systems like IT and finance with the design of the networks that link the people who get work done, they both misunderstand how the work gets done and miss big opportunities for improvement.

For example, though it's not part of the official IT process or in its documentation, Nelson knows that one of the IT techs at MIT's Sloan School, Lamonte "Monte" Collins, can *always* solve his problems quickly and without descending into a bureaucratic tangle. And while Nelson is supposed to call central IT and get issued a ticket when something doesn't work, it's much easier to reach out to Monte directly. Similarly, Harley's firefighting arsonists were able to deliver their projects by leveraging personal connections throughout the organization. Such informal networks often work well when organizations are small but become increasingly ineffective as they get bigger. These workarounds hide the fundamental flaws that emerge in increasingly bureaucratic and overwhelmed processes, allowing the problems to fester and the number of workarounds to grow. Just as Harley experienced as it descended into firefighting, Ron and his team couldn't rely entirely on personal relationships to keep the Toledo refinery running. It had become too complicated and chaotic.

Sophisticated technology and increasingly distributed work, unless carefully designed, further obscure these critical human connections. Before the electronic age, the network of people who got work done was more visible. People along that path were usually in the same or nearby building. Work passed from one person to another either verbally or via paper documents. The path was more visible, and it often left a trail that you could follow to find the error and get to the right person to straighten it out. As computers began to automate work and distribute it around the globe, the chain of people who did that work became increasingly difficult to follow. Today, when we ask students in our Executive MBA program to map the chain of people who touch the work, we often get answers like "We fill out the data and it goes to India."

Used properly, automated systems can reduce effort and improve accuracy. But poorly designed technology often makes it difficult or even impossible to see the work *system*. When this happens, the people who do the work are no longer in control, can't see how their task fits with others', and have no idea what to do when something goes wrong. Like Ron, they work around the system as best they can, but without the big picture, they are just as likely to make things worse as better. No matter how sophisticated the information technology, success requires that the connections among the humans who move work forward be carefully designed to support the desired flow of work.

In Chapter 4, we discussed designing how teams work together to maximize their ability to learn and discover better ways of getting the work done. Building on this point, this chapter details how to design that work so that it flows from person to person to maximize improvement, adaptation, and learning. Conscious processing (or thinking slow) is the ultimate scarce resource in an organization, and success depends on putting that brain power to use at the right times and places. How do we wire hundreds or thousands of people together to interact in the right way and focus on the right things? In this chapter we divide the network of human connections into two interacting pieces: the *work chain* and the *management chain*. We'll show you how to rebuild them and make them function more effectively.

(RE)BUILDING WORK CHAINS WITH HANDOFFS AND HUDDLES

To start, let's go back to Ron and the purchase-to-pay process. When he didn't get all the information needed for a PO, Ron saw only two choices: chase down the requester by email (another electronic system), which took days, or guess at the answer and risk costly rework. At the outset, Ron saw this as a problem in the IT system—it didn't have the fields necessary for all of the information he needed. And he was right. That was a problem. But it wasn't the deal-breaker he thought it was. The IT system may have been inadequate, but the real problem was in the chain of work.

In any system, the *work chain* consists of all the people and all the connections among them needed to pass work from one step to the next. Whether it's lab samples at Broad, guests' experience at a hotel, motorcycles at Harley, or implementation of a strategy, work flows through a chain of people, each doing a particular activity and then moving that work to the next person in line. Because a static approach to design often breaks work and the people who do it into pieces—departments, groups, suppliers, and so on—it's easy to forget that organizations are fundamentally systems composed of people and designed to coordinate human activity so that work gets done. A more dynamic work design recognizes the need to "wire" people together in ways that allow the work to flow effectively among them.

As we see all the time, Ron and his colleagues confused a technology requirement—that the system have the right fields—with a requirement for a well-designed workflow. The work design requirement in this case is simple: the inputs that Ron needed to create a purchase order should equal the outputs of the person making the request. Confusing the design of technology with the design of the work it supports creates a big problem. In an ever-changing world, no computer is going to provide the right inputs to a task without some ongoing human interaction. The output/input match needs to be defined at the outset, and as the business changes, those requirements need to be updated. Without a carefully constructed set of human connections to update the design in an ever-changing world, as Ron experienced, mismatches are inevitable. When that happens, work, like processing purchase orders, will come to a halt if the only option is changing the computer system every time the environment shifts.

Though seemingly basic, the requirement that the outputs of one person's work should equal the inputs needed by the next person in the chain is routinely violated in a wide range of work. One of our former students is a physician at a major cancer center (who asked to remain anonymous). In trying to understand why critical test results were often delayed, she discovered that the form used to request those tests was so old that it didn't have boxes for many newly developed diagnostics. Doctors would scribble the needed test in the margins of the form, but much like Ron's colleagues in the refinery, they would often leave out critical information (the famously illegible physician handwriting didn't help either) and end up delaying potentially lifesaving treatment.

Redesigning the work chain to make sure the outputs of one person's work match the inputs the next person needs and that the people in the chain know each other often yields significant improvements by breaking logjams and getting work moving. Realizing such gains, however, requires recognizing that an effective work chain needs two kinds of transfers: *handoffs* and *huddles*.

Handoffs are effective when the information being transferred is simple and well understood by both parties. No conversation is needed. Nelson's MIT paycheck shows up in his bank account every two weeks. He and MIT both know what it is supposed to be and when it is supposed to show up; no conversation is needed. A huddle, in contrast, is a better choice when the information or material being transferred isn't clear and requires a face-to-face discussion to work through issues to agree on how to proceed. Confusing the two—using a handoff when you need a huddle or a huddle when you need a handoff—can bring a work process to its knees. Conversely, putting the transfers in the right places gets work moving and facilitates ongoing learning and discovery.

Handoffs

Don's first intervention with Ron focused on improving handoffs. Recall that Ron often got incomplete requests and thus was forced to either chase the requester for the missing information or guess at it, both of which led to extra work and delay.

"Ron," Don began, "how many people send you most of the purchase requests you process?"

Ron replied, "Oh, about eight or ten, I think."

Don then suggested that Ron take a few hours away from the high-pressure scramble of processing requests. "Make a checklist of all the information you need to process a request that isn't covered in the IT system. Draw it from the best examples you have, from the emails you get that are helpful. Then take a few more mornings and go visit those ten people in the refinery. Buy them a cup of coffee and tell them that if they send you the information on the checklist by 7 a.m. via email along with the computer request, you will process their purchase order by 2 p.m. the same day. It won't fix the system or all the issues, but I'll bet a lot of your problems will disappear."

Ron sat back, looking up at the ceiling. He knew the system wasn't providing all the information he needed and that it wouldn't get fixed for several years. But because Ron and his colleagues had been confusing technology design and work design, it hadn't occurred to him that the email that some of his buddies in the refinery sent was just another method of getting the right information and could be extended to other requesters. By reconnecting with his customers, he could easily overcome the limitations of the computer system. It would require a bit more work, but that effort would be saved ten times over with the problems it would eliminate. He looked at Don and Mike and said, "That's a damn good idea."

Why hadn't Ron made this leap months ago? The answer lies at the heart of static versus dynamic design. When Ron started working at Toledo, the purchasing group sat in the refinery, close to their customers in the operating units. Thanks to ongoing informal interactions, Ron's customers knew what Ron needed from them, and if there was a problem, it was quickly resolved with face-to-face conversation. However, when Ron's group was moved out of the refinery for safety reasons (out of the blast zone), those connections started to erode. New people came; others left. A new computer system had allowed orders to be entered from anywhere and, by design, eliminated "unnecessary" conversations. But when the technology started to become a bit outdated, the human connections required to adapt to the change had deteriorated, and everyone assumed that the only solution lay in a software update. People were implicitly assuming that the technology design was the same as the design that connected those doing the work.

Ron's experience of losing the human connection with his partners in the refinery is increasingly common. Thanks to both the ever-growing globalization of business and more people working remotely, there are fewer impromptu hallway conversations and random meetings at the coffee machine to ask questions and work through small issues. Not surprisingly, we see the confusion between technology design and work design regularly. As we discuss more in Chapter 7, another company we know well, Fannie Mae, like most big organizations, usually defaulted to fixing problems with new technology, even when there was a far simpler, cheaper fix in the work design. Sometimes a five-minute daily meeting or a few sticky notes on a whiteboard work better than millions of dollars in new IT.

An effective handoff requires a few key elements. Most importantly, both the sender and the receiver should agree on the details of the information or material that is supposed to move between them and when it should be transferred. Ideally, all of the people in a given segment of the chain know one another and the parts they play. They are clear on what the work is supposed to produce (the target) and why their piece is important. When people understand the larger goal and are connected with one another, they are better able to adapt to inevitable changes in conditions and requirements.

The simple checklist defining a good purchase order made Ron's life a lot easier and improved the collaboration between his group and the people in the refinery. It got POs created quickly and also significantly reduced the amount of rework that stemmed from guessing at the information needed to create a PO. Even better, a checklist is easily updated as requirements change or as people invent new, better ways of doing the work. The new IT system, when it showed up, would also help and could incorporate the checklist, but the refinery didn't have to wait for a new system to improve performance.

Note that the magic does not lie in the checklist. Checklists are just one way of making sure that every person is getting the information she needs to do her work. It is the clear human connection that ensures that each transfer results in the downstream people getting what they need to do their work that secures an effective handoff.

Huddles

A handoff is only effective when both parties can clearly specify what is being transferred. Handoffs worked great when Ron was asked to order a standard item that the refinery used regularly. They are not effective when the details of the transfer can't be specified in advance. For example, sometimes Ron would be asked to get a highly specialized item that had never been ordered before. In these cases, nobody knew the exact specifications of the item or the supplier who could provide it. Trying to process these items via a handoff almost guarantees a lot of emailing back and forth, misunderstandings, and consequent rework. Such iteration is far more efficient when it is done in the form of a face-to-face discussion. So, when the work can't be clearly specified in advance, moving it from one person to the next requires more than a handoff; the details need to be worked out in a *huddle*.

A huddle is just a face-to-face meeting to figure out and/or agree upon what the person working downstream needs to get their work done and why. We use the term *huddle* to clearly distinguish this type of meeting from those normally experienced in large organizations. In sports, a huddle is a brief point of connection in which the team determines what they should do next to execute their strategy. It has a specific purpose, and when that purpose is accomplished, the huddle ends. Similarly, when it comes to designing effective work chains, the goal of a huddle is to transfer the information needed to move the work forward. Anything else is a distraction.

In Ron's shop, nonroutine items had been treated just like routine ones and transferred using a poorly designed handoff, leaving Ron to guess at the missing details. Rework was often the result. Ron implemented huddles by leaving his office a few afternoons a week and spending time in the refinery. Each time he got a request for a nonstandard item, he would schedule a face-to-face meeting with the requester during one of these afternoon visits. They would discuss what was needed and come to an agreement, often checking supplier websites and/or getting a customer representative on the phone. The discussions would continue until Ron had enough information to negotiate with a supplier (another huddle) and get a good order into the system.

We have all experienced the consequences of trying to transfer work via a handoff when a huddle is the better choice. Long email chains that circulate among multiple people for days are a common result. In an effort to resolve a complex issue, someone sends an email outlining the problem and soliciting input and solutions. But the ambiguity inherent in such problems requires a lot of back-and-forth to define the problem, arrive at a diagnosis, and surface possible resolutions. While such iteration happens naturally and quickly in a face-to-face huddle, it can be painfully slow and inefficient when done via email or via other asynchronous modes of communication. When Don worked at

Intermatic, anytime he was copied on a long email thread, he would tell other participants to get off email and meet face-to-face, usually resulting in the issue being resolved in a matter of minutes. Trading an ill-structured handoff for a quick huddle led to better and faster resolution.

Ron and the purchasing team also used huddles to improve their connections with accounts payable. Prior to Don and Mike's work with Ron, every time a supplier didn't get paid because of a bounced order, the accounts payable team would send an email to procurement. The person receiving that note would drop whatever they were doing, dig out the purchase order, and try to figure out why it had been rejected by the system. Accounts payable treated a bounced order as something that could be handed off rather than as a problem to be discussed and solved. Procurement was just supposed to fix it. But to paraphrase Leo Tolstoy's famous words in *Anna Karenina* about families ("All happy families are alike; each unhappy family is unhappy in its own way."): every good order was the same; every bounced one was different in its own way and signaled the existence of another problem that had to be investigated to be solved.

It often took multiple emails between procurement and accounts payable to resolve the issue. Each email from accounting interrupted someone in procurement, randomly shifting their attention from processing routine work to solving a complex problem. Such task switching lowered productivity and wasted resources.

Ron and the team redesigned this part of their work by dividing their day into two pieces and clearly separating the two kinds of purchase requests. Routine requests, those that were amenable to handoffs, were quickly processed in the morning, without outside interruption. Later, the purchasing team would sit together with accounts payable to work through the more complex supplier-payment issues. By working together in the same room, questions were answered more quickly as there was usually someone who remembered key information or knew how to solve the problem. With these two design changes— eliminating bad orders from getting into the system and solving invoice issues in a daily huddle—the backlog quickly shrank. Initially, there were enough problem invoices that the team met every day. After a few weeks, they had made so much progress that they needed to huddle only twice per week.

Mixing Handoffs and Huddles

The major flaw we see in most work chains is they don't put handoffs and huddles in the right places. People often don't recognize that different tasks have different levels of uncertainty and thus require a different kind of transfer. Prior to our work with the Toledo refinery, Ron's team relied on handoffs embedded in the computer software. Not only did this create extra work for routine orders, thanks to the software not being capable of transmitting all of the required information, but it also created trouble every time Ron's team needed a conversation to determine exactly what to order. Conversely, some processes rely exclusively on huddles, even when the information being transferred is easily standardized. Precious meeting time, for example, is often spent communicating information that could easily be captured in a good email. At MIT, annual teaching plans are approved and transferred only in a meeting, even when the courses being approved are delivered every year with no material change. Nelson, like everyone else in those long meetings, could often use the time to get real work done.

Hospital emergency departments, in contrast, often mix huddles and handoffs effectively. When the ambulance shows up, the EMTs have a short conversation to bring the receiving medical staff up-to-date on the situation (huddle). Other information, like insurance, is handled separately by filling out forms (handoffs). The doctor makes an assessment in discussion with the patient and the nursing staff (huddle). The staff then orders lab tests and X-rays using forms or computers (handoffs). When the test results return from the lab (handoff), another huddle helps determine the course of action. If something goes wrong and the patient takes a serious turn for the worse, everyone quickly knows about it and moves to respond.

Though the emergency department is often a model of effectiveness, hospitals also provide plenty of bad examples. Trying to decipher a medical bill can feel like an endless series of unsatisfying handoffs as you are moved from person to person or automated system to automated system. Even when you are able to have a conversation with someone, without the key players in the same room it's almost impossible to resolve the competing interests that cross multiple institutions. The issues are pushed around via phone calls and email handoffs for weeks or months, each transaction becoming more frustrating and maddening than the previous one.

More generally, we find that organizations often function effectively when there is a crisis but struggle mightily to execute the work that supports those on the front lines (or that prevent crises in the first place). In the emergency room, the intent is clear, and the work chain needed to deliver that intent emerges naturally. Billing, in contrast, offers almost endless opportunities for improvement. Similarly, Ron had built a sophisticated system of relationships and workarounds to get parts when there was an emergency in the refinery. Conversely, no one, Ron or otherwise, had fixed the underlying system that created many of those crises in the first place. This changed when Toledo started focusing on improving its work chains.

By the time Mark visited, the Toledo refinery's P2P system had improved dramatically. Most orders were now processed the day they were received, and less than 5 percent of them required rework. The backlog of bounced orders was eliminated, and new ones were easily handled in the weekly huddles with accounts payable. Two temporary job positions were eliminated, and Ron and his colleagues went home at a reasonable hour. Within a year, the refinery improved the percentage of invoices it paid on time from about 65 percent to over 95 percent.

CONNECTING THE MANAGEMENT CHAIN WITH PLANNED AND EVENT-BASED HUDDLES

Connecting the work chain is half the story. Taking full advantage of the collective brainpower and experience of the organization to make sure work flows also requires "wiring" together the *management chain*: the sequence of people who support and guide the work. Despite continued advances in software systems for managing workflow and the increasing use of remote, asynchronous modes of working, face-to-face communication remains critical to the rapid adaptation and problem-solving required to be successful in a dynamic world. Unfortunately, face-to-face communication, meaning meetings, is rarely used effectively.

Most managers think they connect to the flow of work through meetings. Weekly staff meetings, monthly one-on-ones, quarterly reviews, and annual off-site gatherings should give managers the opportunity to review the status of the work, deliver new policies or targets, and identify and solve problems. But, despite the ubiquity of such meetings, most people sense that they are not used effectively. When we ask executives to identify the most frustrating things about their organizations, too many meetings and too many bad meetings always top the list. While there's a small industry of people writing books and articles about best practices for running better meetings, it remains an uphill battle with little evidence of progress.

Meetings *can* be one of the most powerful elements of an effective work design. As we saw with the work chain, when designed properly, face-to-face communication allows a real-time flow of information that supports rapid decision-making and problem-solving. But meetings are also one of the most expensive uses of time, so they need to be used wisely. A poorly designed and executed hour-long meeting with ten people amounts to ten hours that are not being dedicated to other kinds of work. Sadly, we see many more bad meetings than good ones. They are usually focused on reviewing metrics and externalizing blame for any shortfalls against the targets. They rarely delve into the state of the work or its design. Bad news is usually not welcomed and is often delayed until reporting it can't be avoided. Once an issue is revealed, the meeting often devolves to finding fault with the people nearest to the problem. Who wants to raise a problem in a punitive environment?

Differences in meeting effectiveness are often attributed to individual style—some managers are extroverts, some are reserved, etc.—but this represents a deep confusion about the nature of effective management and leadership. We tend to deify those few who succeed in poorly designed work rather than highlight good work designs that accommodate a wide range of personalities and styles. Just as a well-designed car can support most individual driving styles, a well-designed management chain can accommodate a range of approaches. Finding the unique personality that can be successful in a poorly designed system is a fool's errand. Designing a system in which most leaders can be successful offers far more leverage.

The essence of designing an effective management chain starts with a simple question: What do managers do to move work forward? The simple answer is that they make decisions and solve problems. When the work is moving, managers don't need to intervene. When the work stops, either something has gone wrong or a decision needs to be made about what to do next (should, as in our Harley example, the engine be optimized for horsepower or torque?). Either way, managers need to get involved. In contrast, managers don't typically need to be involved in handoffs since, by definition, the work is standard. Managerial work happens in huddles, whether they be regular staff meetings, project reviews, or impromptu problem-solving efforts. Management huddles not only keep leaders in touch with what is really happening but are the best vehicle for rapid decision-making, coaching, and problem-solving. They are a critical design element in the management chain. Much as with the work chain, the trick is to get people collaborating in discovery mode at the right moments to leverage the power of face-to-face communication.

Distinguishing between two types of huddles—planned meetings initiated by a schedule and immediate meetings initiated by a specific condition (which we call a *trigger*)—will help get managers and leaders actively engaged in the flow of work at the right places and at the right times.

Planned Huddles

The first type of management huddle is familiar: the regular meeting to evaluate progress and make the decisions necessary to move the work forward. The key to using it effectively is to match its frequency to the speed with which the underlying work generates problems and issues needing discussion and resolution. A disconnect between the frequency of meeting and the speed with which the work generates things that require discussion is, as we will see, a sure sign of poor work design.

Michael O'Sullivan was a product development director for Analog Devices, a major semiconductor manufacturer, when he took our MIT class in 2019. Mike's teams helped develop new chips. As we discussed in Chapter 3, Mike focused his project on the prototype evaluation step, the part of the process centered on measuring the capabilities of a new chip. At that point in time, it usually took Analog Devices three to four months to evaluate the first version of a new semiconductor. Their competitors could execute this step more quickly, making it difficult for Analog to reap the advantage that comes with being first to market.

At the outset of the prototype evaluation process, the team would meet to discuss how they wanted to measure the performance of the new chip to determine the right mix of speed, power consumption, and capabilities. Once they agreed on the specs, an engineering sub-team would build a test bed and assess the chip's performance. Going through several of these iterations is normal for any new product development project.

When Mike dug into the details of how the evaluation work was executed, however, he discovered a big disconnect in the timing between generating test information and the meetings to discuss it. The review meetings to check progress and modify the plan happened on a specific cadence, in this case every other week. But it took the engineers only a few days to build the test bed and a day or so to run the evaluation for each prototype. While the engineers waited for the next status meeting in two weeks, they would break down the test bed and set up and run a test for a different project.

When the larger team finally reviewed the results, they would often ask for more or different tests based on the information the previous tests had generated. Since the engineers had switched to working on other projects, they would wait until they got to a sensible stopping point in the test they were doing, tear down that chip's test bed, and redo the setup for the first project. The every-other-week meeting design was far out of step with the speed at which the work was moving. The biweekly frequency created a situation akin to having a race car wait in the pit while the pit crew finishes planning for next week's race before going to get the car back on the track.

The mismatch between the speed of the measurement work and the frequency of the check-ins resulted in a lot of waiting for one test to finish and even more time and resources wasted on multiple teardowns and setups. Typically, several projects were in process, resulting in repeated setups and teardowns for each one. The time it took for one project to get completely through the process was a significant multiple of the time required for the actual testing. This work design slowed the completion of *every* project. A project that needed three weeks of testing might be in the testing phase for three months.

Managers can easily miss the opportunity to match the meeting frequency with the speed that the work generates new information. Without digging into the details of the work, it looks like things are running well since everyone is busy. Looking at how a specific piece of work or a specific project is moving (or not) can often immediately reveal major opportunities for improving the productivity of the *system*.

Mike's solution was simple. He clarified the purpose of the meeting and its key output—update the management group on the results of the testing so they can give the measurement team guidance on what to do next—and asked the team to meet briefly each day (rather than every two weeks). A quick daily check-in with the full team allowed the engineers to iterate more quickly (daily rather than every two weeks) and eliminated the waste of building up and breaking down the test bed. The four-month evaluation time dropped to less than thirty days. Even better, working on one project at a time eliminated a lot of nonproductive time and increased the lab's total output. *Every* project began moving through this phase faster.

Clarifying a planned huddle's purpose—making sure that it contains the necessary combination of decision-making and problem-solving to move the work forward—and matching its timing to the speed of the work can lead to significant improvements. Most meetings fail to meet these criteria. They are not clearly located within the larger flow of work, and it's often not clear what they are supposed to produce. Words like *oversight* and *review* are too abstract to help participants move work forward. Asking people to explain shortfalls in the metrics puts them in storytelling mode rather than spurring an examination of the work itself to find the cause. Similarly, the frequency of meetings is often dictated by the calendar—weekly, monthly, etc.—with little regard for the pace of the work. For example, prior to their work with Mike and Don, Ron's purchasing team met with more-senior management a few times a year for a check-in, but beyond providing an opportunity to complain about the IT system, little got done at these meetings. In contrast, frequent meetings to investigate and resolve problem POs generated significant gains.

Clarifying a meeting's role in examining the status of the work, moving it forward, and matching the frequency to the underlying cadence of the work is a critical feature of several productivity innovations. For example, consider the increasingly popular *agile* approach to software development. Prior to the advent of agile, software was typically developed using the stage-gate method. The process involved a small number of large stages, each of which focused on a specific activity, such as defining the requirements that the project should meet. At the end of each phase, a large meeting (the gate) was held to review the results of that stage. These meetings happened only every quarter or so. During each stage, teams typically met weekly to review progress.

Agile traded the long stages for a shorter iteration known as a *sprint*. Each sprint lasted two to three weeks and focused on delivery of a specific piece of software functionality. The software development team reviewed their progress with the larger organization at the end of each sprint. Agile also suggests that development teams connect daily in a meeting so short that chairs are not provided. Having no place to sit encourages people to surface and discuss issues quickly so they can get back to their desks. Daily agile meetings typically last no more than fifteen minutes and focus on moving the work ahead, not reviewing and "managing" metrics. Agile effectively increased the frequency of team huddles from weekly to daily and the organizational reviews from quarterly to monthly (or even more frequently).

By better matching the frequency of check-ins to the speed of work in software development, agile produced significant gains in productivity. Whereas in the traditional model a defect or misunderstanding might not be revealed for weeks or months, in the agile approach a defect surfaces far more quickly and is resolved with far less rework. The combination of daily and monthly check-ins has proven to be a better match for the world of fast-paced, highly iterative software projects and has yielded positive results for many organizations.

Agile's success in the software world has, however, led people to apply the frequency of check-ins that works for software development to other types of work. People often confuse the specific practice, such as a daily stand-up meeting, with the underlying principle of matching the meeting frequency to the speed with which the work generates things you need to talk about. Many organizations outside the world of software development now use daily stand-up meetings. But not every type of work requires this cadence. Meetings are a waste of time when not enough has been accomplished to warrant new conversation.

Conversely, in cases like the early moments following a natural disaster, a daily meeting isn't enough. For example, at MIT during the early days of COVID, the situation was changing so quickly and new information became available so often that we needed to check in twice per day. Major accidents sometimes require an even greater flow of information. In some cases the situation is so fluid that the team should just sit together in a perpetual huddle and collaborate continuously, even when it comes at the expense of individual productivity.

How do you know if you are meeting too frequently or not frequently enough? If you find yourself flooded with problems that you learned about through email and instant messaging, then you likely are not meeting frequently enough to keep up with the speed at which the work is generating new information. Conversely, if regular meetings devolve to tedious status reports that don't contain a lot of new information and there isn't a lot of back-and-forth, then you are meeting too often.

Huddles Triggered by Specific Events

When properly designed and located, regular huddles help move work forward. Nonetheless, meetings are overused. We're all burdened with too many meetings, and it is one of the most often-voiced work-related frustrations. One reason for such proliferation is the practice of having a regular huddle "just in case" there is an issue to discuss. These meetings can be eliminated by using a work design element we call a *trigger*: a signal indicating that "we need a meeting." Unlike planned huddles, triggered huddles don't happen at a predetermined frequency. Instead, they are driven by a condition or an event. A trigger brings people together when they are needed.

A huddle initiated by a trigger often has a smaller and more focused scope: solve the specific problem that has stopped the work. Perhaps the most well-known instance of a trigger is Toyota's famous *andon* (stop) cord. When an assembly-line worker sees a problem, he pulls the cord, and the team leader immediately comes to help. If the problem can't be resolved quickly, the line stops. This andon scheme is not random. Toyota carefully specifies both the conditions that dictate pulling the cord and the chain of people who get the signal. In some scenarios the signal can travel all the way up the chain to the plant manager.

While the conditions dictating that the cord be pulled on the factory floor are clear, it's often far less clear when to stop the work in knowledge and service contexts. Individuals and teams are usually left on their own to decide when to raise a hand and ask for help. In the interest of empowerment, or not wanting to micromanage, managers often give subordinates a task and say, "Call me if you need help." But such murky guidance about when and where subordinates should surface technological or other problems almost guarantees trouble. Lacking a clear rule, teams almost always wait too long, hoping they can solve the problem before it causes major delays. As a result, the organization is left with incomplete information about brewing issues that could be easily resolved when small but that quickly become more disruptive when allowed to fester. Defining triggers in advance of doing the work increases the chance that the problems will be surfaced at the right time.

Designing an effective trigger is not the same as saying, "Let me know every time something goes wrong." The key is to define the conditions for a trigger so that more-senior managers intervene when their expertise has something to offer. When a trigger is too loose and when more-senior managers are engaged only infrequently, work gets stuck and major problems surface only when fixing them is very expensive. When a trigger is too tight, managers intervene too often, wasting resources and limiting the contributions of those who actually do the work. Consider the following example of defining an effective trigger.

When Michael Rohleder took our course at MIT, he was the CEO of US oil and gas company Thunderbird Resources. Mike focused his project on a set of wells in the East Texas region that weren't pumping at their maximum potential (and reducing the company's revenue). He hoped to improve their performance by 10 percent.

Onshore wells tend to be spread widely across a basin that can encompass thousands of square miles. Thunderbird, like other companies in the oil and gas business, employs pumpers: technicians who visit the wells on a regular basis to do routine maintenance and adjust the wells to improve the flow of gas.

Mike began by observing how the work was getting done. As we described in Chapter 3, an overreliance on automatic processing often leads to an incomplete investigation into an issue (we think we already know what the problem is) and results in trying to solve today's problem with yesterday's solution. Seeing the work in action is often the only way to get past our preconceptions and understand what is really happening, warts and all. So, Mike spent a few days in the passenger seat of the pickup trucks driven by the pumpers, riding along and watching them work to see what was missing.

When a pumper got to a well site, he would start with general maintenance and then assess the well's performance. If the well was flowing (producing natural gas) as expected, he was done. If not, the well could often be adjusted to improve performance. But before making any adjustments to the well, the pumper had to check with the engineering manager. Gas wells can be dangerously explosive when not managed properly, so the engineering manager required the pumpers to call him and discuss any proposed adjustments before making them.

The charge to call the engineering manager is an example of a trigger. A well not flowing at full capacity combined with the pumper's instinct that it could be improved triggered a meeting (by phone) with the engineering manager. But when a pumper called, the engineering manager might be in a meeting, on another call, or out of the office. The pumper could then either wait for the engineering manager to call back or pack up, head to another well (which could be miles away), and return later. Either way, valuable time was lost, a wasted resource that was not visible to the manager. This was a poorly designed trigger; a well-designed trigger both leverages local knowledge where possible and elicits a timely response when the limits of that knowledge are reached.

To improve the design, Mike brought the pumpers and engineering manager into a room together and asked the group, "Are there things the pumpers can do safely without getting approval first?"

After some discussion, the group identified four adjustments within specified ranges that the pumpers could make without risking well safety. Anything else still required a call. The newly designed trigger gave the pumpers more latitude and, thanks to fewer instances of the trigger being activated, eased the burden on the engineering manager. The session also made the manager aware of the way his behavior was hurting productivity, increasing the chance that when the pumpers did call, they would get a timely response.

The results were dramatic. The new design made it possible for the pumpers to get to many more wells and use their deep experience to safely optimize the flow. While Mike had initially hoped for a 10 percent gain, his project delivered a 110 percent improvement in well productivity.

As Mike's experience highlights, well-designed triggers improve the flow of work by directing help and managerial attention to when and where it's needed. Triggers keep the work moving by signaling when something is stuck and supercharge discovery by exposing issues when they are small and bringing the right expertise to bear in real time. The action Mike took didn't double productivity by teaching the pumpers something new. He just created a system of on-demand huddles that allowed them to put their expertise to work more effectively. Moreover, connecting senior management to the real issues getting in the way of success turns their focus from big one-size-fits-all initiatives to more targeted and effective interventions.

Even when a problem can't be entirely eliminated, triggers help senior teams manage such hiccups more effectively by getting them involved when their help and expertise can prevent a problem from escalating. For example, one student worked to improve the process of building new facilities for her firm, a company that sources and installs solar power systems for homes. Delays in receiving key equipment resulted in wasted resources at the construction site. She inserted a trigger into the project-planning process: anytime a key piece of equipment was shipped late, the leadership team would immediately meet to adjust their activity plan. The trigger helped prevent a lot of delays, but even when it didn't, it gave the team more time to adjust the plan and minimize the impact of the delay. There was no point, for example, in having an installation crew on-site if there was no equipment to install (something that had happened regularly).

Designing Effective Triggers

The key elements of an effective trigger are captured in the design of a fire alarm. Your local fire department doesn't stop by every week for a huddle just to see if something is burning. Instead, there is a clear signal to the fire department that is activated under well-understood conditions: if you see fire or smoke, pull the fire alarm. It is not a personal choice dictated by whether or not you are at fault; it's about the fire. And that signal doesn't go to a random fire department, who may or may not respond depending on how busy they are. A fire alarm goes to a specific fire company that is trained to respond in minutes.

A good trigger starts with clearly defining the condition that requires escalation. When Nelson oversaw MIT's Executive MBA program, he used a simple rule for managing the quality of teaching. As long as an instructor received a rating of 4 or better (on a 5-point scale), the rating didn't need to be discussed. Anything lower than a 4 triggered a meeting with that instructor. With the conditions clearly specified, any session that fell below the threshold got immediate attention and help, irrespective of what might have caused the shortfall.

Similarly, activating a trigger when its condition is met should be an expected behavior, not a personal choice. One of our colleagues in the MIT Executive MBA program might have had a personal challenge that hurt his ratings. Left to his own discretion, he might not escalate the issue ("it was a onetime thing"). But this is a slippery slope that can lead to more significant systemic issues being suppressed. One bad year of teaching, rationalized and therefore left unattended, can easily turn into a string of bad performances. Requiring escalation every time ensures that people don't develop the habit of suppressing bad news.

Triggers are easily adjusted to control the number of escalations. When Nelson first took over the program, the trigger was a 3.5 out of 5. As the overall quality of teaching improved, fewer meetings were triggered and the pace of improvement declined. Nelson simply raised the threshold to 4 so that problems were still being escalated for the team to work on.

When a trigger is activated, the first responsibility of the management chain is to protect the flow of work. This could entail fixing the problem or finding a way to bypass it until it is resolved. When an instructor was really struggling with a particular class, for example, Nelson might consider bringing in a guest instructor to help get things back on track. Once that flow is restored, then the focus turns to redesigning the work to eliminate the problem. The fire department shows up to fight the fire, not to berate you for having a problem. Only after the fire is out and everyone is safe do they send investigators and prevention experts to figure out what happened.

Finally, and most importantly, don't punish people when they activate a trigger. The ultimate goal of dynamic work design is to bring your organization's scarce cognitive resources to the problems and opportunities that matter most. The moment people see surfacing a problem as a waste of time (because you are just going to get a lecture) or, worse, as bad for their careers, your organization is in trouble.

The Broad team used the metaphor of fires to escalate issues. Sheila started every meeting with the question "Is anything on fire?" We've never seen a leader better at creating an environment in which people feel safe to surface issues. For example, in the early days of developing their system, someone at Broad might raise an issue by saying, "Well, it's not really on fire, it's just smoking a little." Sheila would immediately put the issue on the fire board, list their problems to be solved (more on this in Chapter 7), and start talking about protecting the flow of work and then solving the problem. Not only was there no hint of blame, but the person surfacing the issue was praised for his or her courage. It was not a problem to report a fire, but it was a big problem to hide one. Sheila's approach made all the difference and played a critical role in the institute's path to ongoing discovery.

DIAGNOSING BROKEN CHAINS

We can see how broken work and broken management chains can be identified and improved in the case of a second onshore gas producer we worked with a decade ago. The company planned to install several hundred new wells over the space of twenty-four months. The well sites were scattered over several thousand square miles in the western United States. The process of developing each well site was complex, involving acquiring land rights, drilling the well, getting the well technology to work, managing environmental impacts, and connecting the active well to the pipeline network.

The teams responsible for each of these steps were spread over the country. Technology development, geology, and legal were located a thousand miles away, while the land acquisition, drilling, pipeline, and operational teams all reported to different managers and sat in different offices in the region. The project leader was local and tried to coordinate the work among these groups. As a group finished their work on one site, the project leader would have the next site lined up for them. The assumption was that if each party independently did their work well, then all the pieces would fit together and the overall project would go smoothly. Six months in, the company was forty well installations behind schedule, and the financial impact had already reached millions of dollars per day.

Don spent two days with the project manager, asking questions and using the answers to sketch the work chains and management chains on a whiteboard. "Explain how the work moves from team to team," Don asked. The answer took a day and a half: the land team provides legal access and permits; then geology gives the exact coordinates for drilling; then the safety and environment teams prepare the site and ensure that proper safeguards are in place; drilling then drills the well; other teams install additional equipment to make the site operational; the pipelines team connects the flow to the network; and then, finally, the whole thing is handed to operations. It was complex and dangerous work.

Each team was doing what they thought was the right work at the right time, but the pieces didn't always fit together, creating confusion, rework, and delay. For example, drilling would often bring a rig to the site thinking they could start right away, only to find that the site was not yet fully prepared. The drilling team could then either do this work themselves or bring in a contractor. Either way, the very expensive drill rig sat idle until the prep was finished.

Don wrote each of the functions on the whiteboard in a box and lined up the boxes in the order they did their work. On the left side of each box was the input the group needed before they could start work. The right side captured the list of outputs that the group was supposed to complete for the next team. He put them in order and tried to assess whether the inputs and outputs matched at each transfer. Then he and the project lead began calling the heads of each team to check whether the diagram on the whiteboard captured what was happening in the field. The results surprised everyone, including the project leader.

Given their geographic dispersion, the team leads had limited knowledge of their counterparts in the other functions and rarely talked to one another, even when handing over the site from one team to the next. The necessary information was transferred electronically via different software systems and reports, each of which offered a different collection of metrics. Monthly project reports provided overly optimistic assessments and did not highlight issues. For example, though the new technology was supposed to be cheaper and work better, using it in the field was costing three times more than projected. It was also unreliable. But the escalating costs and frequent failures occurred in the field, more than a thousand miles away from the design engineers who had developed it. When Don and the project lead called them to let them know that the new technology was late, over budget, and often failed, the design team assured them that they were wrong. Costs were in line and the technology was working just fine in the lab. The delays must be due to the people in the field.

At that point in the company's history, the pendulum of corporate power had swung toward the functions. The resulting design implicitly assumed that if every function did its work correctly, then the project would be successful. This is the epitome of a static design, the underlying presumption being that the world is so stable and the technology is so well understood that every activity can be defined in advance of doing the work. But, as every project manager knows, this rarely happens in the real world. In this case, well sites often experienced surprises—unique configurations or geology that posed challenges. Similarly, a contractor might be late or understaffed, or might run into a snag doing its work. Each hiccup was likely to ripple from one team to the next, causing everyone to have to do their work a little differently. The project design, however, completely missed the need for the functional teams to adapt to both the environment and one another. They had implicitly assumed that every transfer could be done via a handoff, when a huddle was probably a better choice.

Three interventions helped connect people along both the work and the management chains.

First, they got the leaders from each team in a room together to develop a common picture of the process (starting with Don's initial sketch). They focused on making sure that they all understood and agreed on what needed to be provided when the site was transferred from one team to the next. For example, the group that prepped the site needed to ensure that there were access roads for large drilling equipment and temporary storage ponds for water. Similarly, the team doing the drilling needed to deliver a well capable of the required volume and in a state that made it easy to install the equipment that would link the well to the existing pipeline. This exercise surfaced dozens of gaps, most of which were easily addressed but previously had only been complained about. They also agreed that each transfer from one team to another, from site prep to drilling, for example, would happen at the well site as an organized huddle, not through handing off standard documents that did little to capture the nuances and idiosyncrasies of each site.

Second, they created a trigger mechanism to expose problems and solve them quickly. Team leaders agreed to surface any issue that threatened the schedule by more than two days (anything less was considered to be normal variation), allowing schedule changes to be incorporated into the plans of every team.

Finally, they agreed to move the biggest barrier—the new well technology—off the critical path. Until the new technology could be proven in the field, new wells would use the existing technology, which was proven and reliable. In the meantime, they brought the design engineers to the field (and out of the test lab) to see the high costs and failure rates.

With the interventions, the program that had been forty wells behind was back on schedule in the space of eight weeks.

Though extreme, this project leader's experience was typical. The team had implicitly assumed they could use informal handoffs (in this case just sharing standard documents) between stages of construction when instead they should have used huddles. Having face-to-face meetings to ensure that the site was ready highlighted ongoing issues and helped the project leader stitch the teams together and ensure the activities of one team were closely tied to the activities of the next. Not only did the face-to-face meetings help clarify the basic elements of what the next team needed (or why), but they also provided an opportunity to talk through unexpected details and issues that were unique to the site (and not captured in standard checklists and procedures).

Setting a trigger to expose the issues affecting the schedule in real time also sped the pace of discovery, helping the teams find new methods for working together. Perhaps most notably, the entire team, including the project manager, completely missed the impact of the new technology. Because every team was just looking at their own individual piece, nobody saw how failures of the new technology in the field were throwing the entire project into complete chaos and pushing everyone into firefighting mode.

Using the old technology (until the engineers fixed the new technology) got the work moving immediately. Connecting the engineers to the reality of the front line (that they didn't believe the technology had problems until they visited the well sites) brought critical technical and managerial expertise to help sort out the issues and quickly find a way forward.

While most situations are not quite this severe, poorly designed work and management chains typically reveal themselves via endless chains of emails and instant messages focused on problem resolution. Trying to resolve uncertainty and different opinions asynchronously is slow and error prone, and creates needless, ineffective iteration. We have all had text message chains go horribly off the rails because of a basic misunderstanding of what is being discussed or negotiated. Nelson and his spouse, Karen, having both just landed in Tokyo (coming from different cities), once texted back and forth and looked for each other for almost an hour at the airport before they realized that one of them had landed at Narita while the other was at Haneda. Don't let your work fall into a similar trap. When each question or clarification requires another note, try getting on a call or walking over to have a chat to resolve the issue.

In the early days of the COVID pandemic, Nelson fell into this trap when he needed an out-of-cycle budget allocation to fund an experiment with moving class content to video delivery. He and his colleagues in the dean's office were still meeting only every two weeks to consider the changes needed for the new world of remote teaching. They hadn't yet realized how much the pandemic would affect their routines or how fast they would have to adapt.

When Nelson discovered the new opportunity, he didn't want to wait until the next dean's meeting to get approval. So, he sent an email to his colleagues asking for the money. But this request was too new and too uncertain to be processed as a handoff. The staff had never done this before, and lots of new questions needed to be worked out (for example, does everyone get more money or just Nelson?). The thread totaled more than a dozen emails, many of which veered into unrelated topics. Ultimately, it took two days of unfocused back-and-forth messages to answer a question that could have been resolved in fifteen minutes in a face-to-face meeting.

Ron's experience was similar. Every nonstandard order required multiple emails to clarify details. Despite that time and effort, when that order was wrong because of missing information or a misunderstanding, many more emails were needed to fix the problem.

A deluge of iterations over email or instant messaging is almost always a sign that you need to add a huddle. Get everyone in the same room (real or virtual) and have a face-to-face conversation. You will resolve the uncertainty in a fraction of the time.

The other side of the coin is trying to put things into meetings that don't belong there. As a simple rule of thumb, use two questions to evaluate your meetings: How many decisions were made and how many problems were solved? If the answer to each question compared to the time invested tells you that the meeting was much longer than it needed to be, either fix the meeting or just drop it.

TOLEDO AND BEYOND

At BP, the intervention that turned Ron's scowl into a smile continued throughout Mark's group. Over the next four years, Mark and his leadership team transformed the procurement function. They started with the areas closest to the customer—purchase order processing and invoice payment—and then moved on to the other areas of the operation, such as sourcing and contracting, supplier management, supplier quality, and category management.

With each area, they took the time to clarify the targets and the activities needed to deliver that intent and then, with a discovery mindset, engaged the people doing the work to find better ways to do it. Over four years Mark and his team delivered $1 billion in cost savings, reduced their operating costs by about 30 percent, and delivered the work consistently and predictably. Most importantly, having parts coming in on time, thanks to a reliable system for ordering and delivering them, made it easier for everyone to pay attention to the critical details of running BP's operating units safely and reliably, while delivering more product. Instead of being a huge headache, Mark's group became valuable business partners to the refineries' operating managers. As Mark said, "In many of the areas, the level of improvement was almost embarrassing."

As promised, Ron pushed his retirement back so that he could keep helping Toledo get better. Reflecting on his journey with dynamic work design, Mark said, "Most impressive to me was that this way of working was better, it was sustainable, and it was a much better environment for those of us who worked in it."

Chapter 6

Regulate for Flow

FINISH MORE BY CONTROLLING HOW MUCH YOU START

In 2015, Dr. Abeel Mangi, a cardiac surgeon at Yale University Hospital, decided he'd had enough. All too often, he would finish a surgical procedure and transfer the patient out of the operating room only to find that there was no bed available in the intensive care unit. One of his recent patients had spent over *six hours* waiting in the hallway.

To tackle the problem, Abeel and Diane Somolo, one of his medical students, started by reviewing the data. It didn't take long to realize that hallway congestion was not an occasional occurrence. More than half of the cardiac surgery patients experienced a delay of longer than fifteen minutes between leaving the OR and entering the ICU. Those minutes mattered. Patients who waited in the hallway for long periods of time lost more blood, were 34 percent more likely to be readmitted within the next thirty days, and ended up staying in the hospital about half a day longer. Longer stays cost the hospital more than $2 million a year in forgone revenue because the ICU could not support more surgeries.

Abeel's problem was not unique. The challenges facing the US medical system are well documented and extend far beyond surgical units and ICUs. Costs are growing and capacity is often limited. A recent study found that about 7 percent of patients experienced a harmful event while getting treated in a hospital that could have been prevented.[1]

After examining the data, Abeel followed the *solve-the-right-problem* principle and went to investigate. He watched how patients were moved out of surgery into the ICU and then, later, discharged to other parts of the hospital. He also interviewed doctors and nurses to understand their experience of working in the system to care for patients.

His investigation revealed several useful pieces of information. Most notably, he learned that the ICU staff held a "bed flow" meeting each day at 9:30 a.m. where the team reviewed each patient's status and estimated the numbers of beds that would be available that day. However, surgical teams started operating at 7:30 a.m., long before ICU staff had a reliable estimate of the available capacity in their area. He also learned that there was only one discharge window, a limited period of time when patients could be moved out of the ICU.

Abeel and Diane's findings suggested that Yale's problems were rooted in neither funding nor negligence. Instead, the OR-to-ICU delays were a predictable consequence of the way the work was designed. Yale's leaders had not absorbed the lesson underlying the next dynamic work design principle, *regulate for flow*: a charge to ensure that the amount of work in the system matches the available resources. Maintaining this balance can be harder than it looks. If the entry of new tasks isn't regulated to optimize the flow through the entire system, most work systems will tend toward a state of overload and fire-fighting. Worse, leaders, rather than recognizing the costs of an overloaded, chaotic system, often misinterpret the resulting frenzy of activity as a sign of success.

Many managers believe that they optimize the performance of their organization by making sure that all its members and functions are always working at (or above) full capacity. Yale's cardiac unit, for example, worked to ensure that every surgical slot was full, assuming that scheduling more surgeries maximized the flow of patients through the hospital. But the keep-everyone-busy approach, while seemingly intuitive, rarely optimizes the performance of the system. As we detail in this chapter, getting the most out of a given system requires regulating the amount of work you put into it. The right amount of work rarely results in everyone being fully occupied at all times. When you optimize the flow of work through the system, you automatically maximize individual contributions and create the conditions for discovering problems that, once resolved, lead to even more gains.

Though powerful, the regulate-for-flow principle is counter-intuitive. We all have a natural inclination to give more work to people when they don't seem busy. Filling the surgical sched-ule, for example, seems like a sensible way to utilize the car-diac unit's full capacity. But, as Abeel experienced, adding more work than the system can handle causes debilitating gridlock.

A few simple changes helped Abeel regulate the flow of new patients into the system and improve overall productivity. First, the bed flow meeting was moved to 5:30 a.m. so that surgeons knew the number of available ICU beds before they started their cases. The number of surgeries started each day was then tied to the number of available beds: if ten beds were going to be open, they would do ten surgeries. Second, an additional discharge window was created in the ICU. Patients who were ready could now leave earlier, making another bed available sooner.

Prior to Abeel's intervention, the flow of patients was determined by the surgical suites. Now it was gated by the capacity of the ICU. Though it was a seemingly minor change, performance and capacity of the ICU improved significantly, making room for more surgical procedures. As reported by Abeel, Diane, and Nelson in the *Annals of Thoracic Surgery*, following the changes, the average time required to move a patient from the OR to the ICU fell by about 20 percent (an average gain of about four minutes), and 16 percent more patients were transferred within the targeted fifteen-minute window. Three-quarters of that improvement came from a reduction in those experiencing delays of greater than forty-five minutes—these were the delays that created the most risk for patients and the most chaos for the ICU team.

These gains may seem modest, but their impact was not. Getting patients into the ICU faster meant fewer complications and shorter recovery times. Abeel and Diane found statistically significant reductions in the amount of blood patients lost while in the ICU. The average length of stay in the ICU fell by 0.7 days, going from 3.5 days to 2.8, a change that effectively increased the ICU's capacity by almost 20 percent. Thanks to the shorter average stay, the cost per surgical case fell by 19 percent, a significant achievement in a world of escalating health-care costs. Most importantly, they were able to serve more patients.

THE COSTS OF KEEPING EVERYONE BUSY

Like most people, you probably feel like you have too much to do and that your organization actively conspires against you ever getting it all done. There are too many items on your to-do list, and thanks to endless interruptions and crises, you spend more time reprioritizing them than getting them done. You spend most of your time in meetings, but never seem to reach any decisions. Above all, the more emails you answer, the more messages you find in your inbox. This situation likely afflicts not just you but your entire company; deliverables are late, projects are behind, and everyone seems to be constantly scrambling to meet their objectives.

If life in the modern organization feels fundamentally misguided, you are correct. Many studies have shown that taking on too much work—a phenomenon called *overload*—hurts both individual and organizational performance. Psychologists have long understood that too much stress reduces the ability to perform and learn (a finding first demonstrated at the turn of the last century by shocking rats when they took a wrong turn as they ran through a maze looking for cheese; the fear and stress of being shocked slowed their learning to find the cheese). Similarly, studies of research and development teams show that taking on more projects than they can handle causes people to regularly switch from one task to the next depending on which project is currently getting the most pressure or is facing an imminent deadline. Though its impact can be hard to detect, task switching degrades productivity and leads to error. For example, a recent study suggests that people spend almost 10 percent of their week just switching between different apps on their computers and phones.[2]

As experienced by anyone who has ever had the last doctor's appointment of the day or has tried to drive out of the city on a Friday afternoon in the summer, overloaded systems also struggle to accommodate small disruptions. One late patient or car in the breakdown lane can cause the whole system to grind to a halt.

That said, far too many leaders mistakenly believe that their organizations thrive under constant pressure. They reward managers who deliver under duress and revel in a culture in which the path to the top involves a huge to-do list, long hours, and a willingness to cut corners to get things done. For example, when medical authorities tried to cap the workweek for surgical residents at *eighty hours per week,* many supervising doctors complained.[3] Learning to function while sleep deprived and exhausted was, they claimed, a critical factor in becoming a physician. This claim persists despite research suggesting that the impact on cognitive function of being awake for twenty-four hours is similar to that of having a blood alcohol concentration of 0.10 percent, well over the legal limit for driving.[4] Similarly, at one large company with which we worked, employees regularly told the story of the CEO berating a member of his leadership team for not answering email over the weekend. "If you don't want to work on weekends, I'll find someone who will," he allegedly barked. Whether true or not, this anecdote became a cautionary tale firmly lodged in the company's culture. Our colleague Dan Glusick, after moving on from working at Intermatic with Don, worked for a company that tried to maintain a constant state of crisis. They were explicit in their desire to get "the three best years of your career," knowing that most people could not operate at the company's desired pace for too long. Dan was able to use work design methods to deliver a huge development project in record time and survive more than three years. Adrenaline is not the only path to effectiveness.

The tendency to overload represents perhaps the largest gap between research and practice in the world of management. Psychologists have long argued for the idea of *optimal challenge,* the notion that humans perform best when they are challenged just a bit beyond their current abilities (something that video games manage very effectively). With too little challenge, we get bored and tend to fill in the gaps with our own projects or the all-too-available distractions provided by our smart phones; conversely, facing a challenge far beyond our current ability creates the frustration and anxiety of being held accountable for more work than can possibly be done. Many management scholars have shown the benefits of matching the amount of work in the system to the current capability. But despite the science, little has changed in practice. Following our early work on firefighting in new product development (see Chapter 2), we spent ten years explaining to leaders that by more carefully managing how much work they put into their systems, they could avoid the costs of overload and actually get more done. Despite the nodding heads, most managers returned to work unable to resist the desire to continually push one more important project or task into an already congested system.

Since then, we have come to realize that the propensity to overload work systems is deeply rooted in a fundamental misconception about how work systems perform. Ask a manager who is overloaded what they need, and the answer is always more budget and more people (or its complement, fewer things to do). This answer presumes that overload is solely a capacity problem. But that's only part of the story. Being overloaded *changes* how people manage their work, creating inefficiency and frustration due to constantly changing priorities and task switching. Eliminating these inefficiencies improves productivity to the point that capacity is often no longer a problem. If a capacity gap does remain, it is usually much smaller and more easily quantified and addressed. Conversely, in our experience, until you fix the design, adding additional resources will be largely ineffective. Adding more people without first fixing the design usually makes small problems into major ones. An already ineffective and chaotic system then becomes even bigger and more inefficient.

The Broad Institute's lab provides a vivid illustration of how overload changes the way people execute their work. When we began our work with Sheila Dodge and her team, the lab was jammed with samples being processed. At any given moment, thousands of vials sat between the various steps in the process waiting for a technician to grab the next one in line and move it forward. In manufacturing terms, there was lots of work in process, or WIP—partially completed tasks just sitting there waiting for the next person in the chain. Abeel's patients similarly represented WIP, work that had finished one step in the process (the surgery) and was waiting to start the next one (postoperative care). Your email inbox is likely also full of WIP, partially completed tasks waiting for your attention so that they can move to the next step.

Dynamic work design focuses on getting the work to flow. A system in which work moves quickly is flexible and its direction can easily be adjusted to accommodate a changing world. An overloaded system, in contrast, is slow and difficult to redirect. The bigger the piles, the longer each sample, patient, or email will take to work its way through the system. A system full of partially completed work waiting to be done is the opposite of agile. How many emails do you have in your inbox waiting for you to do something?

At the outset of our work with Broad, the average time to process a sample was over 120 days. The long throughput times created by excess WIP led to two related problems that trap an organization in a state of low performance. You can see the first by considering what you do when you open your email inbox and see more messages than you have time to answer. Like most people, you identify the most important ones and answer them first. This behavior is called local, or *bottom-up*, reprioritization: each person in the work chain imposes their own priorities on their work. Abeel and Diane discovered that when there was a backup in the hallway, doctors and nurses tried to get their patients moved to the head of the line. They wrote, "Certain individuals manipulated the system to benefit themselves, which, combined with delays, caused heightened stress, a constant 'firefighting mode,' and erosion of staff morale."

Local prioritization feels sensible in the moment. However, when different people with different agendas change priorities at every step, the workflow is unpredictable. If a task is prioritized highly by everyone, as often happens in a crisis, it gets done quickly. But if you think a task is important and someone else in the chain does not, it could languish in their inbox for days or weeks. Unless you know how everyone in the chain is going to prioritize a task, it's difficult to predict when it will be completed.

The second problem, the *top-down* version of reprioritization, happens when more-senior managers, frustrated with a slow, unpredictable process, intervene in the hope of making sure critical work gets completed. It shows up as "hot lists" and people tasked with expediting work through multiple steps of the process. Before dynamic work design, such activity was endemic at Broad. The lab team spent the bulk of each day trying to reprioritize the samples to meet the "new" priorities that came from angry researchers or the center director in the hope of moving those deemed most important through the system faster.

Prior to the lean revolution in manufacturing in the 1990s, when companies started to focus on workflow and eliminating the vast piles of work in process, *expeditor* was a recognized job title in many factories. Expeditors started each day with a list of items that were at risk of missing their shipment dates and then hand carried those jobs through the process, interrupting other work already underway at every step, to make sure they got done. Though expediting has largely been purged from the world of manufacturing, it remains almost universal in work done off the factory floor. Despite its ubiquity, expediting is a big engine of inefficiency and a major impediment to discovery. Spending all your time chasing work and manually moving it through the system means that you can't focus on the reasons the system didn't deliver the right work in the first place.

To see expediting in action, consider again your own behavior. What do you do when you have an important task that requires another person's input and you don't want to risk it being lost in his inbox? You try to get that person's attention. You send a text, make a phone call, or stop by his office. Though you feel proactive, efforts to expedite your work risk degrading the overall health of the process. An extra text, phone call, or visit both takes your time and reduces the recipient's productivity by forcing him to switch attention from whatever they are working on to what you want them to do. We all intuitively know that such task switching causes quality problems and drains productivity. In a factory, you could see the work required to switch a machine from one job to the other. Nonetheless, pre-lean factories were often so chaotic that expediting seemed like the only way to consistently meet delivery dates. In the office world, the waste is much harder to see. Asking someone to stop what they are doing and work on something urgent seems normal and to have few consequences. But no one would ever ask a cardiac surgeon to stop an operation midstream because something supposedly more important popped up—we know this is a bad idea—yet we ask knowledge workers to do something similar multiple times a day because the immediate impact doesn't seem onerous.

As we outlined in Chapter 2, left unchecked, fighting fires by working around the system (and not addressing the underlying causes of the fires) quickly becomes the only way things ever get done; it becomes the process. Expediting is just a specific kind of workaround that leads you into the vicious cycle of firefighting. Expediting feeds upon itself by reducing overall productivity and delaying the completion of every other task. Those tasks will soon also need to be expedited, creating ever more chaos and inefficiency. At Broad, attempts by researchers to rush their samples through the process ended up clogging the system, just as efforts by Abeel's colleagues at Yale to get their patients into the ICU created backups in the hallway. In each system, efforts to respond to the chaos reduced overall productivity, which created even more overload, necessitating even more expediting, and creating even more chaos.

There is no other word for it: living in an organization where overload and expediting have become a way of life *sucks*. It's almost impossible to plan your work because you don't know when other needed tasks will get done, and you spend more time lobbying colleagues than you do working. Everything is a rush job, so you often don't have time to review your work or step away from it for a night or two to get a fresh perspective. Defects—ranging from typos to software bugs to medical errors—are the norm and when discovered require even more expediting. Some colleagues, whether they do it consciously or unconsciously, seem to use this chaos to their advantage, always finding a way to game the system so that their tasks magically get priority.

An overloaded system is an effective recipe for mistakes, burnout, and general confusion. The desire to feel in control lies at the heart of human psychology, but overloaded systems work against that need. Recall the quote in the Introduction expressing an all-too-familiar frustration: "I know my organization is in trouble when I start Monday morning by making a list of all the important things I need to do this week. I work my ass off all week, but on Friday afternoon I can't cross off a single item." Not surprisingly, such rushed work is often implicated in major industrial accidents like those experienced by BP (see Chapter 2).

The depth of the inefficiency created by this way of operating is hard to appreciate until you experience the alternative. But before we move on to solutions, let's reflect on one final cost of the overload/expediting trap: it limits an organization's ability to execute its strategy.

During our early work at Harley-Davidson, as noted earlier, the company routinely pushed more product development projects into the system than it had the resources to complete. Projects routinely missed their delivery dates by a year or two, and some waited even longer to reach the market. Delays happen in complex projects (even with the highest priority, Don's engine project was completed two years later than the original schedule), but when unpredictable and major delays are the rule rather than the exception, there is a more fundamental problem. As we discussed in Chapter 2, some project managers, the firefighters, were better than others at getting their projects through the system. As we dug into the work, we discovered that what made a good firefighter was the ability to use social influence to get a project prioritized. It wasn't unusual for a Harley project manager to go to his hunting buddy, the test lab director, and ask him to move his project to the front of the line.

This problem is particularly acute in organizations that rely on a matrix structure—a network of overlapping accountabilities and joint projects—to manage the development of new products and services. Without clear targets for the overall organization, the people managing important functional resources in an overloaded system often impose their own priorities on the sequence of projects that come through their areas. Some projects get fast-tracked, while others seem perpetually stuck on the back burner. Project leaders know this and learn to lobby the leaders controlling the resources they need to get their own work done. Friendship sometimes matters more in making a decision than does a project's official priority. The result is a sticky political mess that contributes to slow and highly unpredictable project-completion times. In this situation, who is really choosing the projects that turn an organization's strategy into action?

We once, for example, worked with a semiconductor company whose CEO constantly pushed his business leaders to make "big bets" and focus on new technologies and integrated systems that offered the possibility of creating entirely new industries. Getting such projects off the ground, however, proved difficult. Facing an overloaded research and development portfolio, product teams tended to focus on projects using incremental extensions of existing technologies. These projects were more likely to deliver a positive return for both the project leader and the company but were unlikely to produce the billion-dollar businesses the CEO so desperately wanted. Regardless of the depth of the commitment that underlies them, impassioned speeches are no match for the pressures of an overloaded system.

THE AIRPLANE DOOR

We can see the utility of regulating the flow and avoiding overload by looking at the way airlines manage individual flights.

Every flight has a finite capacity, which is the number of seats available. Despite the pressure to fill every seat and optimize revenue, the airlines have a clearly established point of no return for confirming the passenger list. When the airplane's door closes, barring an emergency, no one is leaving or boarding the plane. The airline staff at the gate can reprioritize passengers up until that moment—moving people up to first class, offering vouchers in overbooking situations, and so on—but once the door closes, control of the flight switches to the plane's crew, who focus on delivering a safe, on-time flight. There are no more changes; only those who are on the plane are going. Everyone else has to catch the next flight.

Now consider the alternative. What if, to appeal to their high rollers, airlines were willing to bring planes off the taxiway when a frequent flyer showed up late? Though at first glance it seems like a crazy idea, airlines compete fiercely for high-margin customers, and this service might appeal to the perpetually harried business traveler. But think about the instability it would add to the travel system as managers began to interfere with flights after they left the gate. Planes would be in line to take off, come out of that line, get the new passenger, and return to the taxiway. But with the delay, more frequent flyers would show up and also want seats, necessitating another return to the gate. High-value business travelers would soon get used to the idea that planes will wait for them. Worse, when a plane was really late (thanks to multiple returns to the gate), the airline would lobby traffic control to push it to the head of the line, causing congestion in the taxiway and delaying all the other flights. We would never get anywhere.

In a recent meeting, we offered the airline metaphor to a group of software engineers and one of them replied, "Oh, our situation is much worse. We let our 'projects' actually take off and get well on their way. Then we bring them back, unload them, change who is on them and where they are going, and start all over again. It's a miracle we ever get anything done."

Subsequent conversation revealed that the company struggled to stay committed to its strategy and perpetually changed the prioritization of active projects. They would start a project, and the team would work on it until management found a more interesting business opportunity. The existing project was then either abandoned in favor of the new idea or sent "back to the gate" to get completely reconfigured. Both options disrupted the flow of project delivery. Not surprisingly, productivity suffered. Project leaders, unlike pilots and crew, who have the benefit of the airplane door, were frustrated that their efforts to deliver on time were constantly thwarted by changes outside of their control.

In work processes, the airplane door is the point of no return in a work chain, the step beyond which you lock in the scope, ensure the resources are available and assigned, and let the task at hand flow without interruption to the end, without being reprioritized or expedited (as we discuss later, you can cancel work). Creating an airplane door allows you to regulate the amount of work to ensure that once something is started, it moves to completion with minimal delay and disruption. By being more intentional about making sure the highest-priority work is started and allowed to proceed uninterrupted, you ensure that the right projects are active and that they keep moving. This approach shortens delivery times, makes the entire system more productive and predictable, and allows you to deliver more projects.

The key challenge in creating your version of the airplane door is determining when work is allowed through it and into the system. This approach can take different forms, but it should always be guided by a simple principle: work should be allowed through the airplane door only when the system has capacity to work on it. Putting a task into the system when that system is already at (or over) capacity means that people will be forced to stop working on one thing and switch to another. Somewhere work then stops and has to wait, and local reprioritization, expediting, and other workarounds are not far behind. Violating the regulate-for-flow principle slows progress and risks tipping the system into the vicious cycle of firefighting.

In some systems, particularly those dealing with physical work, the ideal workload can be managed precisely. It was relatively easy, for example, for Abeel to identify a simple rule for controlling the workload in his part of the hospital: don't start more surgeries than you have beds for in the ICU. Knowledge work, however, can be both more varied and less precise. It typically doesn't have a single path through an organization, and new work can often enter through multiple portals. Nonetheless, once you understand the regulate-for-flow principle, you can still improve the workflow. Start with congested areas, only let work in when the system has capacity, and gradually develop a set of vital signs that show when work is moving and when it is slowing and you are approaching overload. With time, you will build a more effective way for regulating the flow that fits your unique environment.

To understand the process of learning to regulate for flow, imagine you control the number of cars that enter a long stretch of multilane highway (with no additional on-ramps). Your job is to maximize the flow of cars. It's easy to see that if you allow only one car to enter, its entire journey will be unimpeded, going as fast as physics and safety allow. Something similar often happens when organizations face crises. Only mission-critical projects are allowed into the system, and they flow to completion without interruption. Such a strategy would not, however, optimize the flow of traffic. You'd have lots of unused space in the form of open lanes. If you let a second car enter, it, too, could proceed unimpeded, and you have now doubled the system's output with little to no sacrifice in speed. The same would go for the third car and so on.

That said, as every driver knows, adding more cars only helps get more people where they are going up to a point. Once that threshold is exceeded, each additional car slows progress and reduces overall output and increases travel time. In the extreme case, putting the maximum number of cars on the road—every inch of concrete on the highway is now covered by a car—creates a huge traffic jam and nobody gets anywhere.

Once the traffic jam emerges, the overloaded highway becomes a prime target for expediting, further limiting performance. We are all comfortable getting out of the way for an ambulance, even if it slows our trip home. But how would you feel, as Nelson once witnessed, about a bus full of kids going to a hockey game with a police escort, thanks to one of the dads being the mayor? And, as we mentioned in the Introduction, everybody hates the person who works around the rules and drives in the breakdown lane, completely violating the original intent of the design and inducing others to make similar departures. Something very similar happens in knowledge work. When a system is overloaded, critical work is increasingly expedited, which creates more congestion, slows the progress of every other task, and creates the need for more expediting.

Implementing the regulate-for-flow principle means acting like our hypothetical highway planner. To optimize the flow of traffic, you continue to let cars on the highway until you start to notice congestion. After that, you regularly monitor the system for emerging traffic jams and adjust the flow of new cars accordingly. In knowledge work, if the work is flowing smoothly, you can safely let an additional task through the airplane door. If, however, congestion starts to emerge and key tasks wait for resources (akin to waiting for a clear lane), then the system is probably getting overloaded. The key is to learn your way into the optimal mix of speed and cars on the highway that will deliver what your organization needs.

Spotting congestion in knowledge work can be harder than spotting it on the highway, so the regulate-for-flow principle can take different forms, depending on the nature of the work. In each case, though, it boils down to identifying a set of vital signs for how the work is moving. Monitoring vital signs can be as straightforward as watching the work move (as you can in a factory). Or it can require monitoring metrics like cycle time (how long is it taking to get a piece of work done versus how long would it take if there were no other piles of work waiting?) or staying in close touch with key people in the process and assessing how often they are switching tasks and/or are forced to expedite. Alternatively, if one person is perpetually over-loaded, then she may be the bottleneck. Regulating for flow is a fundamentally dynamic process. Doing it effectively requires constantly evaluating the state of the system and making ongoing adjustments to learn your way to the right amount of work.

Developing ways to spot congestion is also critical in identifying which problem to solve next. Returning to the highway analogy, if every time you let more cars in and the backup occurs in the same place, then you know there is a problem with that part of the highway. Perhaps it's too narrow or turns too sharply. Similarly, if congestion in your product development process always emerges at the testing phase, then it's time to do a deep dive into that part of the process. In contrast, when a system is completely overloaded—it's a traffic jam—then start at the customer and work backward, clearing congestion as you go. You will generate results more quickly and fixing one bottleneck after another allows you to gradually work off the backlog and increase the flow at every step.

REGULATING FOR FLOW IN ACTION

Three examples give a good window into effective approaches for regulating your workflow.

Getting Samples to Flow. The sequencing lab at the Broad Institute was, as we've seen, mired in firefighting and expediting. Demand for the institute's services was falling as researchers began looking for outside labs with faster turnaround times, putting even more pressure on the lab team to deliver to important customers.

To improve their ability to regulate the flow of work through the lab, the institute added an airplane door at the front of the sample analysis process. Sheila Dodge, then the general manager, told the project managers and the institute's director, Eric Lander, that they could reprioritize the pile of samples sitting in front of the process as often as they wished. Once a sample entered the process, however, the door was closed, and that sample would flow to completion without interruption. No more expediting. Not surprisingly, both Eric and the project managers pushed back against this apparent loss of flexibility: Why would you reduce responsiveness when you are already losing business? Their concerns would, however, prove unfounded.

To determine when work was allowed through that airplane door, they used a simple set of visual vital signs to assess the health of the workflow. They created "parking spaces" using cardboard boxes sized to match the plastic trays that the sample vials traveled in and set a specific number of them in between each step of the process. When a sample finished a given step, it would sit in one of these parking spots until the next step was ready for it. If a given set of parking spaces was full, the person running the upstream step would stop working until a space opened. Broad's scheme was akin to the stoplights that sometimes sit on highway on-ramps. Cars are allowed to enter the flow of traffic only when there is space.

This setup made spotting congestion easy and provided a simple guide for regulating the flow of work. If every task had empty parking spaces downstream, new work could be safely introduced into the system. Congestion throughout the process, in contrast, signaled overload. Similarly, regular congestion at a given step signaled the next problem to be solved.

Students of manufacturing will recognize the parking space scheme as a *pull system*: a given step in the process is executed only when there is an empty parking space between that step and the next one in the chain. That empty space (or a card) is a signal to do work and fill the box. In this way, the person needing more work signals the upstream person to produce it, and work is "pulled" from one task to the next until it reaches completion. People work to these signals, not to a fixed schedule. The systems for implementing pull in manufacturing can be quite intricate, but their essence lies in using the accumulations of work between the various steps as signals to regulate the flow of work from one task to the next. Pull systems can be an effective approach to regulating the flow, particularly when all of the work exists in a similar format, such as engines, patients, or samples.

With this system in place, the lab experienced rapid gains. The piles of waiting samples were now small and carefully controlled, designed to be the minimum amount of inventory that covered any natural variation between steps and to keep the work flowing. More samples moved through the now much more efficient process. In the space of a few years, the time required to process a sample fell from 120 to 20 days, and the team's ability to meet promised delivery dates improved dramatically, even as the volume of samples delivered increased. Project managers quit complaining, and the researchers quit calling to check the status of their samples. Now, rather than having to fight over whose sample would get priority, everybody got what they wanted. Samples were now delivered sooner and more reliably. The vicious cycle of expediting became a virtuous circle: as the process became more reliable, fewer requests for expediting were made, making it that much easier to run the lab efficiently.

Broad's success in reducing the time required to process a sample proved to be a significant source of competitive advantage. Prior to 2012, demand for Broad's sequencing work had been declining because of growing competition. But then Broad's industry-leading turnaround times and reliability reversed this trend and allowed them to grow rapidly. The team's ability to quickly spot and resolve problems, and thereby continue to expand capacity, was critical in continuing to match that growth.

As the lab's productivity continued to increase, constraints in the larger system outside the lab started to impede the flow of work, revealing an entirely new set of problems to address. For example, growth in the flow of samples going through the lab led to similar increases in the volume of data being produced. At one point, Broad's in-house data storage facility became so overwhelmed that it literally caught on fire. The team soon moved their operation to a cloud-based service. Later, as the team will proudly tell you, the lab briefly shut down a popular music streaming service thanks to the volume of data they were pumping into the hosting company's servers. No music was just another problem to be solved.

Broad's approach to regulating the flow of work through the lab proved very effective. That said, its success turned on the fact that congestion (fully occupied parking spaces) was easy to see thanks to all of the work being in a similar format. Having standard tubes in standard containers in standard parking spaces made problems visible in real time. Sheila and her team stayed in close touch with the work and responded quickly to problems as they appeared. While Broad's approach—physically moving the boxes of samples through the work chain—is not often feasible in knowledge work, regulating for flow and increasing the rate of improvement is still possible. It just requires a different approach for generating vital signs, as, for example, when a group of managers from Flint Hills Resources, a fuel refining company, realized during a discussion in our MIT class that their maintenance process was mired in overload and expediting.

Getting Maintenance Work to Flow. The maintenance process at Flint Hills started when someone in a production unit identified a new task, such as overhauling a pump. The team member created a work order and put it into the maintenance system. The work order sat in the maintenance function's electronic inbox until the reliability coordinator, often after several increasingly irate emails and calls from the operating units, would determine the scope of the needed work (for example, how many hours, people, tools, and parts would be needed). The job would then go to the planner, who, based on the scope, would determine how long the job would take, who would need to work on it, and how that work might interact with other activities in the same area. She would then release a plan for implementing the work order. Planning required a detailed knowledge of the other work going on at the same time. That plan sat in another electronic pile—the ready backlog—until a maintenance team (again, often after several phone calls and emails from the units needing the work) began the job.

As is often the case when the flow of work is not actively managed and prioritized, thousands of work orders in process sat throughout the system, and the relationship between maintenance and the refinery's operating units had grown increasingly tense. The result, thanks to all the ongoing work and associated long delays, was that reprioritization and expediting were the norm.

Oil refineries are always concerned about operating safely, so when a key piece of equipment isn't working, it can be a big problem. So, when a piece of mission-critical equipment started to misbehave, the operating manager gave it priority one status (meaning that it had safety implications). Seeing a high-priority job, the maintenance team would leave whatever routine activity they were working on and start scoping and planning the more urgent work (the higher-priority job was being expedited). When done, they might be moved to an even more pressing issue. The operating units quickly learned that giving a job priority one status, whether it was needed or not, was the best way to get maintenance's attention. Normal jobs, often focused on preventative maintenance, were rarely completed without interruption and often required more than a year to finish. Doing less routine maintenance eventually created even more urgent work.

Switching jobs midstream hurt productivity in multiple ways. The team had to put the details of the current job on the mental back burner and get up to speed with the new one. When a job was paused, it often had to be entirely replanned, as different work was now underway. And if a maintenance team was pulled off an active job, the equipment they had taken out of service remained idle until the team returned, thereby limiting production. And once the team returned, some work, like pre-job safety reviews, had to be redone, and the team needed to refamiliarize themselves with what they were doing and how far they had gotten.

Not surprisingly, this pattern of behavior both reduced the performance of the maintenance system and created antagonism between the maintenance team and the operating units. The backlog of jobs grew to almost twelve thousand work orders, and the average time required to complete a priority two job (meaning anything less than an immediate safety concern) was three hundred days and growing.

To solve the problem and break the logjam, the Flint Hills team made two changes.[5] First, they added an "airplane door" at the front of maintenance's part of the process. Prior to the implementation of the airplane door, the operating units had grown accustomed to regularly changing their maintenance requests based on the state of the equipment (which made sense given the long delays in the system). These interruptions could happen anywhere in the process, from scoping through execution. Now they were allowed to change the scope of their request only before a job entered the scoping phase (unless there was a true emergency). For instance, they could only say, "We want you to work on this pump, not that compressor" if the scoping work for the compressor had not been started. Once the compressor had entered maintenance's system, however, the airplane door was shut and the job proceeded until it was completed.

Second, they created a simple visual representation that allowed them to see all the jobs currently in progress (we discuss visualization techniques more in the next chapter). Since maintenance jobs exist only electronically in the system and don't have a physical manifestation (at least until they are started), the team couldn't create physical parking spaces like those used at Broad. Instead, they placed a simple schematic of the process on the wall, including virtual parking spaces in between each of the major steps. Each job then went on a card, and those cards were placed in the appropriate parking spaces on the process diagram. Cards for the jobs awaiting planning sat in the planning area and cards for jobs awaiting execution sat in the execution area. When a job was moved from one step to the next, its card was also moved.

The visual system provided useful vital signs to determine whether the current workload was a good match with the available capacity. The team could immediately see whether or not the work was flowing and could quickly spot and address emerging congestion. Being able to visualize the flow of work allowed the team to direct their attention to the portions of the process that were the most troubled. Again, when parking spaces were empty, new jobs could be added without risking overload. In contrast, when every spot was full, it was time to slow the flow of new work until the congestion cleared. Capacity imbalances were also immediately revealed. If everything backed up at the planning stage, then perhaps Flint Hills needed another planner.

The net effect of these changes was to move all of the decisions about what work was to be done ahead of the scoping stage. Once they determined that a given job was the next highest priority and that the system had capacity to work on it, it was scoped, planned, and executed by a maintenance crew. The airplane door was closed, and, barring an emergency, the team was not interrupted. Protecting the maintenance function from the starts and stops that go with endless reprioritization dramatically improved productivity.

Within a few months of making these changes, the average time to complete a priority two work order fell from three hundred to thirty-seven days and overall output increased by 50 percent. *Time on tools*, a measure of productivity widely used in the refining industry (essentially a measure of how much time people spend actually repairing equipment), increased by over fourfold. The site's use of contract maintenance personnel fell by more than 70 percent. Much as what happened at Broad, the vicious cycle of more expediting and longer maintenance delays was reversed. When every job could be completed quickly, the operating units made fewer change requests and made it easier for maintenance to reliably plan and execute its work. With better planning and fewer emergencies, more time could be dedicated to the execution of the routine preventative-maintenance tasks, further reducing the number of emergencies. As the maintenance system stabilized, it grew increasingly effective in delivering properly maintained equipment, improving the performance of the entire refinery.

In essence, Flint Hills created a visual version of the system that Broad used. Being able to quickly spot congestion made it easy to allow the right amount of work through the airplane door. This approach, however, is not always immediately practical or necessary. In some situations, it is nearly impossible to force all the work through an airplane door. Work in office areas is too complex and varied. Trying to capture every on-ramp that allows work into the system would be tedious and distracting. However, combining the principle of regulate for flow with the principle of connect the human chain allows the airplane door concept to be used to get important work moving through otherwise congested parts of the organization, as we can see with Standard Chartered bank.

Getting IT Work to Flow. Standard Chartered is a UK-based bank that provides consumer, corporate, and institutional banking services throughout Asia, Africa, and the Middle East. During David Whiteing's tenure as Standard's chief operating officer, the bank spent over a billion dollars annually on upgrades to its technical infrastructure. Projects ranged from developing new customer-facing applications to upgrading the security of their transactions. Projects typically lasted between two and three years and proceeded through four phases: idea development, approvals, build/test, and implementation. David's team was responsible for the approvals phase, a process that initially took an average of 120 days to complete. Calculations by Standard's finance function suggested that each additional day it took to complete the average project cost the bank over $3 million (USD) in lost revenue. Not surprisingly given the size of the losses, David's organization faced significant pressure to get the approvals done more quickly.

The approvals process was designed to ensure that each new technology complied with all the relevant regulations and did not create unnecessary risk. The key players in the process were sixteen risk owners: experts in different facets of financial risk, such as cybersecurity and data privacy, who were required to sign off on each project. At the outset, project managers were required to work with each of the risk owners individually.

This design created several problems that, by this point, are probably familiar. Following the ideas of connecting the human chain from the previous chapter, interacting with each of the risk owners about a specific project in a serial fashion resulted in multiple iterations. One risk owner might ask for a change that mitigated an issue in her domain but created an entirely new set of threats in another risk area. Consequently, the project managers would routinely cycle among one-on-one meetings with the relevant risk owners until they reached a solution that satisfied everyone. This is a textbook example of the waste that results when making a decision or solving a problem via asynchronous back-and-forth between key players.

The process also suffered from overload and local prioritization. Risk owners often faced significant demands on their time, and, while the bank set high-level priorities, had their own views of which projects were the most important. Consequently, project managers often struggled to get the attention of the risk managers, creating unnecessary delays. As David would later say, "I realized a project was always gated by the risk manager who thought it was the least important." Not surprisingly, project managers invested heavily in lobbying risk owners to get their projects prioritized.

Instead of trying to control the amount of work in process, a difficult challenge in a large "matrixed" organization, David created a weekly hour-long meeting with the project managers and risk owners. That meeting was guided by what David called a *common backlog*, a rank-ordered list of the top twenty projects currently underway. The goal of each meeting was to complete the top one or two projects and get them off the list. Approvals couldn't always be completed in a single meeting—sometimes project managers would be given tasks to do—but the associated project would stay on top of the backlog until it was completed to everyone's satisfaction.

Using the language developed from both the regulate-for-flow and the connect-the-human-chain principles, David's meeting inserted a huddle in the workflow where everyone came together to process the uncertainty that arose from having multiple overlapping risks. While David didn't attempt to directly control the flow of work outside the meeting, he entirely regulated the flow of work into it to ensure that the work kept moving. The rank-ordered list created a strict version of the airplane door. A new project was allowed into the meeting only when it had reached the top of the list. When a project made it through the airplane door, it would be the team's exclusive, uninterrupted focus until they either completed it or discovered a need for additional data. David's weekly meeting was essentially a carefully regulated express lane. All the resources came together to ensure that the most important projects flowed uninterrupted to completion.

David's strategy might feel dangerously close to the expediting workarounds that we have criticized throughout the book. His approach was, however, fundamentally different. It set a global priority and reduced, rather than increased, task switching by controlling how much work entered the system. He focused the entire team on just a few jobs until they were complete, matching the load to the demonstrated capacity. Only then would another piece of work be allowed in, using the meeting to regulate the amount of work in the part of the process for which his team was accountable. Expediting is akin to asking the cars on the highway to pull over so other traffic can come through. David's approach, in contrast, creates the equivalent of a separate, controlled express lane, a parallel process in which work flows uninterrupted to allow the traffic jam to clear without disturbing other work the risk managers are doing.

By eliminating the traffic jam, David's approach improved the flow of work outside the meeting (the main highway). An all-hands huddle with a common backlog meant that each project manager and risk owner knew exactly which project would rise to the top next, and nobody wanted to show up to the weekly meeting unprepared. Work outside the weekly meeting naturally evolved to focus on the common backlog, progressively trading local priorities for global ones.

As this new design started to reduce congestion in the flow of approvals, David added a second weekly meeting that he called an *improvement hour*. An excellent example of Chapter 4's structuring for discovery, the goal of the meeting was to identify a change that could be made in the next week that would improve the approvals process. Barriers identified in the first meeting often provided fodder for discussion about possible changes during the improvement hour.

With these changes, David's team was able to reduce the average time required for an approval from 120 days to 20, helping the company realize well over $250 million of otherwise forgone revenue annually.

Two elements of David's example are worth noting. First, creating a common backlog supported by a regular huddle is a simple and effective first step toward regulating the flow of work in what seems like a very messy system filled with multiple types of tasks and pressures. A common ordering of key tasks eliminates local reprioritization and naturally focuses everyone on the most important projects. If you can help on one of the top three projects, why would you go start a smaller project on your own? If you are on the critical path for the item on the top of the list, you'd better focus on it, or the next meeting will be challenging since you didn't get your homework done. Similarly, this structure forces problems to the surface—a task that doesn't come off the backlog, for whatever reason, is clear to everyone, and it will get the attention needed to get it resolved.

Second, even after generating hundreds of millions of dollars in value, David still faced the occasional pushback on the new design. For example, some people complained that a given risk owner might not have much to contribute in one of the weekly meetings and thus was wasting his time. While certainly true, this complaint confuses individual productivity with system performance. Remember, keeping *individuals* busy doesn't ensure that the *organization* is productive. Sometimes, a piece of the system needs to be suboptimized to keep the work moving. We all have to wait at red lights so that the traffic system keeps flowing. Representing a similar confusion, others complained that given the high-powered attendees, the weekly huddle was a very expensive meeting. While true, the expense was minimal compared with the quarter of a billion dollars the meetings saved each year.

WHY DOES IT WORK?

You may, like many of the managers taking our courses, find the magnitude of the gains reported by Broad, Flint Hills, and Standard Chartered hard to believe. When Don, based on his on-the-ground experience and success with regulate for flow, first started telling Nelson about the results at Harley and elsewhere, the academic in Nelson was similarly skeptical. The fact remains, however, that Broad, Flint Hills, Standard Chartered, and many other companies dramatically increased the speed (cycle times fell by more than 80 percent for all of them) and productivity of their core processes (output increased by more than threefold in each case). We have now supported enough efforts focused on regulating the flow that we are confident that the results are real. For example, both Broad and Harley experienced an approximately fourfold improvement in the productivity of their new product development processes. We have seen significant gains in settings ranging from manufacturing to supply chain management to laboratory testing. Even our personal accountants found ways to make their work flow more smoothly during tax season.

These success stories notwithstanding, we have watched many leaders predetermine failure by trying to regulate the flow without really understanding why it works. Putting in parking spaces, creating a visual board, and implementing a common backlog only work when they are used as tools to manage the collective workload and surface otherwise hidden problems. Using these tools while also still trying to keep everyone busy at all times won't work. Success requires that the organization be able to respond to problems in real time, which requires that capacity be balanced between starting new work and resolving problems that limit the current workflow.

In a similar vein, don't "save" your problems for a monthly or quarterly problem-solving meeting. Where possible, resolve problems as they happen. You will usually be able to fix them quickly while the evidence is still fresh and further improve the system's capacity to safely accept more work. Balancing the team's focus between moving work forward and immediately resolving the problems that impede that movement ensures that you are always focused on the next most important problem to solve and that you don't get distracted by peripheral issues. If something is blocking the flow of work, fix it and you will immediately have more capacity.

Regulating the flow produces two positive effects. One tends to manifest quickly, the other takes longer. The first effect comes from eliminating the waste associated with constant task switching and other workarounds. Task switching and workarounds are the ultimate vital sign, suggesting that a work process is not functioning effectively—the work equivalent of elevated heart rate and high blood pressure. The moment you see task switching and workarounds, you know your organization has too much work going on and not enough clarity about which tasks are most important. Once Broad, Flint Hills, and Standard Chartered created a clear set of priorities supported by a point of no return, an airplane door, they experienced almost immediate gains.

When Abeel first proposed his intervention, his colleagues pushed back, fearing that they would have to cancel long-scheduled surgeries and upset their patients. They failed to realize, however, that performing a surgery when the rest of the system wasn't ready for it guaranteed a workaround to the normal process, causing chaos and confusion as the ICU team tried to treat the patient in the hallway. And this workaround, because it created patient complications and bad health outcomes, reduced the system's overall capacity. Once the flow of patients in the ICU was properly regulated, fewer complications occurred and overall capacity went up, not down. In the short run, doctors ended up having to postpone very few surgeries because the gains were realized in just a few weeks. Even better, in the long run, they were able to do more surgeries, thanks to shorter average stays in the ICU.

The second benefit of regulating the flow comes in creating a better environment for discovery. The combination of too much work, constantly changing priorities, and endless firefighting makes it nearly impossible to see which step in the process is creating the bottleneck or problem. It just looks like an overcrowded highway on a Friday afternoon; nobody knows where to start. A well-functioning flow-regulation system, in contrast, has the opposite effect. Because the goal of a flow-regulation system is to let the work flow uninterrupted, congestion automatically reveals the next most important problem to be solved. If a backup starts to emerge, we know there is an issue. A patient in Abeel's hallway meant something went wrong in the ICU, perpetually full parking spaces at Broad meant that the downstream step didn't have enough capacity, and an approval that never got off the priority list signaled a flaw in the review process.

Put differently, while some inventory is critical to buffer natural variability in individual productivity, too much of it allows everyone to stay busy all the time, even in the face of serious problems, because there are always piles of work waiting. But piles of work don't help you figure out what to work on, and universal busyness makes it impossible to discover which problem should be solved next. Piles of work in process and the universal busyness they enable disconnect system performance from individual performance. With lots of work in process, everyone looks busy, even when the system is completely gridlocked.

Consider another simple analogy: when an orchestra is tuning up, every musician works at their own pace and chooses their own notes. To the conductor this is just noise. When the concert starts, however, everyone is using the same musical score. Even though each musician might be playing different notes, and often is not playing at all, those notes all need to work together to produce beautiful music. When they don't, the conductor can immediately hear a problem. Similarly, an airplane door and a clear set of priorities for letting work through that door create a common "score" for the work. Everyone should be focused on moving the tasks through the system in the order they entered. When something goes wrong, it is usually very easy to see.

Regulating for flow is the single most counterintuitive idea in this book. Managers like to keep people busy because doing so makes apparent sense. If everyone is working as hard as they can, then it seems like the system must be producing at its maximum. But in the complex world of work, this simply isn't true. As we have shown throughout the book, in cases where the system is overloaded, starting less work, regulating it to break the gridlock and improve the flow—whether it be surgical patients, maintenance jobs, genetic samples, or technology development projects—improves the productivity of the work system and delivers more output. When you eliminate the inefficiencies associated with task switching and expediting, which then allows you to direct problem-solving to the highest value opportunities, the gains can be significant.

Nonetheless, getting started with regulating for flow often requires a leap of faith. Doing less to get more is counterintuitive. Based on our experience in implementing and teaching regulate for flow, not every leader will be willing to give it a try. That said, those who are able to temporarily put intuition aside will unlock significant gains and develop a new source of competitive advantage for their organizations.

IT'S ALL ABOUT THE FLOW

As we have highlighted in the previous chapters, the dynamic work design principles build on each other and combine to create a system for making sure the right work flows through your organization to the customer:

- *Solve the right problem* ensures that scarce cognitive processing delivers gains in results and capability.
- *Structure for discovery* matches business targets with the status of planned activities to ensure that the flow of work contains the right tasks, that problems are immediately revealed and solved, that gains are recognized, and that the associated learning is captured and propagated.
- *Connect the human chain* ensures that the inputs and outputs along the path match and that problems generate a quick response.
- *Regulate for flow* controls the amount of work in the system so that the system is not overwhelmed and naturally refocuses attention from firefighting to solving problems as they emerge.

When Abeel left Yale in 2021 to become the chief of cardiac surgery at MedStar Heart and Vascular Institute in Washington, DC, he leveraged all four of these principles to improve MedStar's cardiac operations. He instituted a daily all-hands meeting at 3:00 p.m. (connect the human chain) to review the next day's bed availability and resulting surgical schedule (regulate for flow). Abeel also restructured the system to improve discovery (structure for discovery) by creating a simple feedback system to track and reduce the number of complications experienced during surgeries (solve the right problem).

Once again, there were dramatic improvements, including a 30 percent gain in the capacity of the system and a more stable patient flow. When Abeel joined MedStar, his group lagged behind the national average in six of their seven service lines. A year after his arrival, all seven areas were experiencing fewer complications than the national average. "Everyone now thinks I am a genius," Abeel told us. "But it really came down to understanding the work and applying the principles."

Chapter 7

Visualize the Work

MAKING THE INVISIBLE VISIBLE

Several years ago, we had dinner with three Toyota veterans, one of whom had been an early leader in the company's Lexus program. Over the course of the meal, we quizzed them, hoping to divine the secrets of Toyota's success, particularly how they had adapted their employer's famous production system to work off the factory floor. During our conversation, one of them scribbled two Japanese characters on a napkin. The characters, he told us, translated to "eyes walking around," and next to the characters, he wrote, "Make the invisible visible." We'd be hard-pressed to come up with a pithier expression of the final dynamic work design principle: visualize the work.

As we have discussed throughout the book, the essential challenge facing an organization in a dynamic world is coordinating and leveraging the expertise of all its members to surface and resolve the inevitable mismatches between plans and reality. To that end, the previous four chapters offered principles for reconfiguring the flow of work so that issues are surfaced and resolved in real time. On their own, however, it can be hard to implement these ideas fully when you can't see the work move and, often more importantly, you can't see when and where it's not moving. When the flow of work is hidden from public view, problems are inevitably hidden and allowed to fester. The inability to see work move is a major source of organizational rigidity. The trick to leveraging the first four dynamic work design principles in hidden work is to "make the invisible visible," that is, to create a system that allows everyone to see when and how the work flows.

A system for visualizing work allows leaders and their teams, perhaps for the first time in their careers, to effectively manage their portfolio of activities as a coherent *system*, all affecting one another, rather than just as a collection of individual activities evaluated during performance reviews. When such a system is in place, problems, whether they be small defects or emerging strategic threats, are surfaced sooner and are quickly escalated to the team or teams best positioned to respond to them. People deploy their scarce time and energy far more effectively when they can *see* what to do next instead of having to be told what to do based on a week-old report or the latest "hot list." For many kinds of work, visual management is the "graphical user interface" for the dynamic work design operating system, allowing you to take the ideas far beyond the world of physical things. When people make the transition to managing visually, the gains are often so large and the change so transformative that they are hard to believe. In this chapter, we'll show you how to create such a system for your organization.

INVISIBLE WORK, VISIBLE CHAOS

During Don's first year as a manufacturing engineer at Harley-Davidson, he got firsthand experience with the costs of invisible work when he was asked to substitute for a production supervisor going on vacation. Now one of six production supervisors, Don quickly learned the real rules of the game: sweep any potential problems under the carpet and don't reveal them to your managers unless you are absolutely sure they will otherwise find out.

In the mid-1980s, as part of its much-heralded turnaround, Harley had installed a just-in-time (JIT) production system in its engine factory. It was a huge improvement over its predecessor and had worked wonders for Harley, helping to both improve quality and lower costs. In the years following the installation of the JIT system, Harley's demand grew dramatically. The company's leadership, however, with the memory of being hours away from bankruptcy still fresh in their minds, invested conservatively in new capacity, even though demand had exceeded supply for several years and there was no end in sight. People in the factory focused on squeezing every ounce of production out of their very finite capacity.

The Harley factory was configured so that the assembly line consumed parts faster than the supporting manufacturing departments could make them. So, while the assembly line ran two shifts, most of the manufacturing areas worked a third shift during the night to build up a bank of parts to make sure the assembly line could run two full shifts the next day. Third shift was also an opportunity to recover from any problems that might have cropped up during the two day shifts. In theory, each area had enough capacity to feed the line. In practice, however, almost every day at least one of the manufacturing areas experienced enough of a hiccup that the engine assembly line stopped before the end of the second shift.

Shutting down the main assembly line in any factory is a big deal and was particularly costly for Harley. Harley could easily sell everything it made. Demand was strong; customers were waiting a year or more to get a motorcycle. Every line stop represented lost profit and cash flow that could only be partially recouped by authorizing expensive weekend overtime to get back on schedule.

This should have been an ideal environment for the kind of rapid small-scale problem-solving that we have discussed throughout the book. And, to be fair, Harley's JIT scheme had surfaced and solved many more problems than the system it replaced. That said, it was far from perfect, thanks to a subtle design choice that made the work and any associated problems difficult to see.

Each bank of parts was kept near the area that produced them, in carts that were rolled to the assembly line. In the morning, the carts would all be full and would progressively empty during the first two shifts (since the assembly line consumed them faster than the areas could make them). The carts stayed in the manufacturing area until they were needed by the assembly line.

This design made intuitive sense. Supervisors like Don were responsible for supplying the line, so it seemed sensible to keep the parts in their areas so they could keep track of them. They were the ones accountable for delivering the parts and the ones who got yelled at when those deliveries didn't happen. Plus, parking carts full of parts around the assembly line would cause unnecessary congestion, so the carts were delivered to the line as needed, "just in time."

Supervisors reported on the status of their areas each morning at a production meeting. They shared both the size of the bank they had accumulated overnight and their anticipated ability to keep the line fed during the day's two shifts. This daily huddle should have been the ideal time to surface potential issues and ask for help. However, Don quickly learned that there were few benefits to reporting a problem that *might* shut down the line. Reports typically sounded like "We're tight to the schedule, but should be OK." Surfacing issues just led to more questions. Additional attention from the plant's more-senior leadership often made it even more difficult to catch up during the third shift. Much better to just let the bosses go home thinking everything was fine so you could work in peace.

So, each day the supervisors played a game of chicken in which they would not reveal their area's problem(s) in the hope that another area would be experiencing bigger issues and would shut down the line first. As long as they weren't the ones to run out of parts first (and stop the line), they could catch up without having to worry about additional managerial oversight or "help" that could be more distracting than helpful. Running the area was, after all, their job, and why should they expect others to solve their problems? While this behavior was sensible from the perspective of the supervisors, its net effect was to ensure that problems were only surfaced to the full plant when they had grown big enough to actually stop the line.

When the line did stop, which happened regularly, a predictable flurry of activity ensued. Engineers, operators, and maintenance techs marshaled every resource they could to get production running again, and those who shined during these firefights were rewarded. In the engineering support group "everybody did everything" and a line stop usually got all hands on deck and stole precious time from longer-term projects. The pressure of meeting today's production schedule stretched every department to its max, and with the growing demand from the market, created a by now familiar vicious cycle. As the pressure to meet the schedule grew and as ever-increasing heroic efforts were needed to get the last engine down the line, problems (and work-arounds) grew faster than they were being solved. As he watched people hand carry parts to the line to keep it running late in the day, Don joked, "Our just-in-time system has become a just-in-the-nick-of-time system."

When Don became the plant's manager, he knew the game the supervisors played to survive (having played it himself). Neither platitudes nor threats were going to solve the problem. Initially, Don tried hiring a few new supervisors from other well-run facilities in the hope that they would provide strong role models for how things were supposed to work. But rather than pulling the existing supervisors up, the new hires were quickly sucked into the status quo.

Just as Harley had experienced with their firefighting project managers, the daily game of chicken had little to do with individual personalities. Instead, it had grown out of a work design that was not well matched to the demands of Harley's market. To redirect supervisors' natural problem-solving instincts toward stabilizing daily production, Don's team made the parts banks visible to everyone by moving them to the main aisle and creating specific parking spaces for every cart of finished parts. Now a simple walk through the main part of the plant showed everyone how each area was doing against its hourly schedule. The parking spaces drawn on the floor made it clear how many finished parts there were supposed to be hour by hour for each department.

Now rather than depending on a single report by the supervisor in the morning meeting, complete with "stories," a manufacturing area's performance relative to the daily schedule was visible to everyone in real time. Instead of supervisors being held to a daily schedule (which helped create the game of chicken), they were now evaluated on their ability to meet the hourly schedule painted on the floor. This change to the work design surfaced an entirely new set of issues. As soon as a problem emerged, it showed up as empty parking spaces on the main aisle. With a few hours of buffer built into the plan, this gave the plant a few hours to take action to avoid interrupting the assembly line. Problems that had previously lurked below the radar until they grew big enough to stop the line were now caught sooner and could often be resolved before they created a huge headache. As more problems were solved, the assembly line ran increasingly smoothly, and the new design shifted the culture. The adrenaline-fueled responses were still there, but "crises" were now revealed several hours before the line shut down, when problems were smaller and more time was available to solve them.

As the number of line stops due to missing parts declined, new issues emerged. Line stops from lack of parts had been hiding problems on the assembly line—issues that had been lurking just below the surface. The assembly-line manager now had his hands full tackling the newly revealed issues, which, when resolved, led to further gains.

MAKING THE INVISIBLE VISIBLE

Creating a more visible workflow at Harley was relatively straightforward because the parts that supplied the line had a physical manifestation. Once moved from the manufacturing areas to specific areas on the main aisle of the plant, the parts were easy to see. More complex, less tangible work, such as developing a new drug, executing a large capital project, or doing a merger, poses a more significant challenge. To see these challenges in action and how to meet them (and leverage the first four dynamic work design principles), consider the experience of Caroline Law, the vice president of financial reporting and previous head of one of the accounting divisions of the Federal National Mortgage Association, better known as Fannie Mae.

The Chaos of the Close

Fannie Mae is a leading source of financing for residential mortgages in the United States and is chartered by the US Congress to provide liquidity and stability to the US housing market. Caroline's team played a significant role in making sure that Fannie Mae's books got closed properly each month. In a world enabled by sophisticated information technology, closing an organization's books should be a straightforward operation. In practice, however, just like developing a drug, getting a project done, or finishing a merger, it is often a complex, messy process that requires dozens of skilled professionals from multiple disciplines to collaborate and make numerous judgment calls. Caroline's team had to measure income, expenses, assets, and liabilities with a combination of accounting software engines and manual calculations, record the final results, verify they were correct, and report them. Getting any of these wrong could lead to costly errors, embarrassing restatements, and additional regulatory scrutiny.

At Fannie Mae, the monthly close was a thirteen-day firefight that everyone dreaded. The process was full of starts, stops, restarts, rework, and, in Caroline's words, lots of "hurry up and wait." As in most knowledge work, the root of this complexity lay in the fact that many of the activities in the close were highly dependent on other parts of the process. For example, unusual financial circumstances not anticipated by the designers of the automated accounting system required manual adjustments by experienced accountants. But these adjustments could be made only after the automated system had produced its numbers. If the automated calculations had to be rerun, perhaps because of updates to the input data, then the subsequent manual work also had to be redone. Getting through all of these iterations often required that multiple people work dozens of hours of casual overtime (they were all salaried employees), including working through the weekend.

Caroline's team was responsible for the last four of those thirteen days, and she faced significant pressure from both above and below to improve her team's part of the process. The people reporting to her hated the flurry of activity that occurred during those four days, which eroded morale and made it difficult to retain quality employees. Who wants to work a hectic unpaid weekend once a month? Caroline's boss, Chryssa Halley, Fannie Mae's chief financial officer and controller at that time, also wanted the close to be done more quickly and efficiently, but for an additional reason.

As a government-sponsored enterprise (GSE), Fannie Mae has a role in the mortgage market that has always been controversial. Proponents argue that it plays a critical role in helping young families take an initial step toward a solid financial future by enabling them to purchase a home at an affordable rate. Conversely, critics argue that Fannie Mae is a government bureaucracy that acts as a drag on the otherwise efficient free market for home loans. Fannie Mae's leaders believed that the organization's continued existence turned on its ability to compete favorably with for-profit financial institutions. In their quest for operational parity, the close was a sticking point. For-profit financial institutions could close their books in just a few days. The delays at Fannie Mae slowed decision-making and reporting and made them look uncompetitive.

Caroline's team was a bottleneck; even with forty-five people, their portion of the closing process took longer than the others by several days. She set a target of cutting her group's part of the close in half, from four days to two. She also targeted reducing the amount of after-hours and weekend work by 75 percent as a morale boost for her team.

Caroline expected it would take a year to accomplish her goal. Much to her surprise, the team cut the four-day firefight to a single day and reduced overtime by 80 percent in the first month. There were no major investments in IT, reorganization, or training. Instead, the whole project required about thirty dollars' worth of string, clothespins, and index cards. The staff's enthusiasm soared. Within a year of implementing these changes, the entire Fannie Mae closing process took about six days. As one of the core staff managers said to Caroline, "I had no idea how much we underestimated the capability of our team."

The Close Line

Caroline explains, "We put each task on an index card and hung it on string on the wall using mini-clothespins. It looked like a clothesline in the neighbor's backyard, so we laughed and called it the 'Close Line.' For the first time, we could all see all the tasks at once, just like the neighbor's laundry." Before Caroline's intervention, because they couldn't see what work had been done and what remained, people often had to guess at what tasks could be started next. Guessing wrong wasted time and resources. The Close Line gave everybody the cues they needed to see what needed to be done and when.

Caroline and her team encountered patterns similar to those Don experienced in his initial foray as a supervisor. Her team was composed of smart professionals, but like most knowledge workers, they had never seen all their tasks and problems at once, nor had they understood how they fit together. The work was managing them rather than they managing it. For example, prior to implementing the Close Line, they had no sense of the sheer volume of data they had to synthesize, including information on mortgage transactions, investments, and contingencies. The data were held in several IT systems and overseen by six different groups, each with fifteen to twenty-five people. Successfully closing the books required multiple handoffs, many of which were incomplete or missed (see Chapter 5). Not surprisingly, much as had been done by Don's colleagues, people tended to focus on and prioritize their own part of the work.

"Only a few people professed to know the whole process," Caroline later told us. "And, as we later discovered, much of what they 'knew' turned out to be wrong. The managers met monthly to divvy up our part of the process—the tasks that had to be completed between day nine and day thirteen of the close. The list had no sequence, no prioritization, and no interim deadlines—just a directive to 'get it all done.'"

Those meetings were contentious. Managers, who didn't understand the entire process, made assumptions about the capacity of the other teams and also assigned tasks to their own members without consulting them, often inadvertently giving the same task to a different person each month. The staff, who had to do the work, tried to offer suggestions for how tasks should be assigned, but they were usually ignored. The managers just wanted to get through the few days of hell they faced every month without turning it into a big negotiation. The meeting typically ended with someone mumbling, "Let's just go get it done," and everyone resigning themselves to another inevitable slog.

Once the monthly close process started, nobody knew if they were on, ahead of, or behind schedule. Caroline recalled, "We didn't know when one team would complete a step, allowing another to begin." When sub-teams tried to work ahead, they often discovered that they lacked a vital piece of data and had to start over.

Though these interactions were largely invisible, the outcomes they generated were all too apparent: costs were high, information was wrong, risks were left unattended, and everything took way too long. The whole process was demoralizing. "We knew our work was important for the organization," Caroline said, "and we wanted to get it right, but it was intense, unpredictable, and overwhelming. It was hard work with constant fire drills."

Caroline's experience probably sounds all too familiar to those who live in a world increasingly dominated by knowledge work. Being a knowledge worker often feels a bit like trying to play soccer in a thick fog. You can't see the whole field or the location of the other players. So, when the ball shows up in your area, all you can do is kick it in what you hope is the right direction. Similarly, perhaps the central challenge of managing the flow of knowledge work is that you can't see where it is or when it's moving or predict when it will show up in your inbox.

The inability to see work move creates a host of problems that constantly interrupt the flow of activity. Just as happened on Harley's assembly line, the flow of intellectual work, like accounting, sometimes stops. The issue blocking the flow could be anything: a customer service agent facing a complaint that is difficult to resolve or a bench scientist not knowing the best way to proceed when an experiment doesn't work as planned. Everything stops, but unlike with the assembly line (though similar to Harley's supporting production areas), the problem only shows up locally. Most people can't see or hear the stop. The problem does not generate clear and public evidence of its existence outside of the person or small group affected by it. Consequently, people don't adjust their behavior accordingly or show up to help address the underlying causes. Often, as Harley experienced, the problem just festers below the surface until it becomes large enough to noticeably slow or stop the entire process.

The person who hits a snag may surface the problem to a supervisor. But if they work in an environment where they are supposed to "bring solutions, not problems," they may choose to keep it to themselves and try to work through it on their own. Meanwhile, their other scheduled work comes to a halt. Such private problem-solving often entails adding a workaround, perhaps a new step in the process or a private spreadsheet or checklist that they control. These additions become a permanent part of a vast hidden network of private workarounds, which are typically less productive and more error prone than those that emerge when problems are worked on together. The more these problems are hidden by individual workarounds, the more the way the work actually gets done diverges from how managers think it gets done.

For example, several members of Caroline's team discovered places where two or more software systems produced a different result for a given metric, thus indicating an error, which they then fixed. To make sure a similar error didn't slip by next time, they added a validation step to their individual process, reminding themselves to check the match during each close. Creating the Close Line revealed many such private validation steps that were entirely redundant. There was already an automated test that compared results for all the relevant systems and flagged discrepancies. In the first round of creating the Close Line, they discovered that 13 percent of their tasks were either redundant or simply unneeded.

Because accounting work doesn't have a physical manifestation like a piston or a box of samples, Caroline couldn't just paint some lines on the office floor and move her team's work to those parking spaces. Instead, to manage the flow of her team's activity, like most office work, she needed something akin to the radar screens that air traffic controllers use to manage the flow of planes in and out of the airport. Those screens are not, of course, the real planes themselves but instead are a kind of visual twin that helps everyone see the flow of activity.

A system that makes the invisible visible needs to be easily accessible and widely shared. Only when managers and employees closely examine the specific activities together with the targets to which they are directed do they have a fighting chance of seeing whether they add up to a feasible and effective strategy. Looking at a schedule of milestones that if achieved will deliver a target without examining the underlying "how" is not enough. Relying solely on milestones is akin to a large team scaling a formidable mountain and having just a vague idea of the places they will camp each night. If you don't detail the route from camp to camp, everyone might take a different path, resulting in little ability to work together or share the equipment. A detailed map that visualizes the trek up the mountain or specifies the most effective way to accomplish knowledge work helps everyone focus on desired outcomes and coordinate on the way to achieve them.

A good visualization scheme should also make it immediately evident when there is an issue to resolve. Sheila Dodge, as we saw in Chapter 1, used a visual board to show the status of all the contracts being processed in the Broad Institute's Office of Sponsored Research. It was easy to see when work began to pile up in account creation because that part of the board was overflowing with sticky notes (each of which represented a contract waiting for an account). The board was useful because it was more than a scorecard showing aggregate performance.

Instead, it showed where the work was moving and where it was stuck, helping the team identify the most effective place to intervene.

At Fannie Mae, the Close Line became the radar screen that the team used to visualize the flow of the work through their system. "Before the new system," Caroline said, "when we had a really messy month, a few team members would get together and solve a tough problem. That meant a few people had learned a lot about certain pieces of the process. They became our go-to people when similar issues came up later. But the knowledge was contained in a few heads in a few isolated areas. We needed something much grander. When I first saw the idea of making the work visible, it made so much sense to me. I immediately took it to my team."

The design of the Close Line is captured in the schematic in Figure 7.1. "We reviewed every activity to identify tasks, dependencies, and sequence," Caroline said. As they debated, mapped, and remapped the details, everyone could see the radar screen of the workflow taking shape before them. They used horizontal strings to create three rows that matched the three (morning, midday, afternoon) daily team meetings. Across the top, from left to right, were days. They placed each card under the date where they expected it to be completed. As time progressed, they moved a card from its planned completion date to where it was actually finished. Everyone could see if they were ahead of or behind schedule. Two cards, "dependency," which showed an activity that, when completed, enabled other tasks to be started, and "task," which detailed something that needed to be done, were used. "Loan level processing in accounting engine complete" was, for example, a dependency card. To its right would be the tasks that could then be done, such as the following:

- Complete Manual Journal Entry 1: taxes and insurance adjustments
- Complete Manual Journal Entry 2: cash clearing transactions
- Complete Analytic: unpaid principal balance roll forward
- Complete Controls: review data exception report #1
- Complete Controls: upstream system data compare—review and approve

This is a perfect example of structuring work to enable fast learning (see Chapter 4). Caroline's team could now see and respond to bottlenecks that slowed overall progress and potential "tidal waves" that risked swamping the team. The Close Line structure helped Caroline and her team discover the next problem to solve in real time, and there were plenty of them. The team found themselves questioning long-held assumptions and improving the workflow. Did the dependencies have the right tasks attached? Was the sequence right? Were the time estimates right? "Even the people who knew the most about the process

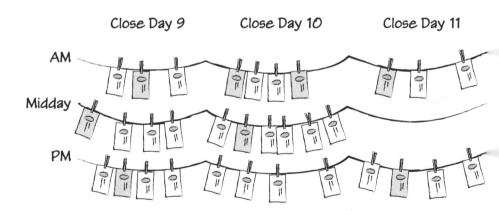

Figure 7.1. The Close Line from Fannie Mae's accounting team

discovered gaps they didn't know about," said Caroline, "and much of what they believed wasn't right."

Caroline's team started their day with a huddle in front of the Close Line to discuss progress. They soon began to invite the other six groups working on the close so that they could better understand how work moved among them. In one roundtable session, a manager from the technology team pointed out that the accounting engine, which analyzed a huge amount of data, took only six days to produce results that Caroline's team needed. Initially, Caroline didn't believe him. "I said, 'That's crazy, that process always takes at least 10 days to give us the results we need.' He persisted and after several minutes of back-and-forth, I finally invited him to tell me more. He explained there were several stages *within* the engine-run: after a specific step, he told me, around day six, our people could start looking at the numbers because the calculations over the following four days were isolated and immaterial. That was a huge eye-opener. For everyone. And, of course, it turned out to be true." Until they tried to map the work together, the manager who ran the engine hadn't been aware that Caroline's team was waiting the additional four days.

As the teams continued to compare notes, these kinds of gaps, often embarrassingly simple, began to surface and get fixed on a regular basis. Initially, the huddles took forty-five minutes, but as regular problem-solving yielded an increasingly stable system, they soon required only fifteen minutes.

The Close Line meetings helped the work flow more smoothly. "We used the huddles to match demand and capacity in real time," recalled Caroline. When their current tasks were completed, the team members could choose their next from the list of items that were ready. They would literally go up to the wall and grab the appropriate card. "They could choose to work on something they knew well or push for more of a challenge. They worked together seamlessly and sorted out who would work on which task in less than five minutes without the managers' involvement." When she needed to get a feel for the flow of work, Caroline simply asked everyone to hold up the card they were working on. It was instantly clear how many people needed work and how many cards were still on the wall waiting for data from an upstream step.

"We eliminated the old task list," said Caroline, "and the bosses no longer needed to assign work to people. Everyone could see it on the wall. People could touch their work, move it around, and feel a sense of accomplishment when the task was completed and removed from the board."

With each iteration, genuine collaboration increasingly replaced infighting and pushback. Managers no longer arbitrarily decided what people would do. Everyone could post issues, and everyone jumped in to work on them. Regular discussions refined metrics and targets. As more data came into view, solutions began to appear. The radar screen grew clearer, simpler, and cleaner. People bought into the new system because they had built it together. Everyone was on the same page about what needed to be done and why. Low-priority and legacy activities disappeared. At every session, the group recalibrated and realigned. Confidence in the plan and its execution rose.

Making the flow of work visible, whether it is putting parts on the main aisle or clipping index cards to a piece of string, can transform an organization's culture. It is hard to keep quiet when everyone is staring at the same set of gaps, issues, and redundancies, and those gaps, issues, and redundancies are staring right back. People naturally join in to put the pieces together. As Caroline said, when asked to reflect on the process,

"It felt like a cross between playing a board game and working a jigsaw puzzle."

GETTING STARTED WITH VISUAL MANAGEMENT

The basic building blocks of visual management are nicely captured in one of its simplest incarnations: the problem board.

In many organizations, managing problems is a problem. Issues that prevent an organization from meeting its targets get surfaced in multiple ways: they are discussed in meetings, mentioned in the hallways, written on tickets, and sent through email or instant messaging. At any given moment, multiple, sometimes overlapping efforts are underway to resolve them. Many problems are repeatedly discussed but never actually worked on. Despite the energy that goes into problem resolution, this ad hoc approach rarely yields satisfying results. Major issues can linger for months or even years, often creating even more workarounds. Every veteran of a large organization has experienced the perennial problem that, while whined about in every meeting, never actually gets resolved.

The "system" that most organizations use to manage problem-solving violates all the principles of dynamic work design, particularly regulate for flow. Problem-solving efforts are not driven by clear problem statements, they are not mapped against overall targets, and they are rarely escalated to the person or group best positioned to resolve the issue. Lack of clear prioritization results in multiple overlapping efforts, each of which is pushed into the system without regard for efforts already underway. The result is wasted resources and counterproductive conflict that is never fully resolved ("but my solution is better"). Lacking clear targets, people invest in tackling issues that, while important to them, are not high on the leader's priority list and often don't get the needed resources. It's a big mess that rarely yields the desired results.

The team running Broad's gene sequencing lab suffered from the syndrome of rarely actually solving problems. Issues were constantly surfacing in the lab—technologies that didn't quite work, samples getting contaminated, software glitches, etc.—but there was no common method for tracking or managing them. No single person was aware of every effort underway, many of which overlapped. Nothing was prioritized. Minor issues sometimes got immediate attention, while major challenges could go unresolved for weeks or longer.

To improve their approach, the team added a simple table to the wall of the room used for their weekly team meeting (Figure 7.2). Each column represents a step in their structured problem-solving process (formulate the problem, investigate, propose experiment, run experiment). Each row captured a problem-solving effort currently underway by members of the team. The current state of each problem-solving effort was then captured by a sticky note listing the issue and placed in the appropriate column. A quick review of this display revealed all the efforts currently in progress and the phase that each one was in, making it easy to see if the work of problem-solving was moving or stalled.

A static display of information then became a dynamic system for managing the *portfolio* of problem-solving by adding two steps to the weekly team meeting. First, the meeting opened with the facilitator asking, "Are there any fires?" *Fire* was the word the Broad team used for a problem and represented any issue that would prevent the team from meeting its weekly targets for sample analysis. When someone raised an issue, it was quickly discussed to determine whether it rose to the level of a fire. Each issue deemed a legitimate threat to the weekly delivery targets got assigned to an owner and a row on the fire board

FIRES

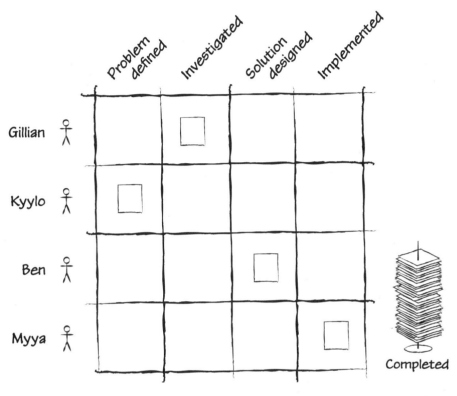

Figure 7.2.

with a new sticky note in the first column (indicating that a clear problem statement had yet to be formulated).

Second, the team would then review the fires already on the board, with the responsible person giving a brief update on each one. When the team agreed that a problem-solving effort had completed a given step, its associated sticky note was moved to the next column. When the team agreed that a problem had been resolved, its sticky note was removed from the board. An effort that was stuck and could not move from one column to the next signaled that the team needed to jump into collaboration mode and offer possible solutions or additional resources to move the effort forward.

This simple protocol brings all the previous four dynamic work design principles to life. The format naturally leads to discovery. The definition of a fire is based on a clear problem statement—for example, a piece of equipment is malfunctioning and jeopardizing the flow of samples—and the visual format allows everyone to see all the activities in progress to solve that problem. Reconciling those activities with the problem statement happens naturally. A brief review of the board allows team members to make their own assessment about whether resolving the problems currently in progress will be sufficient to deliver the week's samples.

The process of reviewing whether sticky notes are moving from one column to the next ensures immediate escalation into collaborative work when an effort hits a roadblock. Much like Don's parking spaces for parts on the main aisle, a sticky note that doesn't move signals that something is wrong and more collaboration is needed. Later, the team would add an even higher and more visible category of escalation (marked by a big stop sign sticker on the board), indicating that the problem had stopped the analysis line. The team would then meet at least daily (note the increased meeting frequency to match the urgency of the problem) until the issue was resolved.

Having all the problem-solving efforts currently underway on the board also helped regulate the flow of work. Putting sticky notes on a wall doesn't prevent people from taking on too much. However, the explicit choice to add (or not) a fire to the board during the weekly meeting created a natural airplane door and an easy assessment of whether something else could be let through it. Don't add new work in the system until someone is ready to work on it. Moreover, when all the problem-solving efforts start to stall—none of the sticky notes are moving—the team gets a clear signal that they have taken on too much relative to the available capacity. Now they either need to be more disciplined in prioritizing which problems to work on or need to find additional resources for problem-solving. As we discussed in the previous chapter, the discipline of focusing on a few important things produces more results than working on ten at once.

For the Broad team, this simple system was almost magical. Dedicating fifteen to twenty minutes in their weekly meeting to reviewing the state of their problem-solving efforts increased collaboration as the team started using its big collective brain to tackle issues that couldn't be solved by a single individual. For example, when a problem-solving effort or project was hampered by an issue with the IT system, another team member was often able to resolve the issue on the spot, thereby saving hours of trying to get the right person's attention. With the resulting focus and collaboration, the team marshaled its scarce resources more effectively, and the pace of problem-solving increased dramatically.

The ability to resolve problems quickly was central to the dramatic improvements that the team produced in the lab. The problem board helped the team balance their resources among doing the work, solving problems, and building new capabilities so that the system performed predictably and the quality and quantity of its output improved steadily.

Visual Management Building Blocks

Visual management can be used to improve the execution of any kind of work and is especially effective in knowledge work since it makes visible what was usually otherwise invisible. Each system for visually managing otherwise invisible work tends to be a bit different, as the system is most effective when tightly tied to the specific work and how it flows. Visual management schemes also tend to evolve over time as both the work changes and the team's understanding of it deepens. Nonetheless, effective systems share four elements:

- **Clear targets and shared intent:** A set of quantified targets and a shared understanding of the intent behind them.
- **Metrics:** Measures that capture progress toward the targets in ways that represent both short- and long-run concerns. A "faster" target, for example, should usually be tempered with a focus on maintaining quality.
- **Activities:** A representation of the actions that are both planned and currently underway to ensure that the metrics reach the targets.
- **Issues:** Visual signals that highlight when the chosen activities are not delivering the targets or when unforeseen problems arise.

Broad's problem board captured these elements in a simple way (and thus makes a good first example of visual management):

- The intent was simply to ensure the regular flow of samples through the lab.
- The metric was, in this case, binary; either the samples were being delivered or they were not.
- Each problem-solving effort was a separate activity with its own specific problem statement.
- Issues were surfaced when a problem-solving effort could not move from one step to the next in a timely manner.

Most visual management efforts are a bit more sophisticated (mostly because the targets and metrics are not an on-off switch), but the core elements are the same. Though, as we mentioned above, each system tends to be a bit different and evolve over time, most of them are a variation of a basic structure that combines the four core elements.

Visual Management in Action

To see how the elements of visual management can be combined to support different kinds of work, here are two examples, starting with the Broad lab's approach to technology development.

Improving Technology Development at Broad. After they finished reviewing the problem board, the Broad team's weekly meeting focused on their technology development pipeline. As mentioned earlier, genomic science is evolving rapidly, and an effective technology development process remains critical to

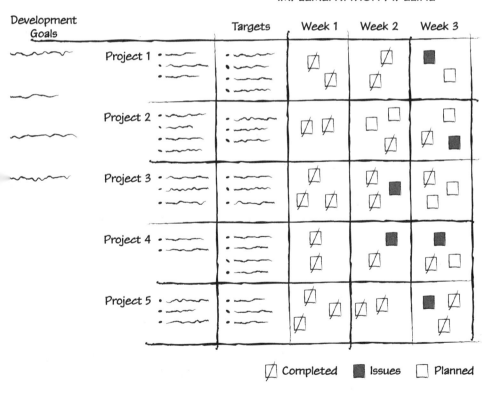

IMPLEMENTATION PIPELINE

Figure 7.3.

Broad's continued competitiveness. The visual representation used to manage this process, implemented with sticky notes and tape on one wall in their meeting room, is shown in Figure 7.3.

Each major project got a row. The sticky notes in a given row captured specific activities needed to complete the project and could include items like "develop a new testing protocol in the lab" or "write the software for a new kind of data analysis." Beyond describing the activity, the sticky note also showed a target completion date and the name of the responsible party. When an activity got stuck and couldn't be completed as planned, a pink sticky note was placed on top of it to signal a problem.

At the weekly meeting, the project's leader would give a brief update based on her row of the board. Activities that were completed without trouble were celebrated by removing their sticky note(s) from the board. Activities that were not moving, those with the additional pink sticky note, were discussed.

This approach allowed the team to manage technology development as a portfolio rather than just trying to push the latest project over the finish line. The entire technology development portfolio, including targets, metrics, activities, and issues, was visible on the wall for everyone to see. Just to the left of the project status were the specific goals the projects aimed to meet. This layout made it easy to compare the targets against the set of activities meant to deliver them and spot problems in the larger plan. For example, as with many organizations, software and data analytics became increasingly central to technology development. Much as happened with the research accounts, the board quickly revealed the imbalance and showed the team where they needed to invest next.

This simple approach immediately revealed severe violations of the regulate-for-flow principle. Just as they allowed too many samples into the lab, they had *way* too many projects in the technology development pipeline. As Sheila put it, the board regularly "went pink," meaning that every sticky note representing an activity had an additional pink note, signaling that it was behind. Everything being late is a sure sign of overload.

The obvious short-term solution was to cancel some new projects, thus bringing the workload in line with available capacity. But anyone who has managed a portfolio of projects knows that almost every project has a cheerleader making the case for why it is important. Broad is staffed with smart, motivated people who have lots of good ideas. While they did cancel projects, they also used a simple method, another manifestation of the regulate-for-flow principle, to counteract the natural tendency to overload the system. They numerically ranked their projects in order of importance, typically one to ten. Similar to the common backlog that David Whiteing used at Standard Chartered, they then regularly repeated the following mantra: "If you are working on project number seven and could be helping on project number two, stop working on seven and focus on two until it's finished." Slowly, the team realized that some of the projects were never going to get attention. Every time an important project finished, someone had an idea for another important project. Everyone began to see that the less important projects, while nice to have, were never going to make the cut. Since everyone could see that these projects never made it to the front burner, the team soon developed a better sense of their available capacity and began adjusting their own choices rather than waiting for more-senior management to tell them that they couldn't do something.

It took almost two years before the Broad team could fully implement the regulate-for-flow principle. Don vividly remembers the first time he saw that all the work on the board was actually moving. "I had been visiting Sheila and her team every few months to coach them on the structure of their visual board and process, each time giving them feedback on how to 'move to the next level.' Time and time again I would tell them the same painful news, 'You have fifty percent too much work on the board,' that they still had a huge traffic jam that was slowing everything down. On one visit, though, I could finally see that all the work was moving well. After about two years of giving them this same tough feedback, I just smiled and told them that the board was finally in sync, the work was all moving, and that they had 'graduated.' There was a palpable sense of relief and celebration in the room, which lasted about three minutes. Then they turned back to the tough work of delivering the work that was still on that board."

As the team finally got the workload under control, the meeting became an increasingly effective venue for surfacing and solving problems. When a sticky note didn't move on schedule (signaled by a pink note), the team knew there was a problem. Did the team need additional resources to move it forward? Was there expertise on other teams that might help resolve the blockage? Often, problems could be resolved in the meeting. If not, they could be added to the problem board described above. IT issues, for example, could often be resolved by someone opening a laptop and granting permission to access a system or changing a few lines of code. Thornier issues were assigned to teams for a more structured inquiry.

The technology on which the labs relied changed every twelve to twenty-four months. Thus, as Sheila explains, being able to redirect their efforts to adopt and use that technology was critical: "We had to be very agile and make sure that we could handle all of the changes in a very dynamic way. That lent itself to using the principles of dynamic work design as a way of grounding us and making sure that those management principles were showing up in all of our work. That became the underlying foundation of how we transformed our labs and created a new line of business. We started to pile on practices and tools that allowed us to use those principles."

Also note that using the problem-solving board and the technology development board in the same meeting allowed the team to naturally balance their resources between resolving blockers in current production (increasing production volume and quality) and supporting new techniques and technologies that advanced the process. If problems in the current production process started to rise, folks from the projects would temporarily lend a hand to get things moving again. If the lab was running smoothly, more effort could be put to advancing the projects.

The lab's sequencing business grew fourfold in just a few years (and helped fill all the capacity they had created in the lab). Sheila's technology development team estimates that by using dynamic work design, they generated a more than threefold improvement in productivity. The productivity gains created so much additional capacity that the Broad genomics labs began several new lines of business, including taking work from researchers outside their own institute. This opened an entirely new universe of customers and helped resolve one of the critical bottlenecks in genomic research today.

Improving BP's Supply Chain. Visual management boards are often very effective in improving R & D processes. Harley used them to make similar gains in their development efforts, also generating a more than threefold improvement in the number of models they could deliver annually. Visualization techniques can also be applied in settings far from the lab or the engineering center. Consider the following.

While Mark Schwiebert was working to improve BP's procurement purchase-to-pay system (see Chapter 5), his team faced another challenging target: reduce cost. With several billion dollars in annual spending spread across five thousand suppliers, they had been given ambitious goals for reducing the cost of materials and services. These savings would come primarily through renegotiating a portion of the over 1,500 contracts that came up for renewal each year.

It was, however, difficult at the outset for Mark to assess whether his team was using their scarce time and energy effectively. Not every contract was a good candidate for renegotiation; some just needed to be renewed. In the system Mark inherited, each procurement specialist chose the contracts that she thought had the best potential for cost reduction and, like the Harley supervisors, only reported problems they thought might cause a major issue. Though the status of each renegotiation or renewal was reported in monthly meetings with polished summaries, the total annual savings was never clear until the final result was posted at the end of the year. Things had worked this way for years, and it proved nearly impossible for Mark to give his boss credible updates. Wild swings in the estimated savings over the course of the year caused endless turmoil in the division's budgeting process. Since everyone was working toward an annual target, major savings would often show up only at the end of the year, thanks to the mad rush to get contracts signed before the end of the reporting period.

Mark needed a more structured and predictable method. He started the year with a new design. An initial meeting with the entire team focused on identifying the contracts that offered the most potential savings. Those contracts were then divvied up among the team members. Each procurement specialist then tracked her portfolio of renegotiation efforts on her own visual management board (literally a piece of poster board in this case) that showed the status of each effort. Efforts at risk of not meeting their savings targets were clearly highlighted. When it came time for the weekly or monthly meeting, each person just picked up their board (shown in Figure 7.4) and brought it to the meeting. Now the statuses of all the negotiations, the projected savings, and the problematic contracts were visible to everyone every week. The new data-driven meetings helped the team spot problems early and marshal the right resources to solve them. The meetings were also shorter and more helpful.

Each stage of a renegotiation was represented by a column on the board, and the rows broke the work into different levels of complexity. Some work was straightforward (bottom row) and moved quickly; some work was complex (top row) and required more thought; other work was somewhere in between (middle row). Each sticky note represented a different renegotiation currently in progress and its status (on track, behind schedule, at risk). The board's funnel shape, captured by the way it's narrower with each subsequent phase, depicts the idea that some projects were not as promising as it was first thought they would be. Those projects would get dropped early and be replaced by more promising ones. Put differently, not every project would make it all the way through the process. The resulting transparency helped escalate emerging issues to Mark's entire team so they could resolve them quickly.

Choosing when to start the negotiations and how many negotiations to pursue at once were important decisions. Following the concept of regulating the flow, they didn't want to start a negotiation that would get dragged out needlessly because there were too many already in progress. The sticky notes in the "ready" column set the priority and showed which negotiation

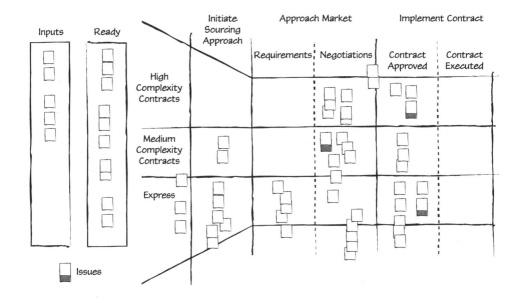

Figure 7.4.

to start next when there was an opening. It was easy for each person to see when they were ready to open another negotiation or when they were too busy, helping to ensure that once a negotiation started, it would keep moving until complete. The team began to produce regular, predictable results every quarter instead of a huge, unpredictable burst of savings at the year's end.

These simple boards bring the first four principles of dynamic work design alive. Taking the work out of spreadsheets, emails, and to-do lists allows everyone to participate in choosing the right set of negotiations to meet the team's targets. The question "Are we negotiating the right set of contracts?" follows naturally and often leads to discovery and new insights ("We do it that way??"). For Mark, a one-hour weekly meeting kept him connected to the work and the people doing it, while eliminating dozens of emails and hallway conversations. Highlighting contracts that were not progressing escalated problems to the weekly team meeting, where the group could use their experience and problem-solving skills to help get it back on track.

Visualizing the work allowed Mark's team to collaborate in new ways that resulted in accurate forecasts of the quarterly and annual cost reduction and eliminated the year-end turmoil in the budgeting process. More importantly, they delivered about 30 percent more annual savings than was previously thought possible, more than a billion dollars in the space of three years, and they did it with 30 percent fewer staff.

MAKING VISUAL MANAGEMENT WORK FOR YOU

Visual management can be a powerful tool for improving the execution of otherwise invisible work. Every effective visual management system, however, is a bit different, and building one requires some experimentation. Four guidelines will help you develop one faster and more reliably.

The magic is in the conversations, not the sticky notes. Most importantly, remember the goal. Visual management is a tool for allocating scarce managerial time and energy effectively by fostering high-quality conversations. A visual board that is simple, clear, and a bit messy is much better than one that is perfectly coiffed and disconnected from the work. A board's sophistication is irrelevant if it doesn't facilitate collaboration. Put differently, the best board in the world is useless if people don't meet in front of it regularly to test their understanding of the system they are managing and then use it to make decisions and solve problems. If your early attempts lead to productive conversations about the status of your organization's work—where progress is being made, where problems are getting in the way of meeting targets, and where lessons are being learned—then you are headed in the right direction.

When teaching visual management, we invariably get questions about using digital tools—one of our Executive MBA students once said, "I get the approach, but the sticky notes just feel so . . . 1980s." Digital representations can be effective and can offer several options that you can't replicate with sticky notes and markers, including integration with other systems, regular backups, and remote participation. But when moving to electronic platforms, don't let the available features distract you from keeping it simple and clear. Digitizing the boards can easily pull you into "automating" the board, and from there it is all too easy to spend more time formatting the board than having the right conversations. Simpler is usually better. In our experience, the biggest risk of moving to digital representations is that people will skip the meetings and say, "I'm busy and can't make the meeting, but I'll check the board later." The moment that happens, you lose the magic.

Starting the board is hard because you don't understand the work as well as you think you do. Your first attempts at visual management are likely to be frustrating. When you start laying it out on the wall, you will likely find that you don't understand the work as well as you think you do. Much as Caroline experienced, few managers really understand the entire system through which work gets done. You may struggle to choose the right representation and to identify good labels for the rows and columns. Initially, everything can feel like a special case that doesn't quite fit the board layout you have chosen. Don't worry, it's a natural part of the process. Each iteration brings new questions and insights, and soon the board begins to look like the work feels.

The board is messy because the work is messy; the work is messy because it has lots of problems. The good news is that seeing the messiness will help you start fixing the work. As discussed in previous chapters, years of living in the firefighting trap results in work processes that are largely ad hoc and undocumented. Efforts to create an effective visual management system will help unearth the targets, what work is in progress and who is doing it, and the issues they face getting it done. Don't shy away from the messiness. Dig in and start fixing the issues you find. For example, creating a visual board often forces leaders to clarify the targets they are giving their teams. Similarly, initial efforts to get all the activities on the wall usually reveal significant overload and start the process of eliminating low-value projects. As each small change improves the system, the workflow will be easier to represent on the board.

Your board will evolve. Once you get a visual system working, don't get too comfortable. In our experience, good visual systems evolve quickly as you improve the work and get better at using the board to guide problem-solving and decision-making. It is a good practice to check in every quarter or so and ask, "Does (do) the board(s) look like the work feels? Does it represent the way our work gets done?" If the answer is no, then it's often time to reconsider them. Every so often, Sheila Dodge would buy a case of beer on a Friday afternoon and invite her team to redo their boards. Sticky notes and tape would come down, and they would experiment with new representations. These are important check-in points that allow people to step back from the day-to-day flux of doing work and revisit the process of how work gets done.

LEVERAGING THE VISUAL SYSTEM

Human beings are visual creatures. Approximately 30 percent of the cerebral cortex is dedicated to processing visual information, and many of our daily activities leverage our ability to process visual signals quickly and accurately. People throughout the world spend hours each day guiding powerful, heavy, potentially lethal machines at high speed in and among others engaged in similar activities. Though driving is far from perfect, thanks to stop signs, stoplights, street signs, painted lines on the street, and instruments on the dashboard, we usually get where we need to go without incident.

Human beings are natural problem solvers, and problem-solving *can* be a major engine of organizational performance. But "solving" a problem with a private workaround often does the opposite. Moving otherwise invisible work out of the organizational shadows through simple visualization tools can redirect our natural instincts in ways that improve the performance of the overall system and open up an entirely new universe of possibilities. "A picture is worth a thousand words" is more than simple folk wisdom. Representing complex work visually conveys more information more quickly and more clearly than trying to do so verbally. It will also challenge what you think you know about your own work and how it all fits together.

Part III

Action

Chapter 8

The Power of Leading
with Principles

STATIC STRUCTURE WILL TAKE YOU ONLY SO FAR

We have now taught dynamic work design to thousands of executives and have worked directly with several dozen companies, ranging from small venture capital funds to large multinational banks and energy companies, to implement its principles. Questions always come up, and perhaps the one that is most interesting and important typically emerges near the end of a session: Does using dynamic work design make your business more prone to being disrupted?

The notion of *disruption* was first popularized by Harvard Business School professor Clayton Christensen, who documented a series of cases in which powerful incumbent firms were slow to respond to technological innovations and ended up losing ground in markets they once dominated. While Christensen outlined a specific set of dynamics, popular use of the term now includes any technology or event that threatens an existing business.

The disruption question turns on the idea that by investing in work design improvements, you might inadvertently make your organization less adaptable and innovative. Perhaps improving efficiency has the side effect of hardening organizational arteries and thus leaving you more prone to competitive upheaval? Being, for example, the most efficient manufacturer of camera film does little to prepare a company for the world of digital photography.

So, do the quality and productivity gains that come with using dynamic work design limit an organization's ability to respond to major changes in its industry?

The evidence accumulated from our experience is that the answer is no. To the contrary, in our experience, using dynamic work design reduces the risk of being disrupted. The foundation supporting our answer captures the essential difference between static and dynamic approaches to designing and managing organizations.

A static approach to improving efficiency and productivity typically relies on narrowing the range of allowable activity and thus can have a negative impact on innovation and adaptability. For example, in the 1960s and 1970s, US automakers (and companies in many other industries) created an intricate system of rules, procedures, budgets, and reporting relationships in the hope of squeezing every ounce of efficiency out of their plants. As Nelson's research documented, by the 1980s, the performance of every machine in every factory was measured and evaluated at every shift. The business case for purchasing a new piece of expensive equipment required showing that it would be fully utilized, thus making its financial return look better, independent of whether all of that capacity was needed.

The consequences for not hitting those utilization targets (now embedded in financial targets) were significant. In the words of one person interviewed, operators who missed their targets knew they were going "to get beat up" by their supervisors, who, in turn, would get beat up by their bosses. Not surprisingly, this approach created deep mistrust between management and those doing the work, who increasingly resorted to surreptitious workarounds to make sure they always hit their targets, even when something had gone wrong. At one plant, operators hid partially completed electrical modules in toolboxes and ceiling tiles so that they could still meet production targets when their machines broke. Don did something similar in his early days as a pieceworker in factories. Operators, with the knowledge of production supervisors (who also wanted some insulation from management's wrath), kept private records of the banks of completed parts, built up on good days, that they could turn in on a difficult day. In both cases, underlying problems with the reliability of the equipment often remained unaddressed.

Thanks to this convoluted, opaque system, when those companies were confronted with newly formidable Asian manufacturers, their existing static approach to efficiency, coupled with an increasingly antagonistic relationship with their workforce, proved to be a serious obstacle to regaining competitiveness. Not only did US companies have a lot to change, but they had few skills for doing so. It would take them decades to regain parity, and two of the big three automakers still required a government-funded bailout in the wake of the 2008 financial crisis.

As we have detailed throughout the book, a dynamic approach creates the conditions for ongoing learning and improvement. More importantly, dynamic work design creates organizational muscles that can be flexed in many ways. It is a kind of general-purpose fitness program that will help you in almost any activity. Many of the organizations we have discussed so far emerged from their efforts to use dynamic work design with a better track record of innovation and more ability to respond to unanticipated changes. Faster, more focused processes staffed by people comfortable with surfacing problems and making adjustments provide a powerful platform for both doing the disruption (innovating) and responding to competitive threats.

That said, the emergence of COVID-19 in early 2020 put this argument to the test in a way that we could never have anticipated. It also provides a definitive demonstration of the dynamic work design approach and principles in action.

"DO WE EVEN DO THIS?"

In the early days of March 2020, Sheila Dodge and her Broad Institute colleagues were busy shuttering the sequencing lab. Universities, including MIT, were sending students home and putting all but the most mission-critical research programs on pause. Without samples to analyze, there wasn't much for the Broad team to do. "I was running around," Sheila later recalled, "figuring out who would be essential, who would stay on-site to keep the equipment running, and how we would keep everyone safe and busy."

During that same period, Doctor Deborah Hung, a Broad Institute core faculty member and a clinician and infectious disease expert at Brigham and Women's Hospital (one of Boston's largest medical facilities), was growing increasingly concerned about the lack of capacity to do COVID tests. Her hospital could process fewer than fifty tests per day, not even enough to regularly test the staff, let alone the patients. In an interview with a local radio station, Hung said, "Testing just wasn't there as we needed it." She had recently experienced immense frustration in arranging a test for *one* patient. "It consumed probably almost twelve hours to make things happen," she said. "Twelve continuous hours of my making phone calls."[1]

On March 9—the day the city of Boston canceled its upcoming St. Patrick's Day parade—Hung had an impromptu conversation with a colleague, another expert in infectious diseases, and they discussed what would be needed to do COVID tests at scale. The requirements included high-volume robotics for fluid handling, expertise in handling biological samples, and the necessary state and federal certifications. Almost immediately, Hung realized that the Broad lab had many of the necessary ingredients. As she said in the radio interview, "And when you think about it that way, there are not that many institutions where all of those converge . . . literally it was two seconds to click."

Phone calls to Broad's leadership—Stacey Gabriel (Sheila's boss) and Eric Lander—followed almost immediately. Stacey, a PhD geneticist, was on her way into a yoga studio. "Stacey, testing is terrible!" Deb said. "You have to help." Stacey stood in the parking lot, rolled-up mat under her arm, listening and trying to understand. "Huh? What do you want us to do? We don't do viral," Stacey responded. Hung explained. "It's PCR, you know how to do it. Use all that infrastructure that you've already built. But it only matters if you can do it quickly, and it's only going to matter if you can do it at high scale." Another lab doing another hundred tests wasn't going to make a difference. "Can you just look at it?" asked Deb.[2] Stacey agreed to look into it.

"There really wasn't a choice," Eric recalled. "Deb Hung called up, and she was so adamant. She said, 'You *have* to do this, you have to let Stacey do this,' and I really didn't have a choice. I said, 'Of course.'"[3]

Stacey and Sheila met that afternoon to discuss the possibility. Sheila recalls her initial reaction: "Okay, we need to think about this, is this our strategy, do we even do this?" Having spent the previous seven years learning to regulate the flow of work and focus scarce resources on the projects most aligned with the institute's strategy, this felt like something very different. Stacey and Sheila went back and forth for several hours on whether shifting the Genomics Platform to COVID-19 testing was possible and the right course of action for Broad.

There were lots of pros and cons. On the plus side, a COVID test is technically simpler to process than a gene sequence. Tim De Smet, another member of the leadership team, said, "Take all the hard parts of sequencing away and you have COVID testing." The lab also had lots of experience with managing large volumes of biological samples. On the minus side, however, Broad had never returned a diagnostic test directly to a patient, something that required both government certification and careful documentation. As we discussed in Chapter 2, although the team had made enormous progress in reducing their turnaround time, twenty days wasn't going to cut it for COVID testing. To be useful, tests had to be done and returned in a day or two, far faster than Broad was used to working. Stacey and Sheila agreed to sleep on it.

Tuesday morning, March 10, Sheila and Stacey reconvened with the team. Sheila landed on the position that "I don't know about this, but it is important, and we're not doing anything else." Eric threw his support behind the effort.

On Wednesday, March 11, in what would be one of their last in-person meetings, Sheila and the rest of the lab's leadership spent the day mapping out a plan, figuring out the chemistry, and identifying the needed automation and which teams would be involved. As Sheila recalls, "We repeated our old dynamic work design process, but focused on this new, even bigger problem."

Small COVID

How do you organize for something you've never done before? Planning was important, but COVID testing represented uncharted territory. They knew they weren't going to get everything right. Success with this new effort would turn on their ability to learn and adapt quickly, skills they had invested in and built up over the last few years. By this point, the lab team was deeply skilled in the five dynamic work design principles, and those principles emerged almost immediately as they started figuring out how to do COVID testing.

Given the inability to make concrete plans, because of both lack of experience and the rapidly changing landscape of COVID, the team knew that iteration and problem-solving would be critical. To that end, within two weeks of their first meeting, the team built their first testing line. The new line allowed them to assemble enough data to apply for state approval. Their application was approved in twenty-four hours. On March 23, the lab started officially doing COVID tests and returning the results to hospitals. On April 9, they started a pilot program with local nursing homes. In the first four days of a pilot program, they handled a thousand tests—more than all of the Boston-area hospitals could process combined—and detected two hundred positive cases of COVID among Cambridge nursing home residents. This was nearly ten times more than the twenty-four cases the city had known about. The information allowed public health officials to move quickly to prevent further outbreaks.

Initially, the test operation was staffed by the most-senior people in the organization, including Stacey and Sheila, who often worked the night shift. This was the ultimate deep dive into the work. Instead of talking to others who were doing the work, they jumped in and got the experience firsthand. A working line staffed by the organization's leaders proved to be an ideal structure for discovering and solving problems. "We were all-hands-on-deck," Sheila said. "It didn't matter whose role was what, we were just getting things done." In a single shift, she might write a hospital contract, reconfigure a lab process, and cut out labels for the sample tubes.

Sheila and the team spent the early days setting up rudimentary processes for all the needed elements (tube filling, label cutting, data entry). For example, multiple tube labels were printed on large sheets and then had to be separated after printing. So, leaders spent a whole day just cutting labels. For each task, she would set up a process, train people on it, and then say, "'Are you okay running this? I'm going to go home for a couple of hours and then I'll be right back here.' That's how we ran it in the beginning, and we said if we don't do it, no one else is going to. So, we did it and we kept up with demand."

Coordinating those problem-solving efforts, however, could be a challenge. Prior to COVID, the team had the luxury of in-person huddles to ensure a connected human chain. Now, state regulations limited the number of people who could be in any room, and some team members couldn't leave their homes because of their own health conditions or those of close family members.

Twice-daily Zoom meetings became the cornerstone of their efforts to reconnect the human chain. Even those coming off night shift made an effort to attend (and then go back to sleep). During these meetings, problems were surfaced, discussed, and assigned. Staff who couldn't risk contracting COVID took on administrative tasks, like assembling test data or writing job descriptions.

Numerous instant messaging threads provided the main channel for escalating issues that couldn't wait for the next meeting.

Having met weekly in front of visual management boards for more than five years, the Broad team was familiar with visualizing the flow of their work. The testing line used the same method for flow regulation that had worked so well with sequencing. Simple parking spaces between steps helped reveal both overload and bottlenecks. Sticky notes and the whiteboard were quickly replaced with an online version that could be easily shared during videoconferencing. The rows represented the threads of activity that supported major goals, such as getting regulatory approval and hiring the staff necessary to accommodate the growing demand. The cards in each row captured specific activities to support those goals. They were reviewed daily and adjusted as the environment changed.

The simple design brought the five principles to life: the initial testing line staffed by senior leaders created an ideal structure for discovering problems; daily videoconferencing and instant messaging threads ensured those problems found their way to the right people; digital visual boards helped everyone see and regulate the flow of work; and structured problem-solving was applied to the most pressing issues. With this design, the team was able to see the gains being made and the next challenge requiring their attention.

For example, the team knew at the outset that supplies were going to be a problem. Most COVID-testing machines used by hospitals are integrated devices. A sample goes in, and a result comes out of a single machine. But thanks to rapidly degrading supply chains, the necessary inputs—swabs, chemicals, etc.—were in exceedingly short supply. Because the Broad team understood the technology, they could take a more modular approach, giving them more flexibility to work around supply constraints. For example, in contrast with the rest of the industry, they chose the tubes commonly used for collecting blood samples as their transport vessel. Initially, COVID samples were collected using the long nasal pharyngeal (or "brain tickler") swabs, which were normally placed in a long tube designed for that swab. Using the blood tube required breaking the stick in half to get it in the tube, thus adding an extra step to sample collection. However, because of their widespread use, blood tubes were widely available (and inexpensive), while the longer containers were in short supply.

Using the visual management board allowed them to track problem-solving on multiple timescales. For example, viral transport media, or VTM, the liquid that preserved the swabs during transport, was the hardest thing to get. The major supplier was a small plant in Italy, a major COVID hot spot in the spring of 2020. For a time, the world supply went to near zero. At one point, Stacey drove three hours to the University of Massachusetts at Amherst to get one bottle. When a new bottle would show up, it had to be put in sample tubes. The team adjusted to the variable supply. Sheila recalls, "When we'd get new VTM, I'd say, 'OK, who's got a couple of hours to come into the lab and help put VTM in tubes?' I would get four or five volunteers, who would otherwise be sitting in lockdown at their homes."

While making do with limited VTM in the short run, the team also tried to solve the problem at a more fundamental level. They did a study comparing samples transported in the VTM with those transported without it. Analysis demonstrated that dry samples were sufficient to detect the presence of COVID, a protocol that was approved by the FDA under an emergency-use authorization. The team performed a similar exercise on the long brain-tickling nasal pharyngeal swabs. Administering them required careful training, and they were very uncomfortable for the patient. Another study showed that a shorter swab that didn't go as deep into the nasal cavity was sufficient for diagnosing COVID. The FDA's subsequent approval of the shorter swab both reduced the discomfort of sample collection and eliminated another major supply constraint.

As the team continued to surface and solve problems, the capacity to process samples grew steadily. Conversations between Eric Lander and Massachusetts governor Charlie Baker led to this new capacity being directed to the state's elder-care facilities. New England's nursing homes were an early and tragic COVID hot spot, leading the Centers for Disease Control and Prevention to recommend that every resident and employee of those facilities be tested regularly. Working with the state to support those facilities created a new set of challenges (and experiences). One day, without warning, members of the Massachusetts National Guard, fully dressed up in hazmat suits and driving Humvees, showed up at the lab to deliver samples stored in beer coolers from nursing homes around the state. The team spent a long night trying to match the labels on the samples to handwritten records and get them into the testing system.

Thanks to the ongoing rapid cycle of surfacing issues, directing them to the right people, and resolving them, by the end of May the lab was able to process five thousand tests per day. The team had played a central role in maintaining the safety of the area's nursing homes, and everyone was exhausted. What the team would eventually call the "small COVID" line had been a big success. As the weather got warmer and as COVID rates slowed, the team looked forward to a respite from the 24-7 schedule that had occupied their spring.

Big COVID

When the lab delivered its one hundred thousandth test in June 2020, Stacey, Sheila, and another colleague, Niall Lennon, had a videoconference call with Eric Lander. Eric remained worried that the nation's testing capacity was woefully inadequate. What would it take, he asked, to get to a million tests per day?

Eric is famous for thinking big, and he views disrupting normal patterns of thinking as part of his role as a leader. As a practicing scientist, he also has a natural inclination toward problem-solving. He explains:

> Stacey and Sheila properly ground me in the reality and complexity of the task because they are the ones who will have to deliver it. They know how to signal me when I am delusional . . . but they will hear me out. I am still a working scientist and will work with them to find ways around blockers they see. But we are always clear on the motivation of the request, and we are working on the same side of the table. We have a shared mission, and we collaborate to find a way if it is possible. There is no magic.
>
> The speed of light . . . I take that seriously as a constraint. But other things, like "there's not enough space," that's not a blocker. It's just an issue, just another problem to solve.

Inspirational leadership notwithstanding, Sheila recalls having a less than positive reaction. "My first reaction was denial: 'Are you crazy?'" says Sheila. Next was anger. "'We've been working our butts off and now you ask us to do this insane thing?' Then I started bargaining with him." After conferring with the team in depth, she returned in a few days with a counteroffer: "We can potentially see a pathway to one hundred thousand tests a day." Eric agreed, and that figure became the next target to go after.

"For us, this was a turning point," Sheila says. "We realized COVID was not going away, and we would be testing for a while. If we were going to do it, we wanted to do it right and not just scale what we had."

The team's hands-on efforts to get to five thousand tests per day had given them a visceral sense of the limitations of the existing system. Data input and management, for example, had been a huge headache. Sheila recalls trying to report results to a hospital in Cape Cod that required that those results be sent via fax. After finding an ancient fax machine in a closet, she ended up calling a colleague at 3:00 a.m. to ask how to use it. Similarly, as previously mentioned, supply chain issues remained a major problem.

The experience of building the small COVID-testing line gave them a clear sense of at least some of the requirements for a new testing line with higher capacity. Samples needed to arrive in standard collection tubes with a barcode already attached. Similarly, data needed to come through a single channel in a common format. As the team discussed where they might most usefully focus their efforts, New England's many colleges and universities emerged as potential targets. MIT and other institutions were working furiously to get their students back on campus safely, and regular testing would be part of any solution. Working with a relatively small number of large entities would help them standardize sample collection and data transfer.

During the summer of 2020, the team designed their "big COVID" line. Building on the challenges they experienced with the small COVID line, the new system eliminated many of the issues that had limited capacity. For example, in the new system, Broad provided sample collection kits to their customers, thus ensuring that they were always received in the same container, with the proper barcode, and that the associated patient information was entered into a single system.

The regulate-for-flow principle was the centerpiece of the new design. The testing line had a clear "airplane door": once samples entered the lab, they were allowed to flow without interruption. To ensure that flow, much as in Don's Harley-Davidson engine assembly line, samples were placed in movable carts. Clearly marked parking spaces for those carts, placed between key steps of the process, immediately revealed interruptions to the workflow and problems to be solved. Over the summer, the team installed web cameras so that the parking spaces (not the people using them) could be monitored remotely. With this setup, Sheila could visually check the status of the sample flow from her phone at any time, from anywhere.

Like its predecessor, the new line facilitated discovery, and the resulting issues were escalated into the daily meeting or via instant messaging threads. For example, some university staff didn't know how to collect samples, so Broad started holding weekly training seminars. "Some people at the colleges were terrified of having the students come back to campus," Sheila said. "They had to set up sites. They had to learn our software. It took an unbelievable amount of energy and effort to help them. We were sending people who had worked in the lab for twenty years out into the field to fix printers. We started hiring a lot more people." Hiring was, of course, also a challenge. Team members who worked remotely jumped in to help.

By September 2020, the lab was capable of processing one hundred thousand samples per day, including those from our home institution, MIT. Without Broad's testing capability, we would not have been able to reopen safely, and, to our knowledge, there was a vanishingly small number of cases among the MIT community. The story is similar for dozens of other institutions. At its peak, the lab performed almost 10 percent of all the COVID tests done in the country, charging far less than their for-profit competitors and returning results for 99 percent of tests within twenty-four hours.

During the fall of 2020, the team also restarted (and tripled) Broad's core business of genetic sequencing, first to track the evolution of the COVID virus and later to relaunch other critical research programs. With both testing and genetic sequencing under one roof, the lab played a critical role in tracking the evolution of the COVID virus and provided critical information to public health officials.

The COVID line was finally shut down in the summer of 2023. At that point, the lab had performed over thirty-seven million tests, with an average turnaround time of less than twenty-four hours. During the three years they performed COVID tests, the lab served approximately seventy-eight thousand people in the state's eldercare and nursing facilities. They also supported over one hundred colleges and universities. The team was able to reduce the cost of the COVID test, initially set at fifty dollars, by almost 50 percent.

STATIC STRUCTURES *AND* DYNAMIC PRINCIPLES

Broad's move into COVID testing is one of the most successful pivots we have ever seen. The lab that had never done a COVID test and that had never returned a diagnostic result to a patient became one of the largest, most reliable, cost-effective testing providers in the country in the space of six months, favorably competing with for-profit diagnostics companies that had been in the testing game for decades. The team's success had many sources. Broad hires talented people and had the full support of its leadership during a national crisis. Eric Lander proved to be remarkably capable in making connections and getting resources. That said, similarly staffed organizations with far more funding have failed to respond to lesser crises. How did Broad do it? The answer gets to the heart of how dynamic work design is more than just a method for improving processes; it is a different approach for thinking about leading and managing, one whose importance will only grow as the pace of technological and societal change continues to increase.

Early in the twentieth century, the pioneers of the Industrial Revolution, people like Frederick Winslow Taylor and Henry Ford, developed the basic technology of mass production. Analyze the work to determine the best way to execute it (what Taylor called the "one best way"), subdivide that work into bite-sized pieces, and then relentlessly standardize each of those pieces. Taylor, in particular, believed that when done in accordance with scientific principles, the initial design of the work was definitive; no further improvement was needed. Ensuring complete adherence to this design required an intricate system of rules and monitoring.

In the middle of the twentieth century, the pioneers of the modern corporate form, people like Alfred P. Sloan Jr., the longtime chairman and CEO of General Motors, extended that approach beyond the factory floor. As we highlighted above, activity and costs were controlled by leaders through the creation of detailed strategies and budgets, to which people were held accountable. The notion that the future is something that can be anticipated and, therefore, planned and managed by a small number of senior leaders remains as central to management today as it did more than fifty years ago.

When confronted with COVID, Broad's leadership didn't sequester themselves in a room and spend months (or even weeks) creating a strategy for processing one hundred thousand samples a day. Similarly, they didn't enshrine that strategy in the form of a PowerPoint slide deck delivered to someone else who would be "held accountable" to build and run it. Instead, Stacey, Sheila, and the rest of the team built a working line in two weeks and ran it themselves. Doing real work, even at two hundred tests per day, surfaced real problems. Real problems were opportunities to make real improvement and build real capability. Growth in that capability revealed the next set of problems to be solved and so on. The team *discovered* their way into being one of the biggest, most efficient testing labs in the country in just six months.

We will never know the exact combination of luck and smarts that created the lab's success. Paradoxically, had they known at the outset that they were capable of one hundred thousand tests per day, they might have tried to plan their way to a solution. Similarly, without the time pressure of a global pandemic and with more time to think, they might have tried to lead with more rules and less emphasis on the work design principles. That said, the lesson remains the same.

Strategy, planning, budgets, rules, and accountability aren't going away. They remain critical parts of the leader's tool kit. But in a rapidly changing world, budgets, plans, and strategies will always eventually become things that need to be worked around. Similarly, being accountable to follow rules and meet targets will always eventually put those doing the work in an impossible position. Perhaps the fundamental question that determines organizational performance is whether these inevitable adjustments are hidden from senior managers or done publicly. A common set of work design principles provides a powerful complement to the more traditional static approaches. These principles transform workarounds from a slippery slope of antagonism, mistrust, and capability decline into an engine of collaboration, results, and capability development.

Throughout the book, we have offered examples of problems that could be identified only by those closest to the work. In direct contrast to Taylor's ethos of managers manage and workers work, building capability through surfacing and solving problems requires engaging everyone in the organization. No system of rules can dictate the novel solution to problems that weren't known when those rules were created. A common set of design principles, not a collection of rules, holds the work together. In an uncertain world, enforcing a set of rules will never be enough. Leaders also need to lead by reinforcing a set of design principles.

Sheila Dodge summarizes it nicely:

As a leader, I always go back to the principles of work design. They're the thing I ground myself in. It's making sure that there's a structure for problem-solving, setting targets, and tracking progress, connecting humans, optimally managing the flow so there's the right amount of work in the system, and making it all visible. When I come up against a problem, I think through the principles. What are we not doing? Most of the time I realize, "Oh! We haven't made the targets clear. We don't have the right people in the room. We've taken on way too much." It's nice for me because it's only five principles; it's not a list of twenty, and these five are straightforward.

Chapter 9

Getting Started

(WITHOUT POSTERS, COFFEE CUPS, OR THREE-RING BINDERS)

Dynamic work design is a set of principles, not a one-size-fits-all system of rules, tools, and rituals. It offers multiple paths for improving the work of an organization, raising the question of how best to get started. We have both, in different ways, grappled with this question throughout our careers, trying to understand it from both scientific and practical perspectives. Our contrasting backgrounds provide the opportunity to share complementary perspectives on taking your first steps toward using dynamic work design to find your own unique path to a better way that transforms your organization.

THE ANTI-INITIATIVE

Nelson: When I met Steve Carboy, he worked at BP as an operations manager in the oil fields on Alaska's North Slope. After spending two weeks with us at MIT learning about the firefighting trap and the basic elements of structured problem-solving, Steve headed back to the Slope, ready to engage his team and start solving some problems. Here's how he reported his first day back on the job:

> I had returned from MIT, and I was discussing with the operators in the control room how BP was changing the way we were going to approach improving and solving operations issues. How we needed the input from experienced operators like them to solve persistent issues, specifically how they had to have more say in how they worked. This is when the lead control room operator pulled out a rather large box of books and binders from the previous campaign and dropped it on the desk. I think he had been saving the material for just this type of conversation. I have to admit, it was a bit deflating.

As we noted in Chapter 3, the basics of structured problem-solving have been around for over fifty years, and almost every company has tried to use them. BP and its associated companies had made at least two efforts prior to their work with MIT. In fact, when I visited the Slope, faded posters promoting the previous effort were still on the walls. Those earlier change initiatives had produced a few significant successes, but they clearly hadn't stuck—and as evidenced by the dropped cardboard box, they had left frustration in their wake.

This experience is not unique. Indeed, it's all too common. I've studied organizational change for much of my adult life. I entered academia in 1990, when the lean revolution was in full swing and Toyota was the envy of every manufacturer. Managers wanted to emulate Toyota; scholars wanted to understand why Toyota was so productive. This was not a crazy desire. Many of the methods that Toyota and other Japanese manufacturers used were well documented, and there was ample evidence that they worked. Nonetheless, most organizations struggled to use Toyota's methods, and very few US companies achieved results similar to their Japanese counterparts. It would take the US auto industry decades to achieve rough parity, and some would argue that they never made it.

As we detailed in Chapter 2, the root of those failures lies not in the tools themselves, but in the strategies used to implement them. For example, most organizations make periodic attempts to introduce new tools and processes, often spurred by the latest fad, and most of those efforts produce little if any sustained change. Company leaders fail to recognize that in most organizations, things get worse before they get better. They pull the plug on change programs that might have worked if the expectations were more realistic. In some cases, the change strategies their leaders used left their companies less capable and more prone to problems than they had been before the effort.

The culture that has arisen around organizational change, aided and abetted by academics and consultants, tends to amplify management's most destructive tendencies. They keep packaging the same management-theory wine in newly labeled bottles, and it never works any better than it did before. Each failed attempt breeds cynicism and disengagement as frontline employees come to perceive such efforts as little more than executive flights of fancy.

That's why BP's Alaskan operators reacted so strongly to Steve's enthusiasm. They weren't just bored or worried about wasted time. In past change efforts they had seen things get worse but never better. Other companies experience a similar dynamic. Harley's employees used to talk about AFPs, an acronym for Another Fine Program, though privately, the *F* often stood for another, less polite word that I don't use around my mom unless I've hit a really bad shot when we play golf.

The biggest concern that Don and I had in writing this book is simply that it would turn dynamic work design into another initiative. The moment dynamic work design is delivered to an entire organization as a two-day training course (with a half-day overview for busy senior executives), replete with posters, binders, and coffee mugs, we know that its impact will be minimal. Ultimately, we think of dynamic work design as the anti-initiative. It is a proven antidote to the bullshit and silliness that so often define the modern organization. But that antidote doesn't work in one big dose. To return to an analogy we have used several times, it is a lifestyle change, not a diet.

The bad news is that temporarily adopting a few tools and language isn't going to cut it. Transforming your organization with dynamic work design requires everyone to manage and lead differently. The good news, however, is that you don't have to adopt its elements all at once or instantly convert your colleagues. Instead, as we have outlined throughout the book, start small, resolve a few issues, calm the system, build a few new skills, and help others think about their work a little differently. With practice, you will be able to generate results faster, and based on those results, your colleagues will start asking you what's going on. These questions become natural opportunities to lead and to spread the approach and principles to other parts of your organization.

Getting started, however, remains easier said than done. Don and I have both experienced the anxiety and uncertainty that come with staring at a messy, chaotic process that requires daily heroics to get work done and not knowing where to start. And therein lies what is perhaps the biggest error in getting started with dynamic work design: in an effort to pick a small problem, you pick one that is not important.

When we introduce our students to dynamic work design and ask them to do an initial project, there is often a strong desire to pick an issue that is not connected to the core work of the organization. This is a normal instinct when trying something new. Try it in an isolated area, away from the real work, so if it doesn't go well, there won't be any collateral damage.

Resist the urge to choose a project on the periphery. One of the core problems that motivated us to write this book is simply that we have too much to do. Working on a peripheral project, while adding to that workload, won't do much to alleviate the firefighting that creates it. And even if it succeeds, a peripheral project won't help you propagate the thinking to your team and organization. In extreme cases, such projects can even do significant damage. When we worked with BP, corporate legend held that a senior manager had once happened upon a team using structured problem-solving to determine the location of two flowerpots. He immediately canceled the entire program.

The essential challenge of getting started with dynamic work design is choosing a starting point that is both small *and* important. Put differently, the key to a successful early effort is choosing a project that will both eliminate a lot of firefighting with minimal effort and reveal the next problem to be solved. Changing an organization is like untangling a messy knot. Pulling the right thread starts unravelling the mess; pulling the wrong one tightens the knot.

The key decision in getting started with dynamic work design is choosing which thread to pull. To help you think about this choice, Don shares an example from his own efforts.

START AT THE SHIPPING DOCK

Don: In late 2004, I left Harley after fifteen years and joined Intermatic, a privately held manufacturing company, as the senior vice president of operations. I was responsible for production, the supply base, logistics, continuing engineering, and quality. The company had been around for over a hundred years; the employees and most of the management had been there for decades.

It was a great job at a really good company, but in retrospect, the timing was terrible. I started in September and had planned to spend the first few months getting my bearings. I also had a long-planned family vacation to visit my sister in Africa in December, with the idea that I would really start to change things when I got back.

For most of its history, the company set the standard for industrial timers and switches as well as small household timers and low-voltage yard lights. In the late 1980s and early 1990s, it was one of the first companies to move production to China, gaining a huge cost advantage. There, it expanded to solar yard lights and other small retail products. Between the products and all the different models of each, we had a few thousand part numbers to manage and a supply chain that stretched from the United States to Mexico and China. The company had grown quickly in the last few years, acquiring small competitors and constantly adding new products and product lines.

The customer base had also changed. It still had the industrial business, but the retail side, the big-box stores, had grown to dwarf the network of distribution centers that supplied the small companies that constituted our traditional business. The big retailers weren't afraid to throw their weight around if they didn't get what they wanted when they wanted it. Every sales season, they threatened to reduce our shelf space if we didn't improve on price and fine us if we missed a delivery. They were also moving to China, creating their own supply chains and in-house brands that competed directly with us.

Change was obviously needed; that's why I was picked for the job. Their family business was making good money, but the way they worked hadn't kept up with the times or the shifts in the market. There were plenty of problems to work on, and I dove in right away. For the first few months, my weekly staff meetings were four hours long. I tried to learn the business and grapple with the constant flux of urgent issues, including several major quality issues and recalls. We made some progress on the basics but definitely were not in control of the situation. It was pretty rough. But suddenly it got much worse.

Operations had become so chaotic over the past few years that the on-time ship metric had slid to nearly 60 percent, meaning that 40 percent of orders were shipped late, and it took multiple attempts to get all the items out the door to complete the order. Suddenly, just as I left for my long-planned vacation, that number got even worse. I tried to keep up while I was gone, but I was in Kenya and often had no phone or internet service. I lay awake at night wondering what I was going to do when I got back. We were already working flat out, so we had to do something differently.

The first morning back after the New Year's holiday, I called my nine direct reports to a meeting. I asked them one simple question: "Why can't we ship the orders today that we are supposed to ship today?"

The room was quiet. Finally, someone asked what I meant. I repeated the question. The directors and VPs started to reply that they didn't know, but they would ask their staff to get us some answers next week. Not good enough, I told them. We aren't shipping product, and we don't know why. I wanted specific answers for every order we were not able to ship, and I wanted those answers by 2:00 p.m. that day. All other plans were canceled.

Off they went. At 2:00 p.m., we reconvened and went through every shipment scheduled for that day, part number by part number. About 5:00 p.m. we sent out for pizza. As we finished around 7:00 p.m. and started packing up to go home, they thought they were done. I told them that we would start again tomorrow at 9:00 a.m., *with answers*. We continued every day. No one was happy, but there was no yelling and screaming and no blaming, just a lot of hard work going through tons of data and figuring out how to resolve the issues one by one, day after day.

Some issues were fixed quickly: wrong part number, wrong location listed for the inventory, paperwork lost. Others took more time and negotiation with the customers. If the parts weren't available, we had to schedule their production. Some parts were delayed at customs in Hong Kong or at the port in Los Angeles; some had quality issues. Product shipment had every problem you could imagine and more. For every problem we found in our own facilities, we also found one at our suppliers'; packaging designs were late or wrong, order numbers were off, and schedules were wrong. Often, the first fix was to call the customer and inform them of a delay and see if we could find a substitute product. Lots of issues that had lingered for years finally got fixed because the execs were out in the shop or at suppliers and were finally paying attention to how the work really got done. So many problems got solved that after a week or two the meetings began to get a little shorter. Asking the executive team to personally dig into the problems got everyone's attention.

One morning, one of the directors reported the reason for a missed shipment as "the woman on the shipping dock dropped the ball." This seemed a little vague compared with the detailed discussions we had been having, so I asked him to stay after the meeting.

At the end of the meeting, I asked the director to come with me. We hopped into my car and made the eight-minute trip to the shipping dock at the warehouse. We went to see "the woman who dropped the ball." After a few pleasantries, I started by asking her to explain how her day was organized and the mechanics of how orders turned into shipments on the trucks. She explained that the "pick sheets" for the day started coming off the printer at about 5:00 a.m. By 7:00 a.m., people were using them to pick and stage orders at the shipping dock so that they could be loaded onto trucks. I asked about issues she had and what worked well and about any changes they had made recently to improve their work. She knew her stuff and had several examples of small changes they had made to make things run smoother.

Then I asked about the specific part number we were looking into. "Oh, yeah, a bunch of people were running around here asking about that number this morning, but it wasn't on our pick list, so I'm not sure where the problem is." When I looked at the manager who had accused her of "dropping the ball," his face had turned multiple shades of red. "OK, can you tell me who puts together the list that gets printed, and we'll go find out why it didn't get on the pick list this morning." She wasn't sure, but she thought it was someone in the sales group. She also mentioned that the constantly broken $125 dot matrix printer frequently delayed the team who picked the orders to be shipped. I handed her my company credit card and sent her to the store to buy two. One to use and a backup for when the first one fails.

We thanked her and off we went, tracing the path of the order backward through the system, person by person. At every step along the way, we had the same conversation we had on the shipping dock, asking people to show us how their job worked and what the issues were and whether they had made any improvements recently.

Along the way, we solved a few small problems and collected a list of issues to bring back to the staff. We learned a lot about how orders turned into shipments. Understandable for me, I'd only been at the company a few months, but the manager tagging along learned almost as much, and he had been there decades. Our several-hours tour ended in finance, far from the "woman on the shipping dock." The order, a piece of paper in those days, had gotten misplaced by the finance team during a routine check of the customer's credit.

Within a few more weeks, things had improved a lot, and like Sheila at the Broad Institute, I got kicked out of the meeting. My staff now ran it with the supervisors and managers in a room down the hall. Finding and fixing lots of little issues and a few very big ones had created a far more stable system. Within two months, the frontline supervisors were running the daily meeting and it lasted only twenty minutes.

By April, our on-time ship metric moved above 90 percent, a number not seen for the business as far as anyone could remember. Our target was still 100 percent on-time ship, but when we hit 90 percent, everything shifted. The customers stopped calling to complain about shortages—calls that had previously caused us to scramble and change whatever we had planned for the day. Similar to Sheila Dodge's experience when the lab team finally got ahead of demand, things calmed down. We began to control what we did every day. Shipments increased. Firefighting nearly disappeared at my level, although I'm sure some adrenaline was still being expended on the front line to hit those numbers every day.

Perhaps more than anything else, that experience crystallized my thinking about making change: pick a problem that, though small, represents the core work of the organization—shipping product was what we were supposed to do—discover how the work generates the problem (you can't print the pick sheet without a working printer), and in doing so, show (not tell!) others what you want them to do.

Prior to my vacation, we'd been doing a lot of problem-solving, but it wasn't getting to the root of the chaos, and it wasn't changing the behavior of my team. The system was still managing us. In contrast, wrestling missed shipments to the ground surfaced all of the problems and workarounds that were getting in our way and changed how the factories operated. Even better, in doing it together, it didn't take my team long before they didn't need me, and I could focus on other parts of the company. And nobody ever accused an employee of "dropping the ball" again (at least not without a lot of data).

FIND YOUR OWN SHIPPING DOCK

We both were raised to be naturally suspicious of senior leaders. Don started as a union member working on the shop floor, while Nelson was raised in a scholarly tradition that tended to downplay the impact of leaders on the organization. Working in and with leading organizations like Harley, Broad, and BP made it abundantly clear that, whether we liked it or not, leaders have an outsized impact on their organizations. But the common image of what leaders do, what our colleague Elsbeth Johnson calls the Hollywood approach, is often counterproductive and leads to many of the problems we have discussed in this book. When leaders focus exclusively on setting high-level strategy and then holding people accountable to the resulting budgets and targets with little regard for the work that delivers those results, they set their organizations up for trouble. Just as changing a bad habit often requires an identity shift, you will not succeed in transforming your organization if you cling to the image of leaders you see on TV and in the movies. You need to engage with the work. Leaders don't just issue commands, they step into the gap and show the way.

But you have a day job and can't spend all day on the shop floor or in the lab. There is no magic here. Transformation is hard work. But there is a lot of magic in *how* you do the hard work, and it comes in resolving an apparent paradox: you need to pick a problem that is somehow both small *and* important.

The resolution comes in realizing that just because leaders have big responsibilities, it doesn't mean that they always have to do big things. Equating a big job with big interventions leads to large-scale change initiatives, and it's the reason why Mr. Oba had to remind Don (see Chapter 3) about the discovery mindset. But this belief represents an incomplete view of how leaders have impact. Yes, of course, the things they do directly can make a big difference. Mergers, technology changes, and market choices all have enormous impacts on the direction of any organization. But leaders also have an equally large impact through the way they act; everyone is watching them to figure out which behaviors are acceptable. Don's effort to chase down one part number might have had a negligible impact on the on-time delivery percentage for that day, but his impact on the behavior of his team was dramatic. He didn't have to ask too many of his direct reports to accompany him to the shipping dock before his expectations were very clear to all involved.

They all quickly learned to do high-quality investigations on their own, to remove blockers for their employees, and to know how the work was getting done (or not getting done). As we all learned in sixth-grade writing class, it is more powerful to show than to tell.

Getting started with dynamic work design often boils down to courage. Problems at the periphery are easy to talk about because they don't really matter. In contrast, discussing flaws in the core work of the organization that happen every day can be challenging. Nobody wants to acknowledge that they might have been partially responsible for maintaining a broken status quo, so we all develop protective mechanisms to rationalize why it's not our fault. Harley executives often claimed that product development was just messy; BP's procurement group thought they couldn't fix anything without a new IT system; and the Broad Institute team thought that chaos was a necessary consequence of being on the cutting edge of technology. In hindsight, all of these claims were clearly wrong—Harley eventually achieved stable product launches; Mark's team saved a billion dollars; Broad's sample-processing lab became a model of efficiency—and confronting these claims produced dramatic gains in organizational performance.

Have the courage to confront the core work of your organization. Find the equivalent of the shipping dock in your organization, the place where the work goes wrong. It could be at the front desk, in the call center, in the emergency room, in the R & D lab, or in the classroom. Start asking basic questions, questions that people may initially hesitate to answer, and work backward until you know why the work didn't get delivered. Initially, it will feel like you are working below your pay grade. You will, however, emerge with a long list of easy improvements, a few hard ones, and a much deeper understanding of how your organization actually works. You will also be a more effective leader.

As the dynamic work design approach gets increasingly embedded in your organization, you'll find that you have little need for change initiatives or their trappings (you'll have to buy your own three-ring binders and coffee mugs). Instead, you will have an organization that constantly senses opportunities in the environment and continually updates and refines its own unique better way.

Acknowledgments

A large number of people have contributed to the development of dynamic work design, and we owe them all a significant debt.

Several leaders at Harley-Davidson not only put up with us but also encouraged us along the way. A special thanks to Tim Savino and the late Ron Hutchinson for introducing us. BP made a similarly large investment in working with us, and we owe a particular debt to Tony Meggs, Graham Cattell, C. J. Warner, Mark Bly, Steve Marshall, John Putnam, Ian Livett, Ronan O'Neill, Susan Kolbush, and all the BP employees who sat in our classroom. People at Fannie Mae were also willing recipients of our teaching and did many fabulous projects. Special thanks to Tim Mayopoulos, Diamond Dubose, and Donna Meador.

This book benefited immeasurably from the opportunity to teach this material to MIT's Executive MBA students, and we are very grateful to the program staff for helping us get the course off the ground and keeping it going for the last decade. A special thanks to program director Johanna Hising-Di Fabio and her crack program team, including Renee Benjamin, Becca Souza, Sorina Brackett, and Katy Radol. Über-assistant Dawn Mackenzie held this whole operation together for many years. This book wouldn't exist were it not for the students who took the class and did the great projects that we describe throughout the book. Similar thanks to the Sloan Executive Education team, who have allowed us to teach our material to many executive audiences. Special thanks to Peter Hirst, Eric Bergemann, Sophie Weintraub, Colleen Berger, Lindy Milton, Janice Gardner, Court Chilton, and Mike Kavanaugh. Similar thanks to all of the students who sat in our classes.

We have also benefited from working with many patient clients. A special thanks to Eric Waller, David Whiteing, Brigit Girshick, and Jim Foster. Longtime collaborators and consulting partners Mark Schwiebert, Mike Plancon, and Dan Glusick have been instrumental in testing and developing the ideas behind dynamic work design. Tom Arenberg, Paula Hogan, Erica Kieffer, and Jamie Repenning generously read the first draft and gave us great feedback.

None of this would have been possible without the ongoing collaboration of our "lead users," the team at Broad. A huge thanks to Tim De Smet, Niall Lennon, Steve Ferriera, Danielle Perrin, Jim "I'm not the IT guy" Meldrim, Tom Howd, Cole Walsh, Emily Moore, Peter Trefy, Deirdre Sheehan, and Justin Abreu. The debt we owe Sheila Dodge would be impossible to overstate. And thanks to Stacey Gabriel and Eric Lander for not telling the factory rat and the social scientist to get the hell out of their lab.

As the idea of writing a book started to form, Art Kleiner and Juliette Powell at KPI provided invaluable guidance and editorial support as we tried to navigate the world of mass-market publishing. Adam Grant, Bob Sutton, and Simon Johnson provided valuable advice along the way, including helping us find our wonderful agent, Giles Anderson. Giles in turn connected us with our incredible editor, John Mahaney. John's patient counsel has made the manuscript immeasurably better.

Finally, the research that led to this book was made possible by generous financial support from the Program on Innovation in Markets and Organizations (PIMO).

Nelson: Since we met in 1996, Don Kieffer has been a constant source of inspiration, support, and friendship. Dynamic work design would not exist without both his deep understanding of the nature of work and his tenacity in figuring out how to turn his insights into action. As I settled into post-tenure life, each new paper started to look increasingly like a slightly recast version of the previous one. Don's enthusiasm and energy for making work better opened up an entirely new direction; he quite literally saved my professional life.

I have also been blessed with an incredible collection of mentors and colleagues at MIT. Most importantly, John Sterman gambled on me as a PhD student and has continued to generously share his deep knowledge of social and organizational dynamics. Bob Gibbons, Rebecca Henderson, Roberto Fernandez, Ezra Zuckerman, Bethany Patten, Jenny Rudolph, Leslie Perlow, and Hazhir Rahmandad have all provided valued insight and feedback along the way. Many PhD and MBA students made important contributions, including Laura Black, Brad Morrison, Paulo Goncalves, Gokhan Dogan, Chris Morrison, Ben Linville-Engler, Steve De Sandis, and Melissa Langley Lawton.

My early collaborators and sponsors at Ford Motor Company played a critical role in setting this research in motion. Thanks to Roger Saillant, Bill Colwell, Laura Cranmer, Tim Tiernan, and Frank Murdoch.

I also owe a huge debt (and more than a few apologies) to the team who kept the MIT Leadership Center running during my frequent book-related absences. Big thanks to Tracy Purinton, Abby Berenson, Nicki Roth, Jennifer Montana, Alison Pepi, Jingwen Yang, and Tracey Mellor. Thanks also to Mario Marzano for patiently helping me in the early days of this project.

I have benefited immeasurably from the patient counsel of many coaches, mentors, and friends. Though perhaps not immediately apparent, the lessons I learned from them appear throughout the book. A lifetime of thanks to Ron Boi, Bob Wright, Esther Redmount, Mark Paich, Bill Weida, Walt Hecox, Lois Eichler, and Adam Myerson. A special thanks to Elizabeth Saltonstall.

Finally, a big thanks to my family, who will probably be very happy when (and if) I am capable of talking about something other than book writing. So much thanks and love to my mom, Caroline (the golf shark); my brothers, Win, John, and Jamie; my kids, Rena and Robbie; and my partner, Karen.

Don: Nelson has been my collaborator in this work since 1996, adding discipline and rigor to my efforts and thinking, clearly elevating both. He also invited me into the world of teaching executive education. Explaining to others what it was that I was doing was hard work; writing it down clearly was even harder. Without Nelson's help, teaching and writing would never have been part of what I do. Together, we have created a framework that is powerful, clear, and teachable.

Many people helped me in my journey from machine operator to executive, but a few folks did so at critical junctures. Larry Scott, the executive at Westinghouse Airbrake, saw value in the shop floor supervisor, former union member, and lathe operator that he fired during a labor strike (and was forced to rehire). He created a position that allowed me to keep working full-time while I finished my engineering degree. Ken Daly mentored me and gave me my first chance to run a factory. Dave Baldwin, an executive OD coach at Harley, took me on as his private project and smoothed many of my shop-floor rough edges (but not all), so that I could survive in the corporate world. Julie Peck gave me the confidence to walk away from a big operations job and go out on my own to find a whole new world of operational problems to understand and solve.

Raising my game at solving problems had help, too. Scott Borg was Mr. Hajime Oba's "number one student"; his patience in helping me understand Mr. Oba's methods and the why behind them helped turn me into a permanent student. Takashi Tanaka taught me the basics of visual management. Toshio Horikiri, CEO of Toyota Engineering Corporation, showed me that there are *always* more things to learn, *always* another door to go through, and *always* a next level to discover. Jamie Flinch-baugh, a major player in the world of improvement and one of the few people who understand the thinking behind Toyota's methods, helped my team at Harley keep moving. Jesper Nytoft Bergmann, at AVT Business School in Copenhagen, supported my teaching dynamic work design to hundreds of Danish MBA students for more than a decade. John Schaller, a "recovering lawyer," former successful Harley dealer, and now budding book editor, made me see just how muddled my writing was and helped me to be clear.

One client whose story did not make it into the book but who deserves a mention is Eric Waller, one of our best students and now a serial entrepreneur. We met when he took on a small project in Wamsutter, Wyoming, while he was employed by BP. He cut the time for getting newly drilled wells online from 120 days to about 10, reducing cost and raising revenue dramatically. He went on to help build and eventually run an oil company that became one of the top one hundred oil companies rated by Moody's, raising $1.4 billion in equity in the process. The walls of his team's offices were covered with visual management boards that were used every day.

To reinforce the contributions of those mentioned in the joint acknowledgments above, my personal efforts have been immensely aided by Dan Glusick, Mark Schwiebert, and Sheila Dodge, who have all been with us in this work for more than a decade. Dan Glusick and I worked together at Harley starting in 2001, and he followed me to Intermatic. He has been both a student and a teacher to me. We worked side by side delivering results and discovering better ways to do it. An expert in operational performance, he has gone on to lead operations and deliver stellar results for several companies. By both my standards and the standards of people at Toyota who spent decades creating the Toyota system, Dan is a world-class leader and practitioner of visual management. Dan remains a valued adviser to me. Mark Schwiebert, one of our best clients for years, jumped over to the dark side of consulting, joining our consulting group in 2018, after decades of success at BP. He now leads our group, and we continue to work closely together. Sheila Dodge, one of the best and strongest leaders I have known, continues to plow new ground in the practice of dynamic work design in her work at the Broad Institute. She and her team have exposed more people to dynamic work design and visual management than any organization I know. She is simply inspiring.

As they say, the teacher often learns more than the student. Every interaction with a client or student has left me wiser, and for that I am forever grateful.

Finally, thanks to my family, Erica, Tony, Maura, Maddi, and Kangway, who have endured talk of "the book" for many years.

Notes

Introduction: The Better Way of Dynamic Work Design

1. Nelson P. Repenning, Don Kieffer, and James Repenning, "A New Approach to Designing Work," *MIT Sloan Management Review* 59, no. 2 (2018): 29–38; James Repenning, Don Kieffer, and Nelson Repenning, "Agile for Everyone Else: Using Triggers and Checks to Create Agility Outside of Software Development" (MIT Sloan working paper 5198-17, MIT Sloan School of Management, Cambridge, MA, June 2017); Nelson Peter Repenning, Don Kieffer, and Todd Astor, "The Most Underrated Skill in Management," *MIT Sloan Management Review* 58, no. 3 (Spring 2017); Todd Astor, Michael Morales, Don Kieffer, and Nelson Repenning, "What Problem Are You Trying to Solve: An Introduction to Structured Problem Solving" (MIT Sloan working paper 5175-16, MIT Sloan School of Management, Cambridge, MA, October 2016); Abeel A. Mangi and Nelson P. Repenning, "Viewpoint: Designing Effective Work in Dynamic Medical Environments" (MIT Sloan working paper 5166-16, MIT Sloan School of Management, Cambridge, MA, April 2016); Sheila Dodge, Timothy De Smet, James Meldrim, Niall Lennon, Danielle Perrin, Steve Ferriera, Zachary Leber, Dennis Friedrich, Stacey Gabriel, Eric S. Lander, Don Kieffer, and Nelson P. Repenning, "Using Dynamic Work Design to Help Cure Cancer (and Other Diseases)" (MIT Sloan working paper 5159-16, MIT Sloan School of Management, Cambridge, MA, June 2016).

2. Peter Coy, "How Waze Changed the Way We Drive," *New York Times*, January 23, 2023.

Chapter 1. When Work Works Well: Getting Rid of Obstacles in the Way of Real Work

1. "Video Game Addiction," Cleveland Clinic Health Library, last reviewed May 27, 2022, https://my.clevelandclinic.org/health/diseases/23124-video-game-addiction.

Chapter 2. The Firefighting Trap: When Just "Getting Things Done" Hurts a Company's Ability to Grow, Thrive, and Compete

1. Daniel Kahneman, *Thinking Fast and Slow* (New York: Farrar, Strauss and Giroux, 2011). The observations and theory of automated and complex systems go back to William James; see Joshua Loo, "System 1 and System 2 Thinking," The Decision Lab, https://thedecisionlab.com/reference-guide /philosophy/system-1-and-system-2-thinking.

2. This example draws on the work of Andrew Jones, "Sustaining Process Improvement in Product Development: The Dynamics of Part and Print Mismatches" (master's thesis, MIT, 1997), https://dspace.mit.edu /handle/1721.1/42625.

3. This section is based on the US Chemical Safety Board's investigation of the incident. See "BP America (Texas City) Refinery Explosion," Chemical Safety Board, www.csb.gov/bp-america-texas-city-refinery-explosion.

4. Clive Cookson, "John Browne: A Man of Science," *Financial Times*, April 26, 2013, www.ft.com/content/9ce25e98-ac7b-11e2-9e7f-00144feabdc0.

Chapter 4. Structure for Discovery: From Tuning Individual Instruments to Playing a Symphony

1. "Welcome to Women's Lunch Place!," Women's Lunch Place, https:// womenslunchplace.org/welcome.

2. Charlotte Hu, "Why Writing by Hand Is Better for Memory and Learning," *Scientific American*, February 21, 2024, www.scientificamerican .com/article/why-writing-by-hand-is-better-for-memory-and-learning.

Chapter 6. Regulate for Flow: Finish More by Controlling How Much You Start

1. Kaitlin Sullivan, "Nearly 1 in 4 U.S. Hospitalized Patients Experience Harmful Events, Study Finds," *NBC News*, January 11, 2023, www .nbcnews.com/health/health-news/nearly-1-4-us-hospital-patients -experience-harmful-event-study-finds-rcna65119.

2. Rohan Narayana Murty, Sandeep Dadlani, and Rajath B. Das, "How Much Time and Energy Do We Waste Toggling Between Applications?," *Harvard Business Review*, August 29, 2022, https://hbr.org/2022/08 /how-much-time-and-energy-do-we-waste-toggling-between-applications.

3. Katherine C. Kellogg, *Challenging Operations: Medical Reform and Resistance in Surgery* (Chicago: University of Chicago Press, 2011).

4. "NIOSH Training for Nurses on Shift Work and Long Work Hours," National Institute for Occupational Safety and Health, last reviewed March 31, 2020, www.cdc.gov/niosh/work-hour-training-for-nurses /longhours/mod3/08.html.

5. During this project, Flint Hills was supported by the ARGO-EFESO consulting firm. For more information, see Brook Vickery, C. J. Renegar, Nelson Repenning, Jorge Mastellari, "Refinery Maintenance: Achieving a Zen State by Leveraging 'Lean Thinking'" (white paper, ARGO Consulting, March 2019), www.argoconsulting.com/wp-content/uploads/2019/04 /Argo-FHR-Pull-White-Paper-1.pdf.

Chapter 8. The Power of Leading with Principles:
Static Structure Will Take You Only So Far

1. Carey Goldberg, "How a Science Giant Pivoted to Coronavirus Testing and Helped New England Colleges Salvage On-Campus Fall," WBUR, October 2, 2020, www.wbur.org/news/2020/10/02 /broad-covid-testing-cambridge-school-reopenings.

2. "2020 Bostonians of the Year," *Boston Globe*, December 10, 2020.

3. Goldberg, "Science Giant."

Index

Credit: Jamie Watts

Nelson P. Repenning is the School of Management Distinguished Professor at the MIT Sloan School of Management. He is the director of MIT's Leadership Center and was recently recognized by *Poets & Quants* as one of the world's top executive MBA instructors. His scholarly work has appeared in *Management Science, Organization Science, Administrative Science Quarterly, the Academy of Management Review, Strategic Management Journal,* and *Research in Organizational Behavior.* He lives in Cambridge, MA.

Credit: Bryce Vickmark

Donald C. Kieffer is a senior lecturer in operations management at MIT Sloan School of Management. He is a career operations executive and cocreator of Dynamic Work Design. Kieffer first operated equipment in factories at age seventeen. He was vice president of operational excellence at Harley-Davidson for fifteen years. Since 2007, he has been advising leaders around the globe in industries as diverse as oil and gas, medical, biomedical, and banking. His guidance was instrumental in transforming both the production and technical development areas of the Broad Institute, a Cambridge-based genomic sequencing organization, now an industry leader. He is founder of ShiftGear Work Design, LLC and also teaches operations management at AVT in Copenhagen. He lives in Somerville, MA, and Burlingame, CA.